'Conor O'Clery is a legend among foreign correspondents . . . His new book will be welcomed by everyone who cares about good writing and about the human stories that enable us to understand the great movements of world history.'

Richard Lloyd Parry, bestselling author of
Ghosts of the Tsunami

'By tracking the hardships endured by one indomitable family, Conor O'Clery takes us into the hidden heart of Soviet Russia – a Russia bristling with vodka and nuclear warheads, food lines and empty shops, full employment and broken dreams ... *The Shoemaker and His Daughter* is an illuminating combination of history, politics, geography and humanity that's personal and close ..'

Keggie Carew, author of *Dadland*

'An absolutely terrific book – moving, informative, an extraordinary story beautifully written.'

Martin Fletcher, former foreign editor of *The Times*

'A tour de force – a sweeping account of the turbulent decades of the Soviet Union and the new Russia, told through the prism of a Russian–Armenian family. The story features love, politics, murder, wars, and the fracturing of ties, personal and ethnic, brought about by Stalin and his Kremlin successors. O'Clery is a gifted writer.'

Luke Harding, *New York Times* bestselling author of
Collusion: How Russia Helped Trump Win the White House

'Brilliant! Conor O'Clery shows more about how people really live in the former Soviet Union than any foreign writer before him. This book is essential reading for anyone who wants to know about today's Russia.'

Fred Coleman, author of *The Decline and Fall of the Empire*

Also by Conor O'Clery

Melting Snow: An Irishman in Moscow
America: A Place Called Hope?
The Greening of the White House
Ireland in Quotes
Panic at the Bank
The Billionaire Who Wasn't
May You Live in Interesting Times
Moscow, December 25, 1991: The Last Day of the Soviet Union
The Star Man

CONOR O'CLERY

The
SHOEMAKER
and His
DAUGHTER

One ordinary family's
remarkable journey from
Stalin's Soviet Union
to Putin's Russia

Doubleday
Ireland

LONDON · NEW YORK · TORONTO · SYDNEY · AUCKLAND

TRANSWORLD IRELAND
Penguin Random House Ireland, Morrison Chambers,
32 Nassau Street, Dublin 2, Ireland
www.transworldireland.ie

Transworld Ireland is part of the Penguin Random House group of companies
whose addresses can be found at global.penguinrandomhouse.com

Penguin
Random House
UK

First published in the UK and Ireland in 2018
by Doubleday Ireland
an imprint of Transworld Publishers

A CIP catalogue record for this book is available from the
British Library.

ISBN 9781781620434

Typeset in 11.25/15 pt Minion Pro
by Integra Software Services Pvt. Ltd, Pondicherry

Printed and bound in Great Britain by Clays Ltd, Elcograf S.p.A.

Penguin Random House is committed to a sustainable future for our
business, our readers and our planet. This book is made from
Forest Stewardship Council® certified paper.

MIX
Paper from
responsible sources
FSC® C018179

3 5 7 9 10 8 6 4

To Marietta

CONTENTS

AUTHOR'S NOTE

M Y WIFE ZHANNA's parents, Stanislav and Marietta Suvorov, and Zhanna herself, are the central characters of this book, so I am hardly a neutral chronicler. Nevertheless, I have done my best to tell their extraordinary story as honestly and accurately as possible, and explain how their personal destiny was affected to a remarkable degree by the epochal events that shaped the Soviet Union and modern Russia, from Stalin's time to the Putin era. I am overwhelmingly grateful to Marietta for her patience in recalling past, and sometimes painful, events, with great clarity, and naturally also to Zhanna herself. Thanks also to Larisa Airieva, Zhanna's sister, and Larisa's son Valera and daughter Zoya, who helped locate documents and photographs. Michael O'Farrell, John Murray, Valera Airiev and Julia Halliday (O'Clery) made valuable comments on early versions of the text. Julia too had to revisit some painful memories. Michael O'Clery drew the maps, and Paul Campbell helped explain to me the craft of shoemaking. I am very grateful to the Irish embassy in Bucharest for hospitality and guidance. In particular I would like to express my appreciation to Eoin McHugh and Brian Langan, formerly of Transworld, who commissioned the book and helped me develop the concept. Thanks also to Andrea Henry, editorial director at Transworld Publishers, whose suggestions enabled me to draw out the emotions that marked the high and low points of the family odyssey, and to Fiona Murphy of Transworld Ireland.

A note on names and spelling. Russian names contain a first name, a patronymic and a surname. To avoid confusion I have tended to omit the patronymic and use the diminutive of first names, for example Sonia rather than Siranush. For the spelling of Russian names and words I have, where appropriate, used the more readable system of transliteration, using –y rather than –i, –ii, or –iy, thus Yury rather than Yuri.

Stanislav died before work on the book began. It was my great privilege to know him. He was a hero of the Soviet Union, in the best sense, and I am proud to own two pairs of shoes that he made for me.

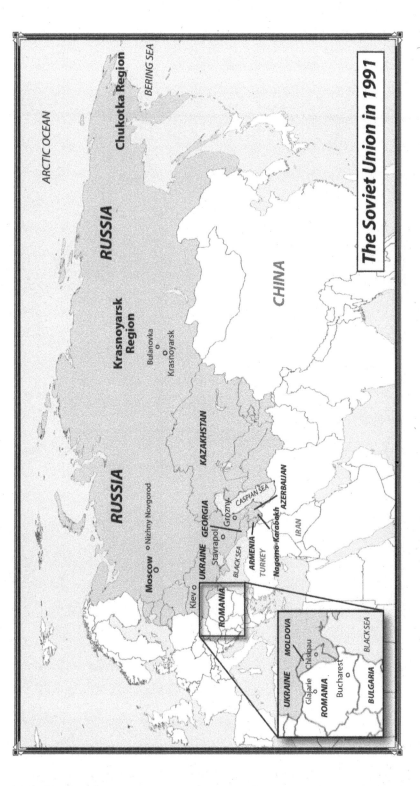

The Soviet Union in 1991

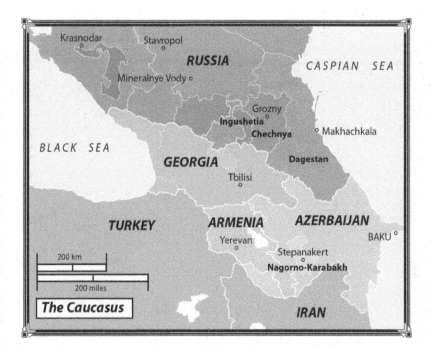

SUVOROV FAMILY

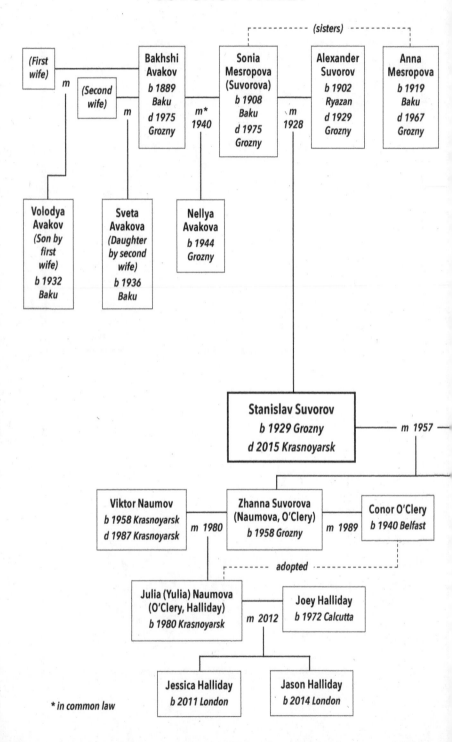

GUKASYAN FAMILY

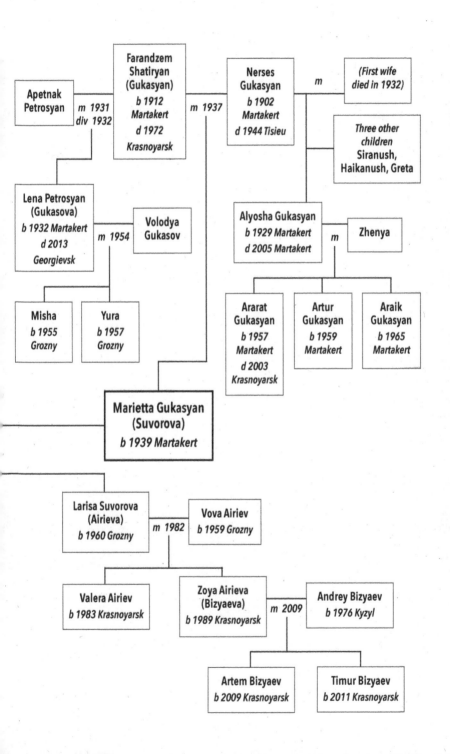

How merry we are with our glasses of wine!
God willing, God willing, not for the last time!
God willing, God willing, that we're drinking not for the last time!

Georgy Stroganov, 'Caucasian Drinking Song'

PROLOGUE

THE LOST LIEUTENANT

O N 11 JANUARY 2017 a diminutive white-haired Armenian woman arrives in Bucharest, and takes a taxi from the airport to the Grand Hotel Continental in Victory Street. The heaviest snowfall in five years has almost paralysed the Romanian capital and she has to pick her way through high snow banks to the foyer entrance after the driver drops her across the street. She is used to severe winter conditions. Marietta Suvorova has travelled from the Siberian city of Krasnoyarsk, six thousand kilometres to the east, where she has lived most of her seventy-seven years and where the winters are long and bitter.

She is joined by me and her elder daughter Zhanna, to whom I have been married for twenty-seven years. We arrive from Dublin the same day. Our purpose in coming to Romania is to find the World War II grave of a Soviet army officer, Lieutenant Nerses Gukasyan, who was Marietta's father and Zhanna's grandfather. He died fighting in central Europe in 1944 when Marietta was five years old and is buried somewhere in Transylvania.

The Russian government estimates the number of Soviet military deaths in the war at 8.7 million, with another 2.4 million missing in action. In the chaos of armed conflict, records were often destroyed, leaving families to grieve without knowing where their loved one was killed, let alone buried. This was the case with Lieutenant Gukasyan. In October 1944 the Soviet army notified his family in the Armenian town of Martakert in the southern Caucasus that he had given his life for the Motherland.

That was it. The letter contained no details of how he died or where he was buried.

The death of her father changed the trajectory of Marietta's life. It meant leaving her birthplace in the warm southern Caucasus and ending up in the frozen expanses of Siberia. Along the way her family suffered the depredations of ethnic wars, economic devastation, imprisonment, murder and the chaos of a collapsing system. Throughout the good times and bad times she was always aware of a void in her life, a lack of closure. As a child she had wept for her father, and as an adult she yearned to one day pay her last respects at his graveside. She never gave up trying to find out what happened to him. She made repeated appeals to the defence ministry in Moscow for information about his burial place. For decades the reply came back, 'Not known.' Her mother, Farandzem, died without ever being able to visit his grave. In 1984 her half-brother Alyosha found out that their father was buried in Romania, but all attempts to find the location, even an appeal to an Armenian newspaper in Bucharest, came to nothing. Then, in 2002, Marietta received a letter from the Russian defence ministry central archives in the city of Podolsk outside Moscow. An archivist had turned up details of the lieutenant's burial place. It was in a village named Tissul in the Reghin district of central Transylvania, three hundred kilometres north of Bucharest.

The letter stated: 'Lieutenant Gukasyan Nerses Arakelovich, b. 1902, place of birth Martakert, Nagorno-Karabakh, commander of rifle detachment, 343 Group, 38th Rifle Division, died of wounds on 30.09.1944. Buried in grave No. 7 by the school of village Tissul, Reghin district, Transylvania, Romania.' However, there is no village called Tissul in Romania. It does not appear on Romanian websites or on Google maps. The letter states it is in Reghin district. Reghin is a town of thirty-three thousand people with numerous villages and hamlets in the surrounding countryside. We made telephone calls to tourist and information offices in Reghin and other nearby towns, but to our frustration no one could locate for us a settlement called Tissul.

As a last resort we have decided to go to Reghin ourselves in the hope of solving the mystery. We suspect the village has been misnamed in translation, or renamed, but we also worry that it has been obliterated to make way for a new development. So while Marietta is in a state of high anticipation, she is fearful that our quest will end in failure.

Next morning we take the fifty-minute Blue Air commuter flight from Bucharest to the city of Cluj-Napoca, the starting point for exploring the landscape of mountains, medieval villages and ghostly castles of Transylvania. We are met at the airport by Ioan Boitos, a soft-spoken Hungarian-Romanian in his fifties with good English, who normally works as a 'transfer expert', shuttling people from the airport to the city. We have contracted Ioan for the day through a car hire agency. We set out in his Mercedes on the road to Reghin, one hundred kilometres to the east. As we drive past isolated wooden farmhouses and vast, snow-covered meadows, we tell him about Marietta's father and how we have not been able to find Tissul on the map. In a stroke of luck, it turns out he has just retired from his career as a police detective, and he readily agrees to help us in our mission.

When we reach Reghin, a town of church spires and wrought-iron balconies noted for its manufacture of violins, Ioan pulls into the side of the road. He scrolls through place names on his satellite navigation system. He suggests that the village we are looking for may be Tyiszó, rendered in English as Tisieu, which lies further east towards the foothills of the eastern Carpathians. The pronunciation of Tisieu is almost indistinguishable from that of Tissul. It is easy to imagine a Red Army officer confusing the two when writing up his report. I am annoyed with myself for not working this out on my own when studying the maps.

We drive along the 153C road for another twenty-six kilometres, past hillsides of leafless grapevines and the occasional roadside crucifix, and find a small signpost pointing left to Tisieu. We cross a little wooden bridge and manage, thanks to Ioan's snow tyres, to make it to the top of a one-lane road deep in fresh snow. Tisieu is just beyond, a hamlet with a narrow *strada principala* and several long lanes leading to a scattering of wooden farmsteads painted in light shades of blue, brown and yellow.

We encounter an old woman in black dress and headscarf stumbling through the snow. We stop and get out. Ioan engages her in conversation and translates for us. We see her nodding her head. Yes, yes, she says. Many 'Russian' soldiers were killed or wounded around here in August 1944. Some of the dead were buried beside the school. We are certain that we have found the right place. Marietta lifts a hand to her face in wonderment and delight. It is a moment of great gratification. It was so easy in the end. In some excitement we ask the villager, through Ioan, to show us the school. It has long since been demolished, she replies. And the graves? Why, Red Army soldiers returned and took the bodies to a different village. She does not know its name.

Our spirits fall. Then a snow plough comes along and the young driver climbs down to hear our story. He starts calling around on his mobile phone. After a few minutes he tells us that all the Red Army dead were collected and buried in Glajarie, a village of about two thousand people twenty kilometres distant.

We set off to find Glajarie. The second half of the journey is along an unploughed two-lane road. We proceed slowly past beech groves and small farms and up a long hill to a neat town with brick houses and wooden chalet-type buildings adorned with satellite dishes. Ioan tells us Glajarie's population is mainly Hungarian. Several communities in this part of Romania are

An emotional moment: Marietta, with Zhanna, finally gets to visit the grave of her father, Lt Nerses Gukasyan, who was buried with hundreds of fallen comrades in northern Romania, 2017.

populated by ethnic Hungarians, a testimony to the shifting borders of central Europe. Northern Transylvania was ceded to Hungary during the war and not returned to Romania until 1945.

We reach a wide, open space at the top of the town where several roads converge. There is a war memorial at the apex of the junction, a grey concrete column listing the names of twenty Romanian war dead topped by an engraved cross. At one corner stands a long white two-storey building with a general store. On the opposite side of the square is an ornately patterned three-storey church building.

Beside it is a small enclosed park, with at its centre, on a raised concrete platform, a slim obelisk about six metres high. It is topped by a red star and bears the hammer and sickle insignia of the Soviet Union.

We hasten to examine it more closely, stamping out a track in knee-deep snow. At the base of the obelisk is an inscription in Russian and Romanian glorifying the heroes of the Soviet army for liberating Romania from its fascist occupiers. Flanking it are eighteen gravestones in two straight lines, and behind the monument are two more gravestones half buried in the snow. We are able to make out the words in Russian: NEIZVESTNYIE SOVETSKIYE SOLDATI (UNKNOWN SOVIET SOLDIERS). Later we establish from a war graves website that the Red Army burial ground in Glajarie contains the bodies of 1,236 unidentified soldiers.

We are certain that we have found the last resting place of the lieutenant. He is not an unknown soldier any longer. The remains of Nerses Gukasyan, Marietta's father, Zhanna's grandfather, lie here, in this mass grave. We stand together, just looking, not saying anything, for several minutes. We are touching history, the history of the family, and that of the great and terrible war that robbed Marietta of her father.

How exactly he died we shall never know but we have evidence he acquitted himself bravely. In 2016 Marietta's granddaughter Zoya discovered an archive on the Internet that lists citations for Soviet army officers killed in World War II. She entered the name Lieutenant Nerses Gukasyan and learned that he had been awarded a Red Star for 'courageously and efficiently' leading his soldiers into battle. No one in his family ever knew this. The red-enamelled five-pointed star, with its image of an alert soldier wearing an overcoat and carrying a rifle, was given for 'exceptional service in the cause of the defence of the Soviet Union'. It is a prized possession among war veterans' families. How proud his wife Farandzem would have been, if only she had known this.

Some months before coming to Romania, Marietta wrote to the Russian ministry of defence asking for her father's Red Star. She was told that the Soviet variety is no longer being manufactured. Instead she receives a card. It certifies that 'Nerses Arakelovich Gukasyan was awarded the Order of the Red Star by decree of the commander of the 38th Rifle Division on 19 September 1944, No. 024n.' It is signed, 'Vladimir Putin, President of the Russian Federation'.

We linger for a while at the grave, taking in the tableau of the obelisk guarded by lines of snow-capped gravestones, in this little memorial park flanked by leafless trees. Marietta feels a great sense of relief, almost joy. Her father can rest in peace, at long last. She is not religious, but like everyone in her family she observes the traditions of her people, fostered through the

Better late than never: the certificate of the Red Star award for bravery to Lt Nerses Gukasyan, issued seventy-two years after his death in action and signed by President Putin.

ages by the Armenian Apostolic Church. Armenians pay special attention to remembering the dead – on the seventh day after death, the fortieth day and annually – and commune with loved ones who have died by visiting their graves.

She can honour and remember her father in traditional fashion now, at least this once, and Zhanna too can pay her respects to the grandfather she never knew.

PART ONE

CHAPTER 1

THE BLACK GARDEN

BEFORE HE BECAME a soldier, Nerses Gukasyan, descendant of a noble Armenian family, was a judge. A tall, dignified man with penetrating eyes, Marietta's father presided over the People's Court of Martakert, a town located in the northern part of an autonomous Armenian enclave called Nagorno-Karabakh inside the traditionally Muslim Soviet republic of Azerbaijan. The name Nagorno-Karabakh translates roughly as Mountainous Black Garden, though its thick beech woods and pastures make it something of a green oasis between the dry plain of Azerbaijan and the snow-clad peaks of the Armenian mountains.

Born in 1902 in Martakert, Nerses studied law in the Azerbaijan capital, Baku, and joined the Communist Party of the Soviet Union (CPSU). In his early twenties he married and had four children, three girls, Siranush, Haikanush and Greta, and a boy, Alyosha. His wife died after the birth of their fourth child.

In 1937, when in his mid-thirties, Nerses marries for a second time. His new wife, Farandzem Shatiryan, a twenty-five-year-old beauty from the same town, with thick black hair, full lips and large almond eyes, was also married before and has a young daughter called Lena.

Farandzem is an independent-minded young woman. She divorced her first husband because he beat her. Few women in the patriarchal society of the Caucasus would have the courage and determination to walk out on an abusive husband. She and

*Farandzem, aged twenty-four, on the left with
a relative, shortly before her marriage to Nerses
in 1937.*

Nerses are ideological bedmates, as Farandzem is also a member of the communist party. Perhaps this common commitment
brings them together in the first place. She must have fallen deeply
in love with Nerses, because to marry him she has to undertake
the care of four stepchildren, while leaving her five-year-old
Lena to be raised by her mother, who persuades Farandzem
that it is for Lena's good. Moreover the judge will not want an
extra child in the house, especially when he and Farandzem
start having babies themselves. The fact is that Farandzem is not
encouraged by Nerses to bring Lena into the household. Perhaps he thinks it is asking enough of his own children to accept
a stepmother. The marriage arrangement suits him well as it is:
he gains a beautiful, hard-working spouse ten years younger

than himself, and he provides his children with a new mother to look after their domestic needs. Farandzem misses Lena terribly, and takes every opportunity to visit her in her mother's house which is within walking distance. At the same time she diligently assumes the role of surrogate mother of the judge's children, who still grieve for their real mother, and who now suddenly find a rival for their father's affection in their midst. They never fully accept Farandzem into the family, especially the oldest daughter. It is the custom for children in Armenian culture to address a stepmother as 'mother' or 'mama', but none of Nerses' children ever do. It is a source of heartache for Farandzem that her husband and his children never invite Lena to come to the house, even for a visit.

On Friday, 24 March 1939 Farandzem gives birth to a girl. They call her Marietta. She will be their only child together. The children of Nerses fuss over their little half-sister, creating at last an affinity between themselves and their stepmother, whose presence in their deceased mother's home has been difficult for them. In material terms, life is quite good for the Gukasyans. The judge has built a fine house in Martakert, a substantial town spread out on low hills, with long lanes and narrow cobbled streets where the older houses have ornamental carvings. Theirs is characteristic of the region, two storeys high with a veranda around the upper floor, and set in a walled courtyard with a large garden at the back for vegetables, herbs, fruit trees and vines. It has four bedrooms and a long low-ceilinged kitchen with a wood-burning stove where everyone eats and socializes. Lighting comes from oil lamps and candles. They draw water from a well and chop beech wood for the stove.

Their standard of living, typical of the Caucasus with its Mediterranean-type climate, is far removed from the miserable conditions endured by the millions of Soviet citizens who live in cramped communal apartments in the northern cities

Postcard showing Martakert in 1970.

or in Ukrainian villages devastated by the terrible famines of the early 1930s. The shelves of the state shops in Martakert might frequently be bare, but for her husband and the children Farandzem can always put home-grown food such as tomatoes, beans, lettuce, beetroot, aubergines and cucumbers on the table, served with discs of unleavened bread stuffed with tarragon, and occasionally a red-finned trout from the full-flowing Tartar and Khachen Rivers nearby, or eggs from the hens and ducks that run around the back yards. The marketplace in Martakert is never short of pomegranates, figs, mulberries, apricots, almonds and plums.

With the help of relatives, Nerses and Farandzem make their own red wine from the Khendorni grapes which hang in great bunches from the vines draped over their outdoor din-ner table. They join in collecting mulberries from which the local vodka, *tutovka*, is distilled. With its yellowish-green tint and pungent smell, it is known throughout the region for its ferocious kick.

If they have an advantage over their neighbours through their party membership, it is occasionally finding out when state deliveries are to be made to the *gastronom*, the name given to the ugly concrete and glass provision store in the town centre. Such insider information is highly valued everywhere in the Soviet Union, where basic goods like flour and sugar are chronically *deficit* (in short supply). With private enterprise curtailed, shops rely on deliveries from state warehouses. Provisions are snapped up as soon as they appear, so people have to know in advance to be at the head of the queue or be friendly enough with the manager to buy goods at the back door.

The judge and his young wife sometimes travel together to Stepanakert, fifty kilometres south along an unpaved road clogged with mule-drawn carts and immense flocks of sheep. There one can imagine them savouring the famous *jengyalov hatz* – flatbread baked with twenty-one different herbs and greens – in the *sahooka*, the city's covered market, or strolling along the wide avenues and enjoying the city's culture, perhaps attending performances in the elegant new theatre named after the great Shakespearean actor Vahram Papazyan, except in winter when it is closed, as it has no heating.

In Stepanakert they also sit in on meetings of the Nagorno-Karabakh branch of the Azerbaijan Communist Party, one of the constituent parts of the CPSU. These are held in the party building on Lenin Square, a vast space dominated by a giant statue of the founder of the Soviet Union with outstretched arm indicating the bright future of communism. They are party members in high standing. Farandzem is the type of person who is always involved in society, organizing and helping. While still in her late twenties she is appointed full-time second secretary of the party in the Martakert district, which covers 1,800 square kilometres, has a population of 20,000, and contains 57 villages, 20 secondary schools and several hospitals. It is a position akin to that of deputy mayor, as the party has the last word in local affairs and personnel matters. Farandzem is given an office at the party building in Martakert's central square, and her work takes her to outlying parts of the district. At least twice a year she travels to Baku for plenary meetings of the party.

She and the judge constitute what in modern times would be called a power couple. It is Farandzem's responsibility to supervise party activity in Martakert, and her husband's job to pass judgment on those citizens who are found guilty of anti-party activities such as profiteering.

Visiting Karabakh decades later, I find myself wondering what made Nerses and Farandzem become members of the party. The Armenians are an independent-minded people of an entrepreneurial bent, with a long history here of land ownership and small farms, and a Christian tradition going back centuries. Yet when Bolshevik rule came to Azerbaijan, including Nagorno-Karabakh, in 1920, the commissars acted ruthlessly to collectivize the larger farms and suppress religion. All Karabakh's two hundred and twenty churches and monasteries were closed and many priests were shot or exiled.

This was a deadly blow to Armenian culture and identity. With its unique architecture, language and music, the Apostolic Church is central to Armenian life. It is called Apostolic because the apostles Bartholomew and Thaddeus are believed to have brought Christianity to Armenians in the first century. Some of the finest examples of its art are to be found in the seven-hundred-year-old Gandzasar John the Baptist Monastery, a masterpiece of ancient Armenian architecture perched on a rocky promontory in the Martakert district. Beneath its pointed dome and stone-vaulted ceilings are relics attributed to St John the Baptist, which are credited with many miracles. The monastery has an exceptional *khachkar*, a carved stone slab characteristic of medieval Armenian Christian art, featuring a cross surmounting a solar disc. Dadivank Monastery in the mountains to the west of Martakert is famous for its double *khachkar* on a memorial bell tower.

Perhaps Marietta's parents, like many Armenians, decided to accept and work within the new order because they truly believed in the promise of a better life through social ownership of the means of production, education for the masses and liberation of the proletariat from capitalist exploitation. On the other hand it may simply have been a means to advance their careers. History provides yet another compelling reason. Bolshevik rule promised stability after a period of war and turmoil when Armenians experienced bloodshed on an unprecedented scale.

Nerses was eighteen years of age when the communists took control in 1920. As a law student in Baku, he was exposed to the revolutionary fervour of the time, which may have contributed to his belief in the socialist model. But more significantly he would have known what had happened five years earlier, when he was thirteen. He would have heard stories of fathers shot in front of their children, bodies left to dry in the sun like prunes, babies snatched from their mothers' arms and dashed to the ground in the mass killings that became known as the Armenian Genocide.

This occurred in the Ottoman empire, where the majority of the world's Armenian population lived. Fearing an uprising by their ill-treated Armenian population when under threat of Russian invasion during World War I, the Turkish rulers had initiated a campaign of liquidation. Up to one and a half million Armenians perished. The Armenians of Karabakh escaped the 1915 genocide by virtue of geography, as they lived beyond the reach of the Ottoman military, but they made little distinction between the perpetrators of the massacres and the majority Muslim population of Azerbaijan, including their own Azeri neighbours, whom they still today call Turks. And in the aftermath of the war they had their own smaller episodes of mass killing, as the newly created republics of Azerbaijan and Armenia fought over Nagorno-Karabakh. The bloodshed ended after the Red Army established Moscow's control over both republics in the summer of 1920, but then came a crushing disappointment for the Armenian population of the disputed enclave. Stalin, in his role as commissar of nationalities, decided that Nagorno-Karabakh should be part of Azerbaijan rather than Armenia. A further strip of land to the west was later ceded to Azerbaijan, so that Karabakh became separated from Armenia proper. In 1923 it was made the Nagorno-Karabakh Autonomous Region within Azerbaijan, with a new capital, Stepanakert, named after Stepan Shahumyan, an Armenian communist executed by anti-Bolshevik forces.

The Armenians never concede the right of Soviet Azerbaijan to administer Karabakh, but no change is possible unless Stalin wills it. Meanwhile the two peoples, one Christian, one Muslim, similar to each other in looks and lifestyle and temperament, and subject to the same master, suspend their deadly quarrel.

This is the state of affairs which the generation of Nerses and Farandzem inherits. Relative peace has descended upon the southern Caucasus. Azeri and Armenian peasants work the land side by side during the communal gathering of the grape harvest and wine making. There are even some rare intermarriages. Azeri peasants come into Martakert to sell milk and cheese, and Armenians go to the black market in the nearest Azeri town of Aghdam to trade in commodities. Yet the Armenians and Azeris of Karabakh inhabit parallel universes. Their interactions are at the fringes of their communities, not at the heart. The territorial dispute continues to be articulated by intellectuals and historians in Baku and the Armenian capital Yerevan, and plans to achieve a resolution are merely deferred until central power weakens, as one day it must.

The issue of the status of Karabakh, one can be sure, is never far from the surface at the party meetings in Stepanakert, which are dominated by Armenians, and in 1936 their hopes are revived. A survivor of the 1915 genocide, the first secretary of the Communist Party of the Soviet Socialist Republic of Armenia, Aghasi Khanjyan, with round face, thick moustache and mop of black hair, announces that he will send a petition to his comrade, Josef Stalin, now undisputed ruler of the Soviet Union, to have Karabakh joined to Armenia.

He catalogues their grievances: the history of Armenia is no longer taught in Armenian-language schools, medieval churches and monasteries are being allowed to deteriorate, sometimes with the help of Azeri vandals, and an influx of Azeris has reduced the Armenian majority from 94 to 88 per cent in the first fifteen years of Soviet rule. He submits that the Armenians can claim an unbroken lineage going back to the ancient kingdom of Artsakh two thousand years earlier. He cites evidence of ancient Armenian civilization, the relics of which are found in great abundance everywhere in Karabakh, such as the two-thousand-year-old ruins of an Armenian fortress founded by Tigran the Great, who was king of Armenia when it was the greatest state east of Rome.

The petition is a rash act at a time when the Soviet dictator is embarking on a purge of those who come to his attention for the wrong reasons. Stalin passes it to Lavrenty Beria, to deal with as he sees fit. Beria, a Georgian and first secretary of the Transcaucasian Communist Party, seizes the opportunity to get rid of the charismatic Khanjyan, who is a rival for influence in the mountain republics.

On 9 July 1936 Beria summons Khanjyan to an office in Tbilisi and accuses him of anti-party scheming. That evening the Armenian is found shot dead. By some accounts Beria pulled the trigger himself, though a distraught Khanjyan may have taken his

Beria, instigator of Aghasi Khanjyan's death, with Stalin's daughter and Stalin in the background (undated).

own life. The Soviet newspapers obediently denounce Khanjyan as an enemy of the people and claim that he committed suicide.

Khanjyan is one of the first victims of the Great Terror, instigated by Stalin in every Soviet republic to unmask and eliminate those he considers spies, provocateurs and other enemies of the people. Under Beria's control in the final stages, the secret police dispatch three quarters of a million victims inside two years, mostly with a bullet to the back of the head, on the slimmest of evidence or on the basis of confessions extracted under torture. They include many old Bolsheviks suspected of sympathizing with Stalin's exiled rival Leon Trotsky, who promoted greater democratization in the party. Millions more die in prison camps.

The killing spree in Azerbaijan is conducted by Stalin's right-hand man in Baku, Mir Jafar Baghirov, a former school teacher with hooded eyes and a Hitler moustache who has risen through the ranks of the secret police to become first secretary of the Central Committee of the Azerbaijan Communist Party. Comrades whom Nerses and Farandzem know begin to disappear, as Baghirov organizes the elimination of seventy thousand people, both Azeris and Armenians, including members of the intelligentsia and the communist old guard. One can imagine the apprehension of the newly-weds from Martakert as they come under Baghirov's gaze at the all-republic party meetings in Baku which they attend together during 1937–8. And how they must tremble at night as they listen for the noise of a car engine and the banging on the door that can signify prison or execution. Perhaps like many in a similar situation they have a cardboard suitcase placed by the door, containing essentials for survival in prison. Nerses is himself old guard, contaminated by association with university friends who rose through the party ranks and are being executed for association with Trotskyites. He knows Baghirov of old and Baghirov knows him: when he joined the party, Baghirov was chairman of the Karabakh revolutionary committee.

Among the Karabakh Armenians eliminated are other old associates of Nerses who have sought high office in different republics. They include Levon Mirzoyan, who heads the party in Kazakhstan and makes the mistake of complaining to Stalin about mistreatment of an ethnic group there; Alexander Bekzadyan, the Soviet ambassador to Hungary, guilty of having been abroad – Stalin is suspicious of anyone who witnesses capitalism working; and Suren Sadunts, first party secretary in Tajikistan. The purge officially comes to an end in the autumn of 1938 with an order signed by Beria cancelling systematic repression throughout the Soviet Union and ordering the suspension of death sentences.

The years immediately following the purge are the happiest for Farandzem since the break-up of her first marriage. With the birth of Marietta in 1939 she is fulfilled again as a mother and more closely integrated into Nerses' household. She is soon able to resume her work as second secretary in the party in Martak-ert. There is war in Europe but the Soviet Union has made a pact with Nazi Germany and their part of the world is at peace. The respite does not last.

Chapter 2

A LETTER FROM THE FRONT

On Sunday, 22 June 1941, Moscow Radio, which is broadcast every day from loudspeakers overlooking Martakert town square, begins its programmes with an item for children, followed by news of record output in factories and collective farms and a series of brisk keep-fit exercises. Then there is an unscheduled burst of martial music and the Soviet Union's most important news announcer, Yury Levitan, comes on the air. In a clipped, dramatic manner, as if reciting blank verse, he says, 'Attention. Moscow is speaking. Today at four o'clock in the morning, without presenting any claims to the Soviet Union, without declaring war, German forces invaded our country.' He ends the bulletin with the words, 'Victory will be ours!'

The announcement is a shock to everyone, not least Farandzem, who undoubtedly feels a sense of betrayal, having assured the people of Martakert, on party orders, that under a non-aggression pact signed in August 1939 the Soviet Union was safe from attack by Germany. Doubtless many townsfolk crowd into the Gukasyans' house to discuss this calamitous news with the judge and his wife over glasses of vodka. Farandzem is then summoned with other party officials to Baku for an emergency meeting at which instructions are issued to mobilize the population to assist the war effort and to be on guard against saboteurs and pro-German sentiment.

German troops sweep across the Soviet border, and advance east and south towards the Caucasus with the aim of capturing the oilfields which supply the whole of the USSR. In Martakert men of fighting age not already conscripted are called up.

Among them is Farandzem's younger brother Suren. They are packed onto trucks and taken to Aghdam to board troop transports bound for southern Russia, there to join millions of recruits being formed into fighting divisions. Nerses begins dispatching offenders to the army rather than to prison. He is exempt himself from conscription because of his age – he is thirty-nine – and his position in society.

During the first months of the war Stalin encourages a new policy of friendship among the peoples of the USSR, with the Russians first among equals. The teaching of Russian is made compulsory in all schools to create a one-nation mentality. Brought up speaking Armenian – an independent branch of the Indo-European language tree with its own distinctive alphabet – Nerses' children find themselves having to study a different tongue with a Cyrillic alphabet. The idea is that over time people will perceive their place in the Soviet Union differently, and that by fighting together in the Red Army alongside scores of other nationalities, and speaking one language, they will acquire a firmer Soviet identity.

Stalin also suspends his crackdown on religious practice to rally popular support, and some churches and mosques are permitted to reopen. Despite the fervour of the early years of Soviet rule and the pre-war terror against 'enemies of the people', religious observance has never been thoroughly repressed in Karabakh. It is rare to find a child born to an Armenian family who has not been secretly christened, even in communist households and even during the 1920s persecution.

In Martakert the Armenian Apostolic Church of Surp Hovhannes Mkrtich – St John the Baptist – is located right across the road from the judge's house. Built in 1881 and topped by a cross-bearing pyramid held up by four columns, it has not been converted into a storehouse or allowed to fall into ruin, the fate of many churches throughout the Soviet Union. Nerses and Farandzem seem to have turned a blind eye to religious observance, allowing the church to be used by believers in full view of their home. Marietta recalls watching a tall, skinny priest conduct rituals in the church in a long black robe, and running after him with other children when he came to conduct baptisms. The priest would fill a bucket of water from a little stream that runs by the church, immerse his cross in it, and sprinkle drops over the child's head. Afterwards women would take bottles of the holy water to bless their houses.

Party figures cannot be seen to be religious, however, and Nerses and Farandzem never invite the priest into their house. They chastise the children one Easter Sunday on discovering they have joined other boys and girls in placing painted Easter eggs around a 'sacred' tree on a nearby hillside.

In the first year of the Nazi invasion, the war goes terribly badly for the Soviet Union. Rostov-on-Don, the last major obstacle for the Germans on the road to the Caucasus, falls to the Wehrmacht in mid-summer 1942. In a battle for the Kerch Peninsula between the Azov and Black Seas, one hundred and seventy-six thousand Red Army soldiers, mostly from the Caucasus, are killed. Martakert loses several of its young men to the fighting. The wailing of distraught wives and parents marks the arrival of each notification of death. Farandzem frets about the fate of her younger brother when his letters stop coming in the post. No word is heard from Suren for several months. He is listed as missing. Eventually a communication arrives from the military with the news that he is dead. Their mother, half-demented with grief, refuses to believe he is not coming back. She takes to wandering the streets, calling out to groups of returning soldiers, 'Have you seen my boy? Is he with you?'

In July 1942, Nerses Gukasyan volunteers for service in the Soviet army. He is old enough to avoid compulsory conscription, but he is also old enough to remember that Turkey fought alongside Germany in the previous war, and the former Ottoman empire is now supplying the Nazi war machine with raw materials. Turkey will undoubtedly come in on the German side if the Nazi armies are not stopped, with bloody consequences for the Armenians of the southern Caucasus. More likely however it is simply expected of him. The beleaguered Soviet Union needs able-bodied men of all ages and is intent on total mobilization.

Marietta aged two in 1941, in Martakert. It is her only childhood photo.

On the day Nerses Gukasyan and other middle-aged volunteers and recruits depart from Martakert on an open ZiS-5 military truck all the townspeople turn out to bid them farewell, many shedding tears. Marietta, three years old and in her heartsick mother's arms, has a vivid memory of people running after the lorries as they roar off in clouds of dust.

War refugees trickle into town. A Byelorussian animal doctor and her younger sister are billeted in the Gukasyan house, and stay until the fighting ends.

In the next two years Nerses comes back twice, for visits of only a few hours each time, once when his mother, who lives nearby, is ill, and once when she dies. On the first occasion he

Farandzem with Nerses before he returned to the front in 1943.

poses for a photograph with Farandzem. He is seated, wearing a lieutenant's cap and ill-fitting summer tunic with shoulder boards and deep breast pockets. He has lost weight and his unsmiling face is gaunt. She stands beside him in a dark costume and necklace, her hair trimmed below the ears in the fashion of the time, her expression equally serious. On the second visit, early in 1944, he appears unexpectedly at the door wearing an unbuttoned greatcoat over his uniform. His face full of emotion, he gathers Marietta in his arms as she rushes to greet him. That is her last memory of him.

Marietta often wonders in later life what suffering her father endured and what horrors he witnessed during his two years fighting with the Red Army. We know that when he joined up he was enrolled in the 38th Rifle Division which had been recreated and re-equipped after being wiped out near Smolensk in the first six months of the war. Based on contemporary accounts he would have undergone a few weeks' basic training, and been issued with a fifty-year-old carbine and a rank-and-file uniform consisting of a cotton tunic, trousers, a soft hat, ankle boots, and metre-long foot cloths. The 38th Rifle Division was attached to the 40th Army which was assigned to defend a sector of the River Don, and for five months Nerses would have seen little action. In January 1943 the 40th Army began a series of engagements, defeating Hungarian and Italian forces near Voronezh, until it was pushed back into defensive positions by a German counter-offensive north-west of Kharkov at the end of February. In July 1943 it was engaged in ferocious fighting against the German 4th Panzer Army at the Battle of Kursk, after which the Germans lost the strategic initiative and began their long retreat.

The 40th Army subsequently helped liberate Kiev in December 1943 and was then deployed south, as part of the 2nd Ukrainian Front under General Ivan Konev. The 38th Rifle Division took part in the capture of Kishinev in the spring of 1944. It then made an unsuccessful attempt to take the key Romanian town of Targu Frumos in May 1944. This was the first incursion by Soviet troops across the land border of the Soviet Union. For three months the front line stabilized and the Red Army built up its strength while successfully fooling the Germans into thinking it was redeploying most of its forces to the north. For Nerses this would have provided a welcome respite from the extreme fatigue, bitter cold, physical hardships and frequent near-death experiences common to front-line Soviet soldiers.

The delay in pushing on into Romania was fatal for most of the hundred and fifty thousand Jews of northern Transylvania, including 3,149 from the Reghin ghetto. On 4 June they were put on trains bound for Auschwitz in Poland, there to be exterminated.

On 20 August 1944, the guns of the Soviet 40th Army, under Lieutenant General Filipp Zhmachenko, opened up all along the northern Romanian front. The 38th Rifle Division advanced westwards through the spruce forests of the eastern Carpathian mountains that form an arc through central and eastern parts of Europe, and engaged German and Romanian forces in Reghin district.

Some time during the week-long fighting Lieutenant Gukasyan was injured. The archives do not reveal how he was wounded or how seriously. But a lieutenant was expected to go ahead of his platoon of about forty soldiers against incoming fire, and the fact that he was subsequently awarded a Red Star would indicate that Nerses Gukasyan led his 343 Group with courage and was most likely shot while doing so. In fact it is remarkable that he had stayed alive for two years at the front, as very few rifle group commanders survived for long in the Soviet army. The casualties were brought to a field hospital in the village of Tisieu. There he lay, fighting for his life, for more than a month.

With immediate medical treatment Nerses Gukasyan might have survived, but conditions at the front were wretched.

Stomach wounds often led to fatal infections. There were desperate shortages of dressings, sterile instruments and cleaning baths in Soviet field hospitals, described memorably by Russian war correspondent Vasily Grossman as places of 'blood-stained rags, scraps of flesh, moans, subdued howling, hundreds of dismal, suffering eyes'.

All around was chaos. Behind the Soviet riflemen came a poorly equipped ragtag army of mainly Ukrainian peasants, recruited from villages devastated by a brutal collectivization programme and a terrible famine a decade earlier. With little political or military training, they had orders to live off the land, which they enthusiastically obeyed. They were by all accounts shocked at the neatness and prosperity of the villages and the dwellings they came across. Some soldiers from poorly managed and wasteful collective farms are said to have wept when they saw the pretty houses, the fattened cattle and the well-stocked barns of the so-called capitalist world, reminiscent of the countryside their parents knew in Ukraine and Russia before Stalin's war on independent farmers. They wept for a way of life and a prosperity that could have been theirs if not for communism.

Nerses may have written to his family, expressing his hopes and saying farewell, as he most likely knew he was dying. On 19 September a senior officer presented him with the Red Star medal certificate for bravery. Eleven days later, on Saturday, 30 September, he died. No letters or documents were ever sent on to Farandzem. His personal belongings disappeared with him.

Those who died in the field hospital or whose bodies were brought in from the battlefield were buried in numbered joint graves beside the school in Tisieu. When one was filled, a new grave was dug. Marietta's father was interred in grave No. 7 alongside twenty-four-year-old Lieutenant Pavel Razbegaev from Georgia, like Nerses a member of the communist party, and Junior Lieutenant Nikolai Yakovlev, aged twenty, from the Tatar Autonomous Republic. There their remains lay as the Red Army raced on through Romania towards the Balkans, until Soviet units returned to exhume the bodies of hundreds of soldiers, including Nerses, from their scattered graves, and rebury them in one place where a future monument could be erected to honour them all.

Marietta learns of her papa's death one day early in October 1944. She is on her way home from kindergarten with her cousin, who is a teacher at the play school, when she sees women in black gathered outside her house. The five-year-old runs inside to find everyone in tears. Her mother wraps her arms around Marietta and says, 'We have lost your papa. Your papa is not coming back.'

A letter from the Soviet army has been delivered. Farandzem knew its contents before she opened it; she has comforted neighbouring women who have received similar messages. The letter from the front does not say where Nerses has died, or how, or where he is buried, only that he has given his life for the Motherland. What follows is now a routine in the death-shrouded town, whose menfolk are being lost one by one in far-away battlefields: word spreads up and down the narrow alleyways, women in black shawls come hurrying to comfort the widow, neighbours bring supplies of bread, vegetables and *tutovka* for the mourners. Bewildered by the sight of weeping adults, Marietta tries to absorb what is happening. It will be some time before she grasps fully that her father is dead. She continues to hope that he will again arrive home one day and sweep her up in his arms. Only later does she come to realize the enormity of what has happened in her life.

Nerses Gukasyan's death is a blow to Martakert. He was the district judge and a party member, and a figure of importance. Farandzem is comforted by party colleagues who come to express sympathy, including the first secretary of Nagorno-Karabakh, a contemporary of Nerses – both were born in 1902 and experienced together the early days of Bolshevik rule.

Farandzem's anguish is compounded by her inability to grieve at the burial place of her dead husband, because there is no body and no grave. She has to cope with her own and Marietta's distress, along with that of the now-orphaned children from Nerses' first marriage, and has to face a new reality. The figure of authority who held the household together is no more. The oldest girls, Siranush and Haikanush, are almost adults; Alyosha is fifteen and Greta is twelve. Farandzem is a twice-married woman living with children not her own. As Nerses' widow, she has claim to the house and this becomes a source of resentment with the oldest daughter who never fully welcomed Farandzem as a stepmother in the first place. Nevertheless life goes on. Farandzem insists on each child getting technical education in Stepanakert after leaving school. She continues to work for the party and enrols Marietta as a Little Octobrist, a member of the communist organization for children aged nine and under, so called for the October Revolution. In the summer of 1945 she sends her daughter to a Little Octobrists summer camp in the old Karabakh capital, Shushi. Marietta finds herself in a frightening landscape of half-ruined buildings. As strong-willed as her mother, she slips out of the camp, determined to go home. As she stumbles down the serpentine road leading to Stepanakert, a kindly adult sees her distress and takes her all the way back to Martakert. Alyosha, ten years Marietta's senior, takes it upon himself to look after his little half-sister in the absence of their father. He carries her on his shoulders when going out to meet his pals. They do chores together, such as picking fruit and vegetables and feeding the poultry. He speaks up for her on occasion, and once begs Farandzem not to be cross when she discovers Marietta has innocently eaten the precious store of sugar put by to serve to visitors with tea. One New Year's Eve when Alyosha, over the objections of the others, insists that it is not too cold to sleep on the veranda, Marietta joins him and they huddle in blankets under the stars, freezing. They form a bond that lasts a lifetime.

Aged ten in 1949, Marietta is enrolled in the Young Pioneers. With her classmates, she promises to study and fight as the great Lenin has instructed and as the communist party teaches.

By now Greta, the youngest of the judge's children by his first wife, is seventeen and has finished her studies. It is probably at this point that Farandzem begins to feel she has done her duty by her dead husband, having raised his children to adulthood, and rethinks her whole life. She is still in her mid-thirties and is an ambitious and active woman. She feels increasingly uncomfortable living with the adult children of her dead husband.

Her daughter Lena from her first marriage, whom she left to her mother to look after, is now almost seventeen. Farandzem has monitored her education and arranged for her also to attend the technical college in Stepanakert. She begins to contemplate a new life for herself and her two girls, but not in Martakert, where she has to wear a widow's weeds and where her daughters' prospects are limited.

Farandzem's future, and that of Marietta and Lena, is decided by a letter from a friend who has spent some years away from Martakert. He writes enthusiastically about life in an oil town in southern Russia. It has plenty of accommodation and opportunities for work. It enjoys a similar climate. It has shops, factories, theatres, good roads and electric trams. There is an established Armenian community of more than ten thousand which is welcoming to newcomers. If Farandzem ever decides to come and take her chances there, he and his wife would put them up until they find their feet.

Farandzem seizes upon the opportunity offered. She announces to her stepchildren that she and Marietta will be going to live somewhere else. She tells them she will lay no claim on the house, which is rightfully hers as Nerses' widow. Instead she will relinquish the house and everything in it to twenty-one-year-old Alyosha, the male among them. The young man is heartbroken that his half-sister Marietta will no longer be around and promises to visit them when they have settled into a new home. For the daughters from Nerses' first marriage it is an occasion of conflicting emotions. They may have resented the presence of their stepmother in place of their real mother but Farandzem has been a provider and has looked after their wellbeing and education, and the tears flow.

Farandzem resigns her post as second secretary in the Martakert party. The news that she is leaving comes as something of a shock to the townspeople who have got used to her organizing presence in their lives.

Farandzem undoubtedly has mixed feelings as the day of departure nears. She is a prominent person in Martakert, with many friends and with family ties. She has known no other life. But after her miserable first marriage, her chance of future happiness and fulfilment died with Nerses. All her emotions and aspirations are now tied up in the fate of her two girls.

The evening before leaving Farandzem packs her few possessions into a cardboard suitcase and a fabric bag. She probably doesn't have much: a small amount of savings, one change of clothes for each of them, some family photographs, and cheese, fruit, hard-boiled eggs, walnuts and sweets for the journey.

It is not hard to imagine that she spends a sleepless night, filled with contrasting emotions: sorrow at parting from the life she knows, fear of what lies ahead, but excitement at being her own person again. Marietta too is fretful, not having any concept of what the future holds, aware only that she is being wrenched away from everything familiar, the house, her school, her childhood friends, and most of all Alyosha, who is so fiercely protective of her and whom she regards, and always will, as a brother, not a half-brother.

Next day, Sunday, 5 November 1950, the two females bid a tearful farewell to Farandzem's mother and older daughter Lena. Farandzem promises that as soon as Lena finishes her technical course in Stepanakert next year she will send the train fare so that she may join them in their new home. Then the thirty-eight-year-old widow and her eleven-year-old daughter board the bus for Aghdam railway station, and begin their journey to a new life, in a town called Grozny.

CHAPTER 3

CITY OF LOST SOULS

IN AGHDAM FARANDZEM and Marietta board an overcrowded train that takes them to Baku. In the Azerbaijan capital they change to a long-distance train for a twenty-hour journey to Grozny. It passes through a hellish vista of leaking and flaming oil wells and industrial waste in northern Azerbaijan. The toxic stench seeps into the carriages. After a stop at the port city of Makhachkala on the Caspian Sea, the train turns west, and for more than two hours passes through a landscape of deserted villages where weeds choke the lanes around derelict cottages. They are now in the Russian territory known historically as Chechnya, situated on the northern slopes of the Great Caucasus Range and bordered by Dagestan to the east, Russia to the north, North Ossetia to the west and Georgia to the south.

When the train pulls into Grozny station it is early on a rainy Tuesday morning. One can imagine them stepping down onto the platform, exhausted and confused, a striking Armenian woman carrying a suitcase in one hand and a multicoloured sack in the other, telling her eleven-year-old child to stay close in the crowd of mostly Russians and Ukrainians on the platform.

The pair make their way through the arch of the two-storey waiting room with its framed picture of Stalin. Their first impression of Grozny is of taxi drivers shouting and trucks revving their engines, and the slightly rank smell of people and petrol and cardboard cigarettes. It is a bewildering, noisy, dirty, muddy world compared to the tranquil, sun-drenched town they have left behind. Here the air is gritty and oily smoke darkens the sky. They take a bus past factories and breeze-block apartment buildings with washing hanging from the windows to the address supplied by her friend. It turns out to be a house in the suburbs. The Karabakh family is expecting them and is happy to accommodate them until they find their own place. Three days after arriving, Farandzem takes Marietta to the local school, where teaching is in Russian. The pre-teen has only a rudimentary knowledge of the language and feels isolated and disoriented until she finds there are a few other children from different parts of the Soviet Union who are also struggling with Russian. In a matter of weeks, however, she is chattering away in Russian with new school friends.

After a month Farandzem finds a single-room apartment in the Oil Workers' Block, a one-storey building designed like a motel, situated halfway along Pavel Musorov Street, a leafy thoroughfare south of the city centre. Their room shares an entrance with another one-room dwelling occupied by an old Russian called Natasha who does housework for local people, including an Armenian woman called Sonia who lives in a fine house across the road. There is not much privacy. People sit and talk on benches right outside their window, and there is always noise with doors slamming and trams clanking past.

Farandzem finds a job behind the counter in a state store. She gets her *propiska*, the document giving her the right to live in Grozny. Unemployment is officially non-existent in the Soviet Union, and the new arrival from Nagorno-Karabakh has to take what is on offer. Marietta is big enough to look after herself outside school hours, and friendly Natasha in the next room can keep an eye on her. The former party second secretary from Martakert registers with the Grozny branch of the communist party, which is almost entirely dominated by Russians, and is readily accepted into their ranks. Of the one hundred or so officially registered nationalities in the Soviet Union, Armenians and Russians get on reasonably well, partly because of their shared Christian background and common antipathy towards Muslims, though it doesn't stop some Russians casually lumping all Caucasians, including Armenians, together as *chyorniye* or *chyorno-zhopiye* – blacks or black arses. With its membership of the Soviet Union guaranteeing security against the Turks, Armenia is the most loyal of the outlying Soviet republics. The Kremlin classifies Armenians as one of five advanced nationalities living inside Soviet borders, the others being Russians, Ukrainians, Volga Germans and Jews. Armenians are perceived to be a clever and intellectual people like the Jews, well represented in intellectual and party life, but because of their Christian ancestry not subject to anything like the lethal anti-Semitic prejudice which occasionally manifests itself in Russia.

Armenians are in fact disproportionately represented in the ranks of the *nomenklatura*, the higher levels of the Soviet bureaucracy that services the party and the ministries. In a backhanded compliment to their resourcefulness and wit, Russians use a mythical Armenian radio station to make sly jibes at the system, citing for example an Armenian radio report proving that the Soviet Union has as much free speech as the United States, because, just as an American in Washington can freely shout 'Down with capitalism!' a Russian may also shout 'Down with capitalism!' in Moscow without fear of the consequences.

Judging by contemporary accounts of communist party activities in the early 1950s, the branch meetings which Farandzem attends in Grozny's party headquarters are taken up with paeans of praise for Stalin and the reading aloud of letters of admiration and adulation from factory and collective-farm workers, which will be sent to the Kremlin to ensure the leader's favour.

Stalin is everywhere in the oil town. His picture looks down from the walls of official buildings, factories, shops and private homes. He is the father of the nation. The newspapers describe him as the beloved leader, the military genius who won the Great Patriotic War and has made the Soviet Union into a world super-power.

Some months after settling in Grozny, Farandzem returns briefly to Martakert where her mother is dying. After the funeral she makes final arrangements for Lena to join her and Marietta. The nineteen-year-old arrives at Grozny railway station on an early summer day in 1951. At last Farandzem's dream of a new life together with her daughters is fulfilled. Lena understands why she could not live with her mother in Martakert and she never feels any resentment. Despite the seven-year difference in age, Lena and Marietta become close. In Martakert they lived under separate roofs. Here they are united with their mother, the lodestone of their lives, and the teenager is delighted to assume the role of big sister and take Marietta under her wing. The younger girl's heart swells with happiness. The three females, living, for now, in one room, which brings them closer together in every sense, must find their feet in a new world and adapt to a new language, which they quickly master, though they will always have slight accents which betray their southern origins. Lena benefits from the technical education upon which her mother insisted in Nagorno-Karabakh and soon secures work as a seamstress.

With her service to the party and her status as a war widow, Farandzem lands a better job. She becomes a conductress on the Grozny-to-Moscow train. Though it takes her away from home for four days at a time – two days there and two days back – this is a coveted and well-paid post, reserved for applicants with a good *kharakteristika*, the official reference document that evaluates the conformity of a Soviet citizen. She comes to an arrangement with Natasha next door to look after Marietta while she is travelling and Lena is at work.

Marietta at sixteen in Grozny, 1955.

Everyone aspires to go to Moscow. The capital city is the centre of the country's political, economic and cultural life and the Soviet Union's showcase to the world. Access is difficult for provincial folk, and special permission has to be obtained to stay for more than one night. The stores are better stocked and cheaper than in the provinces. But even here there are shortages. At stops along the way passengers dismount to buy boxes of fruit and vegetables from peasants to take to Moscow, where delights such as cherries and honey are often *deficit*. Marietta's mother sometimes comes home with boxes of tropical fruits, different types of cloth, cheese, sweets, and – a real treat – chocolate-coated wafers from Moscow's famous Bolshevik Biscuit Factory.

On Friday, 6 March 1953 people gather in the square by Grozny's Lermontov Theatre in anticipation of an announcement of great importance. Then nearly fourteen, Marietta is marched there with all her classmates from school. Lena is somewhere in the crowd too. Radio Moscow is broadcasting solemn orchestral music. The music stops at 2.55 p.m. In a sonorous voice the conveyor of momentous news, Yury Levitan, declares, 'The heart of the collaborator and follower of the genius of Lenin's work, the wise leader and teacher of the communist party and of the Soviet people, has stopped beating.' There is silence. Looking around, the schoolgirls see some people crying. Most just stand there, absorbing the news, before drifting away. Stalin is dead. For thirty years the Soviet people have known no other leader. As the poet Yevgeny Yevtushenko would later say, 'Trained to believe that they were all in Stalin's care, people were lost and bewildered without him.'

Farandzem is on the Moscow-bound train when the news comes through. Passengers weep in the carriage corridors. In Moscow two days later hundreds of people die in a stampede of mourners trying to get a glimpse of Stalin's remains.

The news leaves the Russians in Grozny in a state of shock. Under Stalin's iron rule the city has enjoyed post-war stability. What will become of it now? Will *they* be allowed to come back and reclaim their properties?

They are the Chechens, who for centuries populated the land around Grozny along with a smaller number of related people known as the Ingush, and all of whom disappeared almost overnight at the height of the war, leaving Grozny and the surrounding countryside to be populated by mostly Slavic settlers. They were rounded up and deported in 1944, less than a decade earlier, though it took two years for the Kremlin to acknowledge this, in an item on 25 June 1946 in the party newspaper *Pravda* (Truth) which disclosed that, under a decree issued by the Russian Supreme Soviet, the Chechen and Ingush peoples had been 'settled' in Kazakhstan and other parts of the eastern steppes on the grounds that during the war many had volunteered for military formations organized by the Germans.

Newcomers to Grozny like Farandzem can hardly be blamed for not knowing that the forced removal of the native population had less to do with their role in the war against Germany, which was marginal, than with a decision by Stalin to get rid of a people who for two centuries had thwarted the goal of the complete Russification of the northern Caucasus.

Russian enmity towards the Chechens dates back to the 1780s, when Catherine the Great sent imperial troops to conquer the mountain range stretching from the Black Sea to the Caspian Sea. Under their leader Al-Imam al-Mansur al-Mutawakil 'ala Allah, the Chechens resisted fiercely and kept the Russians at bay behind the Terek River until 1818, when Tsar Alexander I sent General Alexander Yermolov to subdue the mountain tribes. Yermolov, whose disdain for his foes matched his cruelty, established a military outpost and named it Grozny (Threatening). His conquests were romanticized by Russian poets, who saw his bloody campaigns as attempts to civilize barbarians, the 'wicked Chechens' as Mikhail Lermontov, the 'poet of the Caucasus', famously called them. 'Bow down your snowy head, O Caucasus: Yermolov is coming,' wrote Russia's favourite poet Alexander Pushkin.

The Chechens stubbornly declined to bow down and fought a thirty-year war of resistance led by a guerrilla commander called Shamil, who united the tribes by imposing sharia law. Russian forces burned villages and crops and cut down beech forests to deprive the insurgents of cover and in the end they did prevail, although for decades afterwards bands of Chechen fighters wielding sabres continued to raid military encampments, becoming the bogeymen of Russian literature and fuelling the nightmares of Russian children.

The discovery of oil in 1893 made Grozny an important rail and road terminus in the Russian empire, and during the civil war which followed the 1917 Revolution, White Army generals committed atrocities against the Chechens in a struggle for the oilfields. After the Bolshevik triumph in 1920, Lenin established the Mountainous Autonomous Republic with Grozny as its capital, and granted the Chechens considerable cultural and religious freedoms. In 1936 Stalin created the Chechen-Ingush Autonomous Republic but made sure it came under the heel of the Kremlin by executing fourteen thousand Chechens and Ingush who had been opposing collectivization and enforced atheism. Resistance continued in mountain villages, yet Russians living in Grozny were often grateful to the Chechens for supplying the city with food when much of the Soviet Union faced starvation in the 1930s.

During the German invasion of Russia, the Luftwaffe bombed Grozny and German parachutists recruited groups of Chechen fighters in the mountain valleys. A far greater number of Chechens however – thirty thousand – served in the Red Army and some became Heroes of the Soviet Union. When the Wehrmacht's advance stalled, the rebellion in the mountains petered out.

Sure of winning the war, Stalin resolved to succeed where Yermolov had failed. With the world distracted he would get rid of the troublesome Caucasian tribes for good by transferring them to the wilderness of the eastern Soviet Union. He gave the job of uprooting and deporting the Chechen and Ingush to Lavrenty Beria, who had done Stalin's bloodletting for him in the purges of the late 1930s. Beria was now in charge of the political police, the NKVD, and had expanded it into an army of two hundred thousand personnel including a military force, secret police, border guards and a detachment known as SMERSH (Death to Spies) notorious for shooting Soviet soldiers who retreated in battle.

The planning involved extraordinary duplicity. In the winter of 1943–4 Beria deployed tens of thousands of NKVD troops in the northern Caucasus on 'exercises'. All inhabitants were ordered to gather in village and town squares at dawn on

23 February 1944 to celebrate Red Army Day. No one had any knowledge of what was about to happen, though there were hints: in one village the evening before, a soldier told an old woman to stop cutting wood as she was wasting her time. That fateful day, as heavy snow fell, troops herded Chechen and Ingush people at gunpoint onto thousands of Studebaker five-ton trucks brought in through Iran as part of America's contribution to the Soviet war effort and began taking them to Grozny central railway station.

Even Chechens and Ingush who had cooperated with the NKVD and served with distinction in the Soviet armed forces were bundled onto the transports, having been extracted from their units at the front with the promise of home leave. Those considered to be 'untransportable' were liquidated. In the village of Khaibakh, 704 men, women and children were burned to death in a barn on the orders of a NKVD colonel because thick snow made moving them difficult. Sixty-two patients were taken from their beds in the Urus Martan hospital and shot.

At the station the stunned and bewildered victims were transferred to unheated wooden freight cars and disease-ridden cattle wagons which had been brought in from all over southern Russia, each numbered and stamped with the hammer and sickle and the letters USSR. Every day for the next six days, up to thirty trains, some consisting of one hundred wagons, pulled out of the station heading east, taking men, women and children to the arid and freezing steppes of Kazakhstan, where they were unceremoniously dumped.

Such a large operation, going on around the clock, could not go unnoticed. Scores of Grozny citizens waiting to go over the level crossing on Prospect (Avenue) Lenina witnessed the passing of the carriages with their human cargo. Among them was a fourteen-year-old native of Grozny of mixed Russian and Armenian blood called Stanislav Suvorov. The teenager had been

Last glimpse of home: Chechen children being deported in 1944 to Kazakhstan.

required to leave school the previous year to take the place of a worker at Shoe Factory No. 1 who had been called up for military service. Stanislav and his mother, who worked in the factory as an accountant, commuted by tram from their home on Pavel Musorov Street to their workplace across town. Every day they had to dismount at the level crossing and walk over the railway line to board a tram at the other side. That week their journey was disrupted several times as the long trains shunted slowly by, gradually picking up speed, the shrieking of their steam whistles drowning out the cries of the people crammed inside. In this way Stanislav and his mother witnessed Stalin's crime. They did so in silence, I imagine, standing in the trodden snow, avoiding eye contact with other people. In Stalin's Russia no one spoke to strangers about matters that did not concern them. Later Stanislav went with some friends to a Chechen village to see for himself what was happening and was distressed to find the house where a Chechen friend lived empty and looted. He knew that the families of his Chechen and Ingush friends had nothing to do with helping the Germans. Some of their fathers had died in the Great Patriotic War fighting for Stalin. The sense of injustice affected him deeply. His Chechen school pals had done nothing wrong as far as he was concerned. They were just as frightened as he was when the Nazi bombs fell on Grozny, destroying much of the city centre.

Over the next two months the trains returned empty and then steamed off in the opposite direction, carrying livestock rounded up from Chechen and Ingush holdings for delivery to collective farms in southern Russia and Ukraine.

Years later historians established that some four hundred and eighty thousand Chechens and ninety-six thousand Ingush in total were deported and that an estimated third to a half of them died on the hellish journey to Kazakhstan or shortly afterwards. Their absence accounted for the deserted villages which Farandzem saw from the windows of the train when she first came to Grozny. After their forced departure, Chechen settlements, mosques, libraries and artefacts were systematically destroyed, their gravestones torn up from cemeteries for use in road building. All references to the Chechen and Ingush peoples were excised from a new edition of the thirty-volume *Great Soviet Encyclopedia*. They were never mentioned in the newspapers. They ceased to exist in their own homeland. What Stalin did was an attempt to destroy the essential foundations of the life of an entire group, an act which qualifies for the term genocide as defined by the Polish lawyer Raphael Lemkin in the late 1940s.

When the operation was completed, and Grozny had become a city of lost souls, Stalin abolished the Chechen-Ingush Autonomous Republic and divided its territory among the adjoining republics. On Beria's instructions a statue of Yermolov was erected in the city centre, inscribed with the general's opinion of the Chechens: THERE ARE NO OTHER PEOPLE UNDER THE SUN MORE VILE OR DECEITFUL.

The Great Patriotic War ended on 9 May 1945, and homeless people from devastated parts of Russia, Ukraine and Byelorussia – today Belarus – began arriving and occupying the empty houses in and around Grozny. Any feelings of guilt they might have had were assuaged by assurances that the Chechens were traitors to the Motherland who deserved their fate.

But now, with Stalin gone, their world is no longer quite so secure.

CHAPTER 4

THE SHOEMAKER

STANISLAV ALEXANDROVICH SUVOROV was born in Grozny on 26 February 1929. His father, Alexander Suvorov, was a highly qualified Russian mechanic who came to the Caucasus from Ryazan to do specialized work repairing German-made sewing machines. His name is the same as that of a famous eighteenth-century Russian military leader, the only tsarist general never to lose a battle and incidentally Yermolov's role model.

A work collective at Grozny sewing machine repair factory in 1927. Alexander Suvorov, Stanislav's father, is second from left.

In Grozny Alexander met and fell in love with Siranush – whom everyone calls Sonia. She was a member of a prominent Armenian family and her father forbade her to marry a Russian, but Sonia defied him. Stanislav was their only child. Seven months after their son was born, the sewing-machine repairman contracted pneumonia and was admitted to hospital. On discharge he made the mistake of drinking cold beer with a friend and suffered a relapse. Alexander died aged twenty-seven, leaving Sonia a widow.

Thereafter Sonia's life is so full of drama that in later years she likes to joke that she will give the details to Mikhail Sholokhov, author of the literary sensation *And Quiet Flows the Don*, so he can write a novel about her. It is a story of family turmoil and changing allegiances. First she meets another Russian and moves with him to the Black Sea city of Sochi, but he is abusive to little Stanislav so she leaves him and comes back to Grozny. There she

Stanislav as a child in 1931, with his mother Sonia.

begins work as an accountant in Shoe Factory No. 1 where in 1940 she finds a new partner in the shape of a fellow employee, a tall, slim, gaunt-cheeked Armenian cobbler called Bakhshi, nineteen years her senior.

Originally from Baku, Bakhshi has endured a life marked by family discord and tragedy. He divorced his first wife, an Armenian, with whom he had a son, Volodya. His second wife, a Jewish woman with whom he had a daughter, Sveta, met a violent end: she was murdered when travelling by train from Baku to Leningrad by a fellow passenger for the money she was carrying.

Though they do not marry, Stanislav's mother and her new partner start a family. They have a daughter, Nellya. They also have a son but, in another tragedy for the Baku shoemaker, and for Sonia, the boy, barely into his second year, dies from sepsis contracted from a stick which he pokes into his own eye.

Stanislav's stepfather Bakhshi, half-sister Nellya and mother Sonia, 1952.

Stanislav with his stepfather Bakhshi, mother Sonia and Sveta and Nellya in 1955.

Bakhshi builds a rambling one-storey brick house for his new family, Sonia, Nellya and Stanislav, on Pavel Musorov Street in Grozny and the young Stanislav is happy to regard Bakhshi as his new papa. The union of Bakhshi and Sonia is an attraction of opposites. Bakhshi is a modest man with a wry sense of humour, who works hard and says little. Sonia is a loud-voiced woman who has accumulated considerable wealth in the form of crystal glasses, antiques, silver cutlery, brass candlesticks and a wardrobe full of fine clothes, though she wears old dresses and lets the house fall into disrepair. She hates spending money and is notorious for buying the cheapest things, such as tomatoes fit only for cooking. Sonia's talents lie in dealing. She dominates the neighbourhood committee, and people turn to her for advice and letter writing and small cash loans. Nicknamed the commissar, she earns some extra income on top of her salary as an accountant by leasing out three small rooms with separate entrances at the back of the house, one of which is used by an Armenian tenant as an unofficial barber's shop.

All of this makes Sonia something of a *bourgeoise* in communist Russia. She even has a Russian housemaid, Natasha, an old woman from a one-room apartment in the Oil Workers' Block across the road, who does occasional cleaning for her. Unsurprisingly Sonia is not a member of the communist party.

Stanislav's mother Sonia in her early thirties, 1938.

By contrast, Sonia's younger sister Anna Mesropova, Stanislav's aunt, is a party member of high repute, a graduate of the Rostov-on-Don Railway Institute who will one day be elected to the Supreme Soviet in Moscow, the highest legislative body in the Soviet Union. She is, as they say, a 'capital-letter person'.

Stanislav grows into a sturdy broad-faced schoolboy with thick dark hair parted in the middle and a sunny disposition that matches his willingness to turn his hand to anything. He is usually taken for an ethnic Russian because he has inherited his father's Slavic looks and his famous Russian surname. At school he makes friends easily among his Russian, Armenian and Jewish classmates, and also with the small number of Chechen and Ingush pupils whose parents have migrated from the villages to work in the factories and oil installations. These native children hold themselves aloof, and the others generally avoid them because they are fierce and hit back without mercy in a fight.

Stanislav is a good student and an avid reader, but his future is determined by his new stepfather. Bakhshi converts an outhouse into a cobbler's workshop and sets up a small business making and mending shoes in the evenings and at weekends. Stanislav starts spending time with him there, watching in fascination, and helping when asked. Bakhshi impresses upon him the dignity of the profession, and how it was ennobled by the Roman brothers Crispin and Crispinian, the patron saints of shoemaking who were martyred in the early days of Christianity. Working with Bakhshi, Stanislav learns the first principles of bespoke shoemaking: how the foot is an arch composed of a series of bones with elasticity in the sole so that the weight of the body is thrust down on the arch, and how it is the shoemaker's responsibility to enable the free action of the tendons and muscles and to allow for the spread of the toes and the elongation of the foot when walking. Bakhshi emphasizes to him the importance of making precise measurements with a compass and of having a good hardwood last to replicate the foot, and how to adjust it by tacking on strips of leather. He shows the teenager which way to use a feather knife to put grooves in the leather, and if he cuts himself accidentally – it happens to Bakhshi all the time – how to close the wound with a Russian medical glue called BF-6, which he shouldn't confuse with the industrial version used for repairing shoes and boots.

His mentor lets Stanislav experiment with discarded bits of leather on his sewing machine, and teaches him how to use the various hammers and pincers and nail removers, and the difference between an in-seaming awl and a fine-closing awl, and how to make laces by waxing thread and how to cut patterns for the sole. Above all, Bakhshi stresses the significance of 'reading' leather, demonstrating how the skin of the breast and the stomach of the cow tends to be flabby, and the leather of the neck is always coarse, but skin from the ribs has the best texture – and even then to look carefully for flaws caused by barbed wire or thorns.

In 1943, when aged fourteen, Stanislav has no choice but to exchange his school books for wartime replacement work in Grozny's shoe-manufacturing enterprise. The factory is working flat out to deal with a chronic lack of footwear for millions of soldiers. It is mass-producing military boots made with kirza, a combination of artificial pig leather and compressed layers of cotton fabric, based on a formula developed in Kirov at the start of the war, and considered in hindsight to be as important an invention as the Katyusha rocket launcher in achieving victory over the Germans. By the end of the fighting an estimated ten million Soviet soldiers will be wearing kirza boots. The switch in production in shoe factories of course means that the shortage of civilian footwear becomes acute.

Stanislav does not return to school after the war ends in September 1945, but stays on at the factory to complete his formal apprenticeship. Two years later, upon reaching the age of eighteen, he is conscripted into the Soviet army to do his national service. The young Russian-Armenian packs his shoemaking tools with his kit and sets off to Mineralnye Vody, a town three hundred kilometres north-west of Grozny, where he has his hair cut short and undertakes basic training. He is then put on a military aircraft with other recruits and flown across the vastness of Russia and Siberia to serve in Chukotka, the Soviet region nearest to Alaska. It is a time of rising international tension between the United States and the Soviet Union. In Berlin Russia has blocked rail and road access to the sectors under Western control, in a struggle by the victorious powers to shape Europe according to their competing ideologies.

Stanislav finds himself serving in a coastal defence division almost within sight of the enemy. Red Army soldiers posted to Gvozdev Island, known to the Americans as Big Diomede Island, can see the Stars and Stripes flying on Little Diomede Island just under four kilometres away, separated not just by language and ideology but by the International Date Line, so that the two outposts are also known as Tomorrow Island and Yesterday Island.

It is so cold in Chukotka – the temperature stays below freezing for eight months of the year – there is a pressing need for warm boots, which the system is striving to provide and which explains why Stanislav is sent there. The sturdy youth with skilful fingers is given a space and put to work making and mending boots for the officers. He becomes proficient at fixing up officers' kirza boots with calf leather toes and soles of wear-resistant rubber and nails, and with pimples to provide traction; these are very popular with men assigned to tough terrain.

Because it is a sensitive military zone, no one is allowed leave during their service, and it is three years before Stanislav, no longer a youth but a strapping young man, is able to return to Grozny. Now twenty-one, Stanislav resumes work in the shoe factory, which is one of the largest enterprises in Grozny. Friends of the family get to know of his exceptional talent with footwear. They begin to ask him to do repairs privately and to make bespoke shoes, as the quality of mass-produced shoes in the Soviet Union remains very poor. Protruding nails, inadequate waterproofing, cardboard vamps – uppers – and even heels tacked on in the wrong place are common complaints.

Bakhshi and Stanislav become a small boot-and-shoe enterprise, toiling out of sight at the back of the house. They have a friend, also working on the side, who carves wooden lasts for shaping shoes to individual feet. While risky, such small-scale private enterprise is widely practised in the USSR, thwarting the state's aspiration to own and control all the means of production. The two restrict their services to those customers they know, as the authorities could impose a substantial tax or even haul them before the courts if they find out and if the inspectors are not

A walk in a Grozny park for Stanislav and Bakhshi, with Bakhshi's daughters Nellya and Sveta.

amenable to reason in the form of a free repair job or a small contribution. Stanislav cheerfully works at home every evening after a long day at his official employment, and turns over his earnings to his mother. He gets a reputation at the factory as a 'one-plus' shoemaker – he can make two pairs of shoes a day, where one is normal.

Unlike many of his Russian friends, Stanislav does not smoke, and he restricts his drinking to a small glass or two at

Already the businessman: Stanislav aged twenty-four, in Grozny, 1953.

the dinner table. He likes dancing and going out but his biggest indulgence when relaxing is to read. He devours any books he can get, and peruses every column inch of the four-page newspaper *Groznensky Rabochy* – the *Grozny Worker*. Like most of his circle he avidly plays chess, and throughout his life he takes on all comers who are happy to challenge him.

A chance encounter on the No. 7 tram as it trundles towards Pavel Musorov Street from the city centre has far-reaching consequences. Farandzem and Bakhshi recognize each other as neighbours and, given their Armenian origins, they get talking, following which the two families become friends. Marietta and Stanislav are soon acquainted. As time goes by, the good-looking and cheerful young man attracts the romantic attention of the girl from the Oil Workers' Block, who has grown into a very attractive teenager, with brown eyes, curly hair and a sense of humour. Stanislav has his eye on her too, it transpires. A romance between them begins at a wedding reception for his stepsister Sveta which the Gukasyan females attend. He doesn't like it when he sees that an Armenian youth is trying to court Marietta. He takes her aside and says, 'Let me drive you home.' She climbs into the car with him and they return together to Pavel Musorov Street. In this way he declares his intentions to her and everyone takes note. From then on they are inseparable.

It is the old story of falling in love with the girl next door, or in this case, the girl across the tramlines. Despite the age difference they are smitten with each other. After a short courtship and with the assent of their respective mothers, as both are fatherless, Stanislav and Marietta arrange to get married the following year when she reaches the minimum age of eighteen, which is not uncommon in Armenian culture.

By now Marietta's older sister Lena is already married, to Volodya Gukasov, a tender-hearted and obliging metal-factory worker with a neat moustache whose nationality is unknown but who is almost certainly Armenian, as he was abandoned as an infant at the door of a childless Armenian family in Grozny who raised him as their own. They have moved in with Volodya's adoptive parents in Boghdan Khmelnitsky Street, named after a Ukrainian hero of the seventeenth century.

Farandzem herself is still an attractive and personable woman and has several male admirers. Marietta makes it her business to discourage them in whatever way she can and if possible see them off. Whether this works, or whether none of the suitors is ever sufficiently worthy to replace her lost husband, Farandzem never marries again. She has other things to distract her, with her party responsibilities and her service on the train to and from Moscow.

Party activity is mainly concerned with the upheaval in Soviet politics resulting from the death of Stalin. Beria tries to grab power but is arrested and given his favourite treatment for

Nikita Khrushchev in 1959.

others, shot while on his knees and begging for mercy. A new leader emerges in the rotund shape of Nikita Khrushchev, who becomes first secretary of the Communist Party of the Soviet Union. Ordinary people dare to hope that this is the end of repression and there will be a political thaw.

Farandzem is at home on Tuesday, 6 March 1956 when all Grozny party members are summoned to an emergency meeting at the regional headquarters in Grozny's central square. So too is Stanislav's aunt Anna, a rising star in the party.

When they take their seats in the main hall, they are addressed by the Grozny first secretary, forty-five-year-old Alexander Yakovlev, a Russian freshly appointed to the post. He informs them that two weeks previously Khrushchev made an unpublicized speech to a closed session of the Twentieth Congress of the CPSU. Yakovlev has just received a transcript. He holds up a thirty-eight-page booklet with a red cover inscribed SECRET. He has been instructed, he says, to read it to them. No one is to take notes. The contents must be absolutely confidential.

The comrades listen in growing disbelief as they hear Khrushchev make a furious assault on the character of Josef Stalin. He accuses his predecessor of rejecting Lenin's principles, committing crimes against innocent people, inflicting mass terror on party members, failing to prepare for the German invasion in 1941, mismanaging the war – which he allegedly followed on a globe – and plotting a new purge of Jewish doctors. Khrushchev denounces in particular Stalin's cult of personality. Everything that has gone wrong since 1917 is not the fault of the communist system but of the maladroit comrade at its top who accumulated too much power and misused it. Khrushchev reveals that Lenin himself condemned Stalin in his final and still unpublished letter.

One can imagine that Yakovlev's voice shakes a little as he reads out such heresy and that there are gasps and cries from the audience. How can good party members possibly come to terms with what they have just heard? They have been taught to hail Stalin as the noble, inspired, indispensable genius, the hero who built socialism, who led the Motherland to victory, who transformed the Soviet Union into an industrialized superpower. His portraits hang everywhere. His embalmed body lies beside Lenin's in the Kremlin mausoleum. Now they are being told he was a mass murderer. They are conditioned to accept without question the line from the Kremlin. But now perhaps cries of 'Shame!' or 'Slander!' are uttered.

One section of the speech might even have caused some commotion in the hall. Referring to the Soviet Union as a model multinational state, Khrushchev condemns as monstrous Stalin's deportation of the Chechen and Ingush peoples, and also of the Crimean Tatars, the Balkars, the Karachai and the Kalmyks. This, he declares, amounted to mass repression of women, children and old people, including good communists, exposing them to misery and suffering. Ukrainians, he adds, only half in jest, would have met the same fate for cooperating with the Germans, only there are too many of them.

It must occur to some of the shocked party members that if the deportations were an injustice, the victims might be allowed to come back and reclaim their properties. The words of the poet Anna Akhmatova on learning of the secret speech have a particular resonance in Chechnya: 'Now the prisoners will return and the two Russias will look each other in the eyes; the one that imprisoned and the one that was imprisoned.' The Grozny communists, mostly Russians and Ukrainians, are in a quandary. How can they go along with Khrushchev's views? All had expressed their adulation of Stalin at some time or other; some in attendance at the meeting no doubt colluded in his actions. To criticize Stalin now is to pass judgement on one's friends and neighbours, and on oneself.

Hundreds of thousands of Stalin's victims are soon post-humously rehabilitated, including Aghasi Khanjyan, the brave but foolhardy Armenian party secretary who raised the hopes of Armenians in Karabakh in the 1930s, only to be eliminated by Beria. Some of Stalin's bloodthirsty provincial sidekicks are themselves now shot, among them the Azerbaijan party chief, Mir Jafar Baghirov, who had caused Farandzem and Nerses fearful and sleepless nights. He is executed by order of a Soviet military tribunal.

The speech does not stay secret for long. As many in Grozny feared, especially those living in houses belonging to deportees, Khrushchev restores the Chechen-Ingush Autonomous Repub-lic, and the survivors of the genocide begin returning, at first in a trickle, then in large numbers. Some Chechens and Ingush pitch tents outside their former homes until the occupants are intimidated into leaving.

Russians, Ukrainians and others who took over empty prop-erties depart to start a new life elsewhere. Some slip away in the darkness from the farms they have appropriated, rather than face an angry young Chechen armed with a *kinzhal*, the curved Cau-casian dagger. But in other cases, Marietta remembers, the Slavic occupiers simply hand over the keys and are thanked by the Chechens for taking care of their properties. To ease tensions, returning deportees are given modest government grants to buy back their houses from the settlers. Those leaving are encour-aged to resettle in republics such as Latvia and Estonia, Baltic states annexed by the Soviet Union after the war and subject to Russification by Moscow.

Stanislav's family home is not affected, as it was built by his stepfather, Bakhshi; the Armenian family never occupied Chechen or Ingush property. The young shoemaker is, in fact, delighted at this reversal of history. A wrong has been righted. Deported children come back as hardened adults, many already married with children. He welcomes the returnees, some of them his former school pals, including an Ingush called Bashir who becomes one of his closest friends.

Because of their high birth rate, more Chechens come back than were deported. Within a decade the population of Grozny rises from two hundred and fifty thousand to three hundred and sixty thousand, of whom a third are Chechen or Ingush, where there were none before. Despite their return, the party refuses to order the removal of the insulting statue of Yermolov, the first conqueror to attempt their genocide, which continues to dominate the centre of Grozny.

Most of the thirteen thousand-strong Armenian population were integrated into the life of Grozny before 1944 and, like Stanislav's family, did not take over abandoned homes. Despite their Christian background they have always coexisted on reasonably good terms with their Muslim neighbours in this part of the Caucasus. As a native-born citizen of Grozny who lives like an Armenian but looks like a Russian and has a Russian name, and also has a tolerant and cheerful personality, Stanislav experiences no animosity. As a witness to the genocide of the Chechens, he is gratified by the secret speech and the decision to reverse the deportations.

The year ends with Soviet tanks crushing an anti-communist rising in Hungary, and a summons to party members to hear the contents of another secret letter, this time from the Central Committee of the CPSU. It demands vigilance against criticism of the Soviet system because of events in Eastern Europe and heightened condemnation of the USSR from democratic countries. Stalin may have been discredited but socialist restrictions and taboos still apply.

CHAPTER 5

THE GOOD LIFE

O N 15 JUNE 1957, twelve weeks after her eighteenth birthday, Marietta Gukasyan marries Stanislav Suvorov, aged
twenty-eight. The festivities take place in the grounds of Sonia's
house with music from a *sazandar*, a traditional Armenian band
with percussion and wind instruments. Marietta wears a white
dress run up by her sister Lena, and white shoes made, naturally,
by the groom. One hundred and fifty friends and relatives turn
up, mostly from Grozny's Armenian community and also some
from Nagorno-Karabakh. Stanislav, or Stasik as Marietta calls
him fondly, also invites an accordion player. As is the custom,
the dancing guests throw money at the feet of the *sazandar* players, who much to the groom's dismay refuse to share it with the
accordion player, and he has to pay him separately.

The newly-wed couple settle in Grozny. Despite the pollution
from the oil refineries and other heavy industries and the unsta-
ble nature of society following the return of the native inhabitants, the couple have many advantages starting out in married
life in Chechnya. Stanislav has two jobs, at the shoe factory and
in his backyard working with Bakhshi, and he has money that
he gave to his mother to save in the years before his marriage.
The climate is mild. Their diet is good with consistent supplies
of fresh fruit and vegetables. There is no shortage of work. The
same cannot be said about conditions in other parts of the
Soviet Union, in particular the northern cities where people are
crammed into communal apartments and are subject to harsh

Facing the future together: newly-weds Stanislav and Marietta in 1957.

winters and frequent shortages of fresh produce. The energetic young shoemaker builds a small house for his bride on a hillside outside Grozny, where they live until their first child, Zhanna, is born in May 1958, after which they move into his mother Sonia's house on Pavel Musorov Street.

Stanislav, on the left, with friends who are helping to build his first house in Grozny, 1957.

Young mother: Marietta at nineteen, pictured in Grozny in 1958, the year Zhanna is born.

Sonia Suvorova is a Christian believer at heart who wears a small crucifix around her neck, and she takes it upon herself to have the infant Zhanna baptized in the Russian Orthodox church of St Michael the Archangel, the only place of worship for any religion allowed to operate in the whole Chechnya region – where the most fervent believers are Muslims. None of the family is a practising Christian but like Armenians everywhere they are respectful of old traditions and rituals. Besides, furtive baptisms are common in the USSR, usually arranged by old people, even prominent party officials, as afterlife insurance for their grandchildren. Despite an official policy of atheism, many Soviet citizens also observe some of the customs associated with religion such as making pancakes on Shrove Tuesday and painting

Polina, the religious flower-seller, posing with Stanislav and his stepsister Sveta in Grozny in 1955.

hard-boiled eggs on Easter Sunday. Sonia's neighbour, an elderly Ukrainian woman called Polina, defies the anti-religious ortho-doxy of the times and keeps a silver-framed icon of the Virgin in a corner of her living room where there is often an aroma of burning candles. She is intensely devout, and callers sometimes find her kneeling in front of the icon, nodding and blessing her-self. On Sundays she worships at St Michael's.

In August 1958 Russian resentment over the returning deportees erupts after an Ingush kills a Russian sailor in an altercation over an Ingush girl. Russian mobs wearing red headbands take control of the streets for a week, demanding the Soviet authorities send the native peoples back to Kazakhstan or they will be 'torn to pieces'. Only when the crowds take over Grozny railway station to block trains bringing Chechens home and begin looting government buildings does the Soviet military intervene to restore order. During the unrest, Stanislav and Marietta stay at home looking after their newborn. No Armenians venture out into the dangerous streets. With complexions darker than those of the Slavic people, they might easily be mistaken for Chechens or Ingush. After the insurrection is quashed, many more Russians simply abandon the city.

That year Stanislav organizes the construction of a larger dwelling for his young family in the grounds of his mother's house. Farandzem contributes to the capital cost from her savings, while the shoe factory management helps by buying the bricks and timber he needs, and deducting the cost from his salary. By Armenian tradition relatives, friends and neighbours come to lend a hand, digging the foundations, putting up the walls and roof, fitting the doors and painting the wooden window frames.

When completed the red-brick house with tiled roof has three bedrooms, a dining room, a bathroom and a living room, with shiny dark red hardwood floors. Stanislav installs a flush toilet, a real luxury in a city where most residents make do with a pit in the back yard. He also puts in a natural-gas boiler which heats big radiators in every room and digs out a cellar to store potatoes, vegetables and fruit. The house is typically Caucasian, built in two parts, with toilet, workshop and kitchen in one section and bedrooms, bathroom and living room in the other. Between the two buildings he creates a courtyard paved with tarmac. He adds a large garage with windows on the side, which makes it more like a conservatory. Here Stanislav will keep his car.

For some years the shoemaker has been driving a GAZ-M20 Pobeda (Victory), a small hump-backed automobile which has been mass-produced since 1946, and is the first Soviet car to have electric windscreen wipers and turn signals and a heater. GAZ stands for Gorkovsky Avtomobilny Zavod – Gorky Automobile Plant. It is not, strictly speaking, Stanislav's car, as it was purchased on his behalf by his mother. On the roads around Grozny there are always *militsia*, as the police are known, waving down drivers with their black and white sticks for the slightest offence, and a policeman might be interested in where he got the cash to make such a big purchase on a young shoemaker's wages.

With a wife and mother and mother-in-law and other family and friends to ferry around, in 1958 Stanislav trades up to the best vehicle available for ordinary citizens, a GAZ-M21 Volga saloon, which has recently started production. Much coveted

Grozny's municipal swimming pool – the city reservoir – in 1960. Stanislav is holding Zhanna, with stepsister Sveta in the middle.

by members of the *nomenklatura* as an official car, the Volga is equivalent in status to the Cadillac in the United States. Sonia some time previously paid a deposit of 1,350 rubles to the automobile sales office – the required 25 per cent of the purchase price of 5,400 rubles – to get on to the waiting list for the Volga, a considerable sum given that the average Russian worker earns eighty rubles a month. They have no access to credit, but Stanislav's mother is wealthy by Soviet standards, and her son has his private business making bespoke shoes and boots. Sonia returns to the sales office once a month, as is required, to confirm her place on the list, until the day comes when Stanislav takes possession of the blue Volga sedan.

Designed to imitate an American saloon, with bench seats and a leaping deer mascot on the bonnet, it has three-speed automatic transmission and several features new to Soviet cars, including a cigarette lighter, three-wave radio and fold-flat front seats. It feels smooth on the few tarmac roads in and around

Stanislav in Grozny at the wheel of his first Volga, with Zhanna, 1961.

Grozny, and can cope well with unpaved roads. Stanislav uses the Volga to drive to the market and on shopping trips, but he is always careful to have a few rubles for the *militsia* and to park the car inside the garage when at home.

After settling into their new house, Stanislav and Marietta plant tulips and narcissi around the courtyard and erect a metal trellis to support vines, which will provide shade and grapes for making sweet wine. They cultivate a small garden at the back for lettuce, cucumbers, aubergines, tomatoes, herbs, raspberries, and apricot and plum trees.

Farandzem leaves the single-room apartment across the tramlines and moves in with them. The couple's second daughter, Larisa, is born in 1960, and Farandzem helps look after the two little girls. The house is put in her name, partly out of consideration for her contribution, but also out of prudence: it avoids

New Year celebrations in Grozny, 1959: Volodya, Stanislav (holding Zhanna), Marietta, her mother Farandzem, sister Lena, Lena's son Misha, and friends.

questions about how a cobbler just turned thirty can afford it on his modest official income.

On one of her train trips to Moscow Farandzem manages to travel on to Riga, the capital of Latvia, where good-quality furniture can be bought, and finds a suite in walnut for the new house. The manager of the store prepares it for transport to Grozny but the Latvian police, motivated perhaps by national resentment at their republic being annexed by the Soviet Union after the war, intervene to claim he does not have the authority to export furniture to another republic. Farandzem goes to party headquarters in Riga, tells the pro-Kremlin comrades there that she is a member in good standing, a former second secretary and a war widow, and that the furniture is for her own house in Chechnya. She is given a transfer certificate, and the set is dispatched to Grozny.

The walnut table is placed in the front room, always with a bowl of sweets on it for visitors. The matching sideboard is adorned with framed photographs. The bookcase with glass doors is filled with Russian classics in gold-inlaid bindings – Dostoyevsky, Tolstoy, Pushkin, Turgenev and Chekhov – and translations of novels by Thomas Mayne Reid, Mark Twain and James Fenimore Cooper.

Khrushchev has relaxed censorship, and Stanislav manages to get his hands on the most daring new novels. These generally confirm his own evolving views on Soviet society – especially *The Thaw* by Ilya Ehrenburg, which gives its name to the post-Stalin period – dealing as they do with Soviet life in a realistic way. Marietta too is an avid reader. They pass between them the sensational novel *Not by Bread Alone* by Vladimir Dudintsev, which becomes the literary symbol of the cultural thaw. Published in instalments in the journal *Novy Mir* (*New World*), it promotes the individual's right to challenge officialdom, a notion close to Stanislav's heart. Its hero finds himself in a Kafkaesque nightmare when he is accused of giving the secrets of his revolutionary invention to his lover, but he is not told in court the details of the charge, as the secrets must remain secret even to him, and he is sentenced to eight years in a prison camp.

Occasionally Stanislav and Marietta go out to cheer on the Grozny football team, Terek, named after the river that flows through Chechnya to the Caspian Sea, or to weekend dances or to watch the new films shown in the Grozny Kinoteatr just along from the Oil Workers' Block. Everyone raves about *The Cranes are Flying*, the only Soviet movie ever to win the Palme d'Or at the Cannes Film Festival. It depicts the cruelty of war and human issues of betrayal and guilt, with less focus on the glorious exploits of Soviet forces, as was typical of Stalin-era productions. A film which Farandzem finds particularly relevant and moving is *The House I Live In*, as it demonstrates how the failure of a soldier to return from war – an experience shared by millions of Soviet families – can have devastating consequences for those left behind.

There is no end to Stanislav's acquisitiveness when it comes to his new family. He is one of the first in Grozny to purchase an electric refrigerator, a Minsk-1 with a chrome car-door-style handle. He gets his hands on a Zenit camera made in Krasnogorsk and a record player on which he likes to play Tchaikovsky's *Nutcracker Suite* with the windows open. He obtains a television set – a big wooden box with a tiny screen – and a washing machine and everything else needed for a comfortable life, other than a telephone; the telephone network serves the needs of institutions and government rather than the public and private calls have to be made and received at a telegraph office. In the cash-only Soviet economy he pays for everything with bundles of high-value ruble notes and uses his contacts and popularity to avoid the long waits experienced by those who sign up for the lists.

Going places: Zhanna and Larisa with horse tricycle in Grozny, 1962.

Stanislav Suvorov exploits to the full the informal economy which thrives in Grozny, as in so many Soviet towns. He makes friends with the people who matter: officials who know when registration for a washing machine has started or scarce items are being put on sale such as shampoo, sturgeon or chocolate. Such connections are known as *blat*, and Stanislav has good *blat*. Just as Farandzem experienced in Martakert, information is as important as money.

Distracted by the inter-ethnic tensions, and with the loosening of restrictions in the new Khrushchev golden age, the authorities largely ignore much of the irregular commerce going on under their noses. Indeed officials are often part of it. Rising expectations of a better life in the post-war years leads to an imbalance between the demand for consumer items and their supply, and this, along with centralized pricing, makes a flourishing and widespread black economy inevitable. People give tuition at home, do repairs and renovations, barter with each other, and buy and sell products, all outside the state's purview.

At the upper end of the scale factory officials sell manufactured goods not recorded on their books through accomplices in state shops. At the lower end people sell their own produce, like the Suvorovs' neighbour – Baba Polina, as the children call her – who grows gladioli in her garden and takes them in white enamel buckets to sell at the market.

The market is a sprawling open-air expanse of stalls at the junction of Prospect Mira (Peace) and Prospect Svobodi (Freedom), where everything is on sale, from fresh eggs, skinned rabbits, whole chickens, *smetana* (thick home-made cream), honey, sauerkraut, pickles, mushrooms, potatoes, onions, beetroot, herbs and seasoning, to metal busts of artists and Soviet heroes, bags of nails, bits of car engines and wedding dresses.

Such markets are tolerated by Khrushchev to make up for state shortages, as long as stallholders offer only their own things for sale. Any hint of a middleman or profiteering risks a visit from the *militsia*. Occasionally party officials make an example of offenders. The neighbour of a sick widow who kindly takes her potatoes to sell at the market is fined and stripped of his party membership. A Chechen has his greenhouse smashed by the *militsia* when he is accused of employing young men to sell his tomatoes.

Khrushchev, impetuous and undisciplined, complicit himself in many of Stalin's crimes, nevertheless has a sense of social justice and is an authentic reformer determined to improve living standards. He pressurizes state enterprises to produce more consumer goods to satisfy people's higher aspirations. Wartime armaments factories begin turning out toys and vacuum cleaners and other household goods. Engineering works scale down the production of tanks. More private cars are assembled but waiting lists are for ever. The Soviet Union is producing no more than one hundred thousand cars a year for a population of two hundred million. There is ideological resistance to manufacturing cars on a large scale – shared by Khrushchev – and a preference for expanding public transport. Moreover the roads aren't equipped for a sudden rise in automobile traffic.

As the proud owner of one of the few private sedans in Grozny, Stanislav likes to take his family out for picnics of shashlik in the woods by the River Terek. The route takes them past the oil derricks and jets of burning fuel that roar into the air, and on towards the hills where, in the tranquillity of oak and beech forests, they pick snowdrops and wild asparagus, and forage for damsons and miniature raspberries and fat, juicy blackberries, depending on the season. Coming home in the dusk the pillars of fire cast an unearthly light over the oilfields. On a spring day in 1961 Stanislav drives them as far as Makhachkala, which everyone still calls by its old name of Petrovsk, where Zhanna, barely three years old, gazes in wonder at the turquoise waters of the Caspian Sea stretching to the horizon. She is allowed to sit in the front seat of the Volga, licking chocolate-covered Eskimo ice cream while he plays tricks on her, lifting his hands from the steering wheel and pretending the car drives itself. Their father laughs a lot and loves telling stories.

In creating a home and a good life for his family, Stanislav brings to his mother-in-law a measure of happiness at last. Farandzem arrived in Grozny a grieving war widow and still occasionally writes to the ministry of defence for news of where her husband is buried. As she planned, she has given her daughters a better start in life than they could have expected in Martakert. Both now have fine husbands. Farandzem has four grandchildren, two boys by Lena named Misha and Yura, and two girls by Marietta, Zhanna and Larisa. She also has a job she loves on the railway, is a woman of good standing in the party organization, and once more lives in a fine house, with a son-in-law who loves and respects her, indeed shows her more affection than to his own mother. In ten years her life has been transformed, and she has no reason to think that there will be any more upheavals in the future.

CHAPTER 6

HOMO SOVIETICUS

To MAINTAIN HIS family's comfortable lifestyle, Stanislav spends many evenings, sometimes until after midnight, measuring, cutting and hammering in the well-equipped workshop behind the kitchen, using a leather-stitching Singer sewing machine he bought in the market, to produce bespoke footwear. Khrushchev once said that in his early days in tsarist Russia 'every villager dreamed of owning a pair of boots. We children were lucky if we had a decent pair of shoes.' Boots and shoes are available to the masses now, but are so inferior that any top official who travels abroad heads straight to the nearest shoe shop.

Stanislav's young wife proves to be a talented seamstress and also works hard in the hours of darkness, making garments not just for the family, but eventually also for neighbours and friends. The couple think nothing of running up a couple of pairs of men's trousers in an evening for private sale. Lena often comes by to contribute to the success of the little garment work-shop with her own sewing skills. The house on Pavel Musorov Street becomes a microcosm of the Soviet Union, a centre for people of different nationalities who call in to place orders and be measured. On any given evening one might find a Russian, a Tatar, a Ukrainian, an Armenian or a Chechen leafing through magazine pictures of the latest fashions. A lonely Jewish piano teacher sometimes comes with a modest order and lingers to chat. Her family was exterminated by Hitler, though she never

The Suvorovs' house in Grozny, with the garage where Stanislav kept his Volga, pictured in 1991.

speaks about it. Stanislav and Marietta take care to tidy away their materials afterwards in case of official prying eyes.

At home, during dinners to celebrate birthdays and anniversaries, Stanislav always insists on making toasts: to women, to health, to peace in the world, to friendship among the nationalities of the USSR. He likes to sing a song which is often broadcast on the radio and becomes his party piece. Composed in 1939 and sung in Russian by a famous Azerbaijan singer and actor, Rashid Beybutov, the 'Caucasian Drinking Song' is about internationalism and friendship among Armenia, Azerbaijan and Georgia, and it eulogizes their capital cities, Yerevan, Baku and Tbilisi. Everyone joins in the chorus:

> How merry we are with our glasses of wine!
> God willing, God willing, not for the last time!
> God willing, God willing, that we're drinking not for the
>   last time!

The idea of Soviet man, *homo sovieticus,* is promoted by Moscow, and widely accepted even in troubled Grozny. Ethnicity matters less when everyone can accept the way things are and share a sense of pride in Soviet achievements, such as Yury Gagarin's space flight in April 1961. A ditty to capture the national mood becomes popular.

How good it is that our Gagarin
Is no Armenian or Tatarin
No Jew, no Lett or Moldovan
But just a simple Soviet man.

Stanislav identifies with such sentiments, having a Russian father and Armenian mother and a network of many ethnicities exemplified by his friend Bashir.

An Ingush of proud bearing who customarily wears a tall grey lambskin *papakha* hat, Bashir has prospered in Grozny since his return from Kazakhstan. He first moved back into his former apartment beside the cinema in the centre of Grozny but has since become manager of the city granary and built a fine house to accommodate his family of eleven children.

Uncle Bashir, as Zhanna and Larisa call him, occasionally invites Stanislav's family to dine at his home, which they consider to be a mansion and which contains a prayer room with many carpets where he and his Muslim friends worship secretly. Grozny's mosques were wrecked during the deportations, and permission to rebuild has been withheld. Bashir entertains the Suvorovs in a lavishly decorated dining room with wallpaper of large green leaves tinged with gold. His wife Fatima serves the meal but by Ingush custom does not take a seat at the table when receiving guests. Wearing traditional long sleeves and a headscarf, she joins them afterwards, occasionally glancing nervously through the window in case a relative drops by and finds her

mixing with infidels. The visitors are impressed by how respectful the children are – when an adult walks into the room, the
youngsters immediately get up.

Both Stanislav and Bashir manage to give their families a
standard of living equivalent to that enjoyed by the post-war
middle class in developed countries like the United States, with
the added benefits of free education and healthcare – such as
they are in the USSR. They enjoy new movies like *And What If
It's Love*, which breaks taboos by portraying entrepreneurs and
speculators almost as ordinary people. They are not members of
the party but typical of a generation of reform-minded citizens
who believe that education, culture and science can contribute
to a perfect society.

One of the imperfections of society in Khrushchev's Soviet
Union is the excessive consumption of vodka, which causes lost
production, frequent work accidents and abuse in the home. It
is not uncommon for party officials, factory bosses, collective
farm managers and workers, if they can afford it, to spend much
of their time comatose. In an effort at reform, drinking songs
are banned from the radio, including Stanislav's favourite and
another long-popular number, 'Beethoven's Scottish Drinking
Song', sung by Mark Reyzen, an opera singer with a beautiful
bass voice. They are never heard again on the air.

Khrushchev begins to regret his encouragement of private
economic activity and obsesses about a return to 'Leninist
norms of socialist legality', an ill-defined concept combining a
legal structure to combat crimes against the workers' state with
the abolition of bourgeois ideas of civil liberties and private
property. He publishes a decree reducing the permitted size of
the private plots on which peasants grow fruit and vegetables
for sale. Prices soar because of reduced output and the increased
risk of prosecution. In 1960 he oversees the writing of a new

criminal code to be applied in Russia. It is based on the suprem-
acy of socialist ideology, which requires all laws to adhere to a
centralized planned economy and command administrative system. At its heart is Article 154, which criminalizes speculation,
the private resale of goods for profit. Speculation is anathema
to the socialist experiment. It was condemned by Lenin as freedom for the rich to get richer and the poorer to starve. Setting in
motion a campaign promoting 'socialist morality' Khrushchev
rails against speculation, complaining about the 'private property mentality' of citizens. As a warning to everyone conducting
business *na levo* (on the side), *Groznensky Rabochy* carries reports
of trials arising from the clampdown on speculation. The most
sensational of these is a two-week criminal trial in Moscow in
June 1961 at which speculators called Rokotov and Faibisenko
are given fifteen-year prison sentences for acquiring enormous
quantities of gold coins and banknotes by trading in foreign
clothing and currencies. Wanting even harsher punishment,
Khrushchev then has the law changed to raise the maximum
penalty to capital punishment, as a consequence of which the
unfortunate pair of businessmen are retried and shot. The law is
imposed retroactively, which is against legal norms. The rights
of Soviet citizens do not apply to speculators and profiteers. The
party leader is particularly concerned about the black-market
trade in second-hand cars. These are being sold privately under
the pretence of being given away or loaned, instead of being
bought from official outlets known as commission shops. Courts
are given new rights to punish speculators by confiscating cars
or even pulling down improperly acquired houses. Party leaders
in the republics are encouraged to show their loyalty by making an example of wrongdoers and getting prosecutors to come
down hard on speculators.

Khrushchev also campaigns against officials employed to cut
through red tape to expedite the supply and delivery of materials

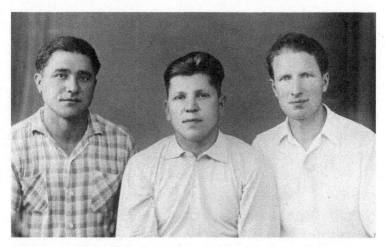

Stanislav in 1956 with Sasha Ryzhov, the expediter, left, and friend Franz Kostovsky.

from one state enterprise to another, whom he regards as 'shifty people'. These expediters help managers to avoid the worst inanities of the centralized system, such as material from one factory being shipped to Moscow and then sent to the factory across the road which has requested it. Stanislav and Bashir share a Russian friend, Sasha Ryzhov, who expedites several products, including vodka, milk and grain. He is a valuable connection. They regularly have dinner in each other's houses. The children know him as Uncle Sasha and his wife as Aunt Lisa. Little Zhanna is so charmed by her father's friend that she tells him she wants to marry him when she grows up. Uncle Sasha is arrested in a sweep of officials but released after two days and recognized as a *chestnyi chelovek*, an honest and straightforward person. It is clear, however, that anyone suspected of gaming the system needs to take great care.

As a wheeler-dealer in the underground economy, flying close to the sun with his private enterprise and lifestyle, Stanislav is usually on his guard. He can't afford to do anything careless.

But just at this time the Grozny shoemaker decides to sell his car through unofficial channels, at a profit. Strictly speaking it isn't his car; it was purchased in his mother's name, and he doesn't do the transaction himself: he lets Sonia conduct the sale as she is good at bargaining, and she gets much more at the market than the unrealistically low price set by the state.

After the sale Stanislav takes possession of a new car, a second-series Volga. The very latest model, it has a seventy-five-horsepower engine, ten more than before, a smart chromium-plated badge in place of the leaping deer bonnet ornament, windscreen washers, a wider grille, cloth rather than vinyl trim, and tubeless tyres. It is delivered by the state supplier on 1 June 1961. The new car is his pride and joy. He uses it sparingly, for outings and for weekly visits to the market. When it gets dirty on Grozny's muddy roads, which is quite often, he drives it into his garage and washes and polishes the metal and chrome. He never leaves it on the roadside, where it might draw the unwelcome attention of zealous officials or passing thieves.

Later in the summer Stanislav and Marietta treat themselves to a holiday. They go to Leningrad where they stay with a friend while they explore the palaces and museums, and then travel on to Moscow to spend some days with another acquaintance.

The only upset in their lives that year occurs when Bakhshi, then aged seventy-two, falls in love with another woman and goes to live with her. Stanislav is dismayed at the behaviour of the man he calls 'papa'. His mother rages against her former partner. What a disgrace! And such an embarrassment to be the subject of gossip among the other members of the neighbourhood committee, who know her mockingly as the commissar. But when the other woman tries to persuade Bakhshi to sell the house which he built and in which he and Sonia lived together for over twenty years, the septuagenarian cobbler concludes she only wants his money. He bids her goodbye, and returns to Pavel Musorov Street after only a few weeks away. There is an enormous row. Sonia refuses to let him back into the house. The normally timid Bakhshi refuses to be cowed, and moves into rooms at the back where he resumes his work as a cobbler. His relationship with Sonia is over, but after tempers cool he takes his place at her dinner table every evening as if nothing has happened.

Chapter 7

PROFIT AND PUNISHMENT

On Monday morning, 1 October 1961, Stanislav Suvorov does his usual stretching exercises, has his breakfast of buckwheat and tea, kisses Marietta and the children goodbye, and leaves the house to take the tram to the shoe factory to begin another week's work. He never gets there. The *militsia* are waiting in the street to arrest him. They put him in the back of a patrol car and drive him to the central police station. They leave behind two officers who bang on the door of the house and demand the keys of the Volga, which they drive away.

One can imagine the fright this gives Marietta, and the terror when she learns that her husband has been arrested. Farandzem is in shock, and tries to comfort her daughter. Three-and-a-half-year-old Zhanna is terrified by the rude uniformed men who invade their home, shout at her mother and take her papa's car away.

There is panic in the house after the police leave. Who knows what is really going on? Are the family being targeted not just because of the car sale but because they are making shoes and garments for private sale? Bakhshi hastens to hide the cobbler's tools he and Stanislav use in the evenings and make the workshop look like a storage room. The evidence of Marietta's sideline as a seamstress is also secreted. Sonia frets that her private dealings and her sublets will bring the wrath of the socialist state down upon herself.

Stanislav is held for a night and much of the next day in a cell, with nothing to eat. The next afternoon he is visited by an investigator for the Grozny procurator, who has prepared a charge sheet. He is accused of an offence under Article 154 of the Criminal Code of the Russian Soviet Federative Socialist Republic, enacted in 1960, which forbids speculation, defined as 'buying up and reselling of goods or any other articles for the purpose of making a profit'. Stanislav *has* made a profit – that is, he got more than the state commission price for his old car – but that was not his purpose when through his mother he bought the first Volga in 1958. He kept it for over three years and only sold it to trade up. Someone has evidently tipped off the authorities. Stanislav has no enemies that he knows of and suspects the buyer has got into trouble and informed on him to save his own skin.

Family gather around Marietta after Stanislav is jailed: at rear, Volodya Gukasov, Farandzem and half-sister Lena, with Zhanna and Larisa, 1962.

Marietta tries to find out where he is being detained. No one will tell her, but she learns that arrested people are taken to a remand centre, where they are held, without visitors, until a trial date is fixed. So begins the most fraught and miserable period in the life of the young couple. Marietta will not see Stanislav again until he is brought to court for trial, which could be many months away. Still only twenty-two, the young Armenian mother feels lost and helpless, but she must show strength through her tears for the sake of the children. Her beloved Stasik always provided for the family and took care of them; now he has been snatched from them and is being branded a 'speculator', one of the most pejorative words in the communist lexicon, making him out to be an enemy of the people. Her mother urges her to go out and face the neighbours. Some Armenians and Russians whom she considered her friends cut her dead, even walking across the road to avoid her. Others go out of their way to ease the pain. Big sister Lena and husband Volodya rally to her side; Lena becomes like a second mother to Zhanna and Larisa, and often takes them to stay overnight in her house. Sasha the expediter and his wife come around often, and never empty-handed.

Conditions in the Soviet Union's remand centres are wretched, and it is possible to reconstruct Stanislav's experience from contemporary accounts of prisoners awaiting trial. He is put in a cell with a dozen other men, some of them violent offenders. They have nothing to do for twenty-three hours a day but sit or lie on a few bunk beds made from planks, on which they have to take turns, a severe ordeal for the hyperactive shoemaker. There is little ventilation and the cell stinks of urine, vomit, sweat and burning tobacco from cheap cardboard cigarettes. Meals consist of buckwheat with bread and tea for breakfast, cabbage soup for lunch, and fish soup in the evening.

Inmates are allowed to exercise for one hour a day in an open space measuring seven metres by ten. Some of the accused men sit around during this break, but those determined to keep in shape, like Stanislav, who always exercises at home in the mornings, use the sixty minutes to walk up and down and flex their muscles. Detainees are denied any correspondence or contact with their families, and are restricted to one package every four weeks, which may not contain books or papers. The only reading material allowed in the prison is *Pravda*. Stanislav no doubt reads it from front to back despite the dim lighting and the tedious content.

Marietta hires a member of the College of Advocates, a Jewish lawyer widely respected for her knowledge of the Soviet penal code, to defend Stanislav and to secure the lightest possible sentence should he be found guilty.

The family has little doubt he will be found guilty. Being arrested is a presumption of guilt, and the burden of proof of innocence is on the accused. Even the government newspaper *Izvestia* (*News*) admits that only one in a hundred criminal defendants is ever acquitted in Soviet courts. Stanislav's chances of a fair trial are also prejudiced by undoubted pressure from Moscow on the new first secretary of the Communist Party of the Chechen-Ingush Autonomous Republic, fifty-nine-year-old Alexander Trofimov, to make some examples of people abusing the system in Grozny, where things are getting out of hand.

The day of his trial comes on Thursday, 11 April 1962, six months after his arrest. Marietta is allowed into the courtroom, with Lena and Volodya for support. Stanislav's mother Sonia is not there, perhaps because of the shame of her son being on trial or because the car was in her name and it is better to stay away. They take their seats facing the circular gold hammer-and-sickle emblem of Soviet Russia hanging from a nail in the wall. They recoil in dismay when Stanislav is brought in. He has lost weight and developed a prison pallor.

The judge begins proceedings by asking Stanislav if he is *partinyi* or *bez partinyi*, a party member or, literally, 'without party membership'. He replies that he is *bez partinyi*. He is not a communist. Whether being a party member might mitigate the severity of his sentence he will never know. It could equally make it worse. The official investigator presents his summary of accusations, and although the Volga is in the name of his mother, Stanislav acknowledges that it was sold on the market as his property.

His lawyer then submits that under Article 154, for there to be a crime, the intent to sell for profit must be present at the time of purchase of the goods. Stanislav Suvorov has had the vehicle for three years. He has used it as a family car, to go to work or to the market or on longer outings, and if he had bought the Volga to make a profit he would surely have sold it soon afterwards. She also submits that if the prisoner is found guilty, the sentence should be at the lighter end of the scale. Article 154 provides for different punishments to fit the crime: a fine not exceeding three hundred rubles, correctional tasks not exceeding one year, or deprivation of freedom for a term not exceeding two years, with or without confiscation of property. Only speculation as a form of business or on a large scale merits the most severe punishment: deprivation of freedom for a term of two to seven years with confiscation of property. She argues that Stanislav Suvorov is a valued and skilled worker with no previous charges against him, that selling the car is a first offence and that there was obviously no criminal intent at the moment of purchase.

The judge confers with the male and female people's assessors, sitting one on either side of his chair. These are citizen judges with no legal training, there to give a lay opinion. Defence attorneys call them nodders because they never disagree with the trial judge. After nodding their agreement, the judge announces the verdict.

'In the name of the Russian Soviet Federative Socialist Republic, the judicial bench of the Grozny City Court finds Stanislav Alexandrovich Suvorov guilty of violation of Article 154 of the Russian Soviet Federative Socialist Republic Criminal Code and sentences him to seven years deprivation of liberty and confiscation of property.'

Seven years! Shock is inadequate to describe the reaction of Marietta and other family members as they hear the sentence. It is so manifestly unfair and unjust. By no stretch of the imagination can Stanislav be deemed to have engaged in 'speculation as a form of business or on a large scale'. Her Stasik has hardly enriched himself very much by selling his car on the market rather than through the state outlet. Now they will put him in jail and will seize all the property for which they have worked so hard.

Stanislav is not the only person that year to receive a harsh sentence for selling a state-supplied car on the open market. The smell of politics hangs over the courts' decisions. The judiciary is subject to directives from the Kremlin on penal policy, and Khrushchev is on the warpath. Judges serve five-year terms, and their continued careers depend on the party's assessment of their conformity. First secretary Trofimov can report to Moscow that the judges at the Grozny City Court are fulfilling their socialist duty and making an example of big-time speculators.

Stanislav's new Volga is now officially confiscated. It will go to some functionary in the administration, of that he has little doubt. Perhaps this was the plan all along: a scheme to steal the comfortable sedan from an uppity shoemaker for a self-important official who is tired of using factory trucks for his transport. Stanislav will never know.

The police come immediately after the trial to seize Stanislav's other property and evict Marietta, her mother and the two little girls from the house on Pavel Musorov Street. They demand the house deeds. However, the residence is in Farandzem's name and they cannot claim it. She contributed to the cost of construction and furnishings, and Stanislav and Marietta put everything in her name. That decision now saves them from destitution but they have to endure a few minutes of terror as the police poke around the house. They do not find any of Stanislav's shoemaking and leather-working instruments, as they were well hidden as soon as he was arrested.

After sentencing, Stanislav is taken to a prison situated among the oil derricks on the outskirts of Grozny. It is a strict-regime labour camp and consists of low brick buildings surrounded by barbed-wire fencing. He is put in a cell with three Armenians and a Georgian who have committed various non-violent crimes.

It is a small consolation for Marietta that her husband has not been sent to a faraway jail or even to a camp in Siberia. Under Stalin, whose era ended a mere nine years earlier, a man could get five years for buying a bottle of vodka in a state shop and selling it on the street, and anyone sentenced to more than three years in prison was automatically sent east. Khrushchev has closed the system of camps and high-security prisons in Siberia known as the Gulag, and thousands of political and criminal inmates have been released and in many cases rehabilitated, but ordinary prisoners are often sent to the detention centres there. It saves building new prisons and finding fresh staff.

On 14 April 1962, just a few days after Stanislav's sentence, while Marietta is still trying to come to terms with losing her husband for seven years, she puts a pot of water on the electric stove to boil. Her religious neighbour, Polina, comes by to sympathize. She reminds Marietta that it is Easter Sunday in the Orthodox Church and that it brings bad luck to work on a holy day. Shortly after Polina leaves, eighteen-month-old Larisa, playing in the kitchen, accidentally pulls the boiling water down over

Zhanna, aged four, puts a protective arm around her mother, holding Larisa, shortly after her father's arrest in 1962.

herself. As her mother frantically tears the scalding clothes off the screaming child, the skin peels away, leaving lifelong scars on her arm and leg. Never again will Marietta, a convinced atheist, work on an Easter Sunday.

Zhanna, who turns four six weeks later, is barely able to grasp why her father is not at home and her mother is crying. She accepts for a long time that her papa has gone on a trip but realizes the truth when she is a little older and sees her mother disappear for whole days carrying a big bag of food. In time Marietta tells her what has happened and her eldest daughter develops the unshakeable belief that her father has done nothing wrong and that he is being punished for trying to do his best for the family.

The imprisonment of her son-in-law is a personal and ideological upset for Marietta's mother. Farandzem Gukasyan believes in the communist party, despite living through the

1930s terror and having her world turned upside down by Khrushchev's denunciation of Stalin. Her life in Martakert and that of her husband centred on party activities and involved taking punitive measures against those who offended against Soviet law. Now she is the mother-in-law of a 'criminal', though no one in Stanislav's family will ever call him that, and she will support him through his long ordeal. She does not lose faith in the system, but her trust in those administering it at the top is eroded.

The affair is also a severe blow to Stanislav's aunt Anna. A determined, heavy-set woman with hair pulled back in a bun, she is a senior official at the railway headquarters in Grozny. More importantly, Anna Mesropova has just been elected to a four-year term as a member of the USSR Supreme Soviet, officially the highest legislative body in the Soviet Union.

The Supreme Soviet, consisting of twelve hundred unpaid members, holds sessions in the Grand Kremlin Palace at least twice a year. Its members sit at shiny black-walnut desks in a chamber the size of a football field, facing an eighteen-metre-high statue of Lenin, the largest in the country, and elect an executive committee called the Presidium, which makes laws, issues decrees and selects a council of ministers. In reality, the Supreme Soviet merely rubber-stamps the decisions of the Central Committee of the Communist Party of the Soviet Union, provides legal status for members of the government and the supreme court, and appoints the procurator general of the USSR.

The current procurator general, Roman Rudenko, is the highest law officer in the land. He can order a court judgment to be revisited. Aunt Anna has access to him because of her status as a deputy. She determines to lobby him for a review of the trial, though it means drawing the attention of the Kremlin to the fact that her nephew is serving time in prison for speculation. She

A capital-letter person: Stanislav's aunt Anna, member of the USSR Supreme Soviet, with her son Sasha.

makes an appointment for herself and Farandzem at a time when Stanislav's mother-in-law is in Moscow for work, so they can go to the Kremlin together.

One can imagine the procurator general peering rather incredulously at the two Armenian party members who arrive into his cavernous Moscow office, where a large portrait of Lenin hangs on the wall – a little to one side of his desk as only the first secretary of the CPSU can have an image of the nation's founder directly behind him. Corpulent, bald and wearing rimless glasses, Rudenko is a formidable figure: he was chief Soviet prosecutor at the Nuremberg trials of Nazi war criminals and was the judge who decreed that Beria should be shot in 1953 and who sentenced the American CIA pilot Gary Powers to ten years' hard labour in 1960 for spying on the Soviet Union. Rudenko also has a name for rebuffing appeals to speed up the rehabilitation of thousands of former camp inmates.

No mercy: Roman Rudenko, USSR procurator general, who spurns Aunt Anna's personal appeal for clemency for Stanislav.

He hears the women out, then stands up and starts to escort them to the door, saying there is nothing he can do. He can intercede only if a court has made a decision not conforming to Soviet law. The judge has applied the law and his verdict must stand. 'There is no method by which we can intervene without consequences for Soviet power. If we reopen the case, it means that everyone in charge, the investigator, the procurator, the judge, acted wrongly and will have to be disciplined.' He dismisses their argument that speculation is only a crime if the item is bought to make a profit.

It is Nikita Khrushchev's wish to come down hard on speculation, and even the highest party connections are of little use.

There is another factor against them. Their visit coincides with a brief period of serious unrest in the Soviet Union. Khrushchev, advised by his economic thinkers that the way to combat shortages is to make essential items more expensive, orders a rise of 30 per cent in the price of meat and 25 per cent in the price of butter, and at the same time cuts the pay of workers by increasing the minimum production quotas in factories. On 1 June 1962, in Novocherkassk in central Russia, workers from the Budyonny Electric Locomotive Factory stage a mass protest about price rises and their generally wretched lives under the communist system. They refuse to disperse when ordered and are cut down by gunfire. Twenty-six are killed and eighty-seven wounded. The event unnerves the Kremlin and the amelioration of workers' conditions becomes a priority for Khrushchev. Concessions are made – there will be no more price rises in the Soviet Union for a quarter of a century – and new measures are put in place to crack down on individuals who are drifting towards a capitalist lifestyle and causing discontent among the masses. There is no sympathy at the Kremlin for imprisoned speculators.

Appealing to Rudenko is therefore a courageous act by the two women. They have risked their own reputations and have demonstrated that family is more important to them than party standing.

Marietta faces up to the challenge of raising the two girls without Stanislav's regular income for the next seven years. Her mother is now the de facto breadwinner, but Marietta is able to bring in extra money from her own private work. Already skilled in dressmaking, she becomes highly proficient at running up good-quality pleated skirts, which are currently in great demand. As her clientele builds, she works long hours – cutting fabric strips for waistbands, sewing buttonholes, measuring folds for pleats, stitching and pressing late into the night.

Her greatest concern is that Stanislav should not be ill-treated in prison. She makes shirts and trousers for the prison officers and pleated dresses and other garments for their wives, whom she invites to the house for fittings, all without charge. Their expediter friend Sasha provides litre bottles of vodka to give to the Russian and Ukrainian prison guards. Marietta is consequently given permission to visit her husband twice a month, instead of once as per regulations. She is also able to persuade the guards to pass on to him the books that he craves and fruit and vegetables to keep him healthy.

In return for her gifts and sewing services, the guards undertake to look after Stanislav's wellbeing. They do not mistreat him or subject him to the worst indignities, such as spells in the punishment cell, which typically in Russian prisons consists of a tiny, dank space with stucco walls and a plank for a bed, to which prisoners are sometimes confined for weeks. Stanislav's sunny disposition finds expression even behind bars, and he shares whatever he gets from outside and never complains. He is popular with his fellow prisoners and their custodians. He is excused from labour detachments and allowed to do leather work, for which he is even paid a few rubles a month. Some of the boots he fashions go onto the outsize feet of his guards.

Their mother and grandmother try to shield the children from the shame of their father being in prison and to ensure that life goes on as normally as possible. Zhanna starts school when she reaches the age of seven, in the third year of Stanislav's sentence. She is enrolled at School No. 4, a five-minute walk from the house. On her first day she wears a pleated skirt made by her mother and is given a posy of Polina's gladioli for the teacher. Seeing other children arrive with both parents, she is acutely aware that her papa is absent at this important moment in her young life and, not for the first time, she implores her mother to tell her when he will be coming home. She begins attending music classes in the afternoons after primary school. Two years Zhanna's junior, Larisa also starts school and music lessons in due course. One of the last things their father organized before his imprisonment was the purchase of a black Rostov-Don piano so that his children can practise in the house, and Larisa quickly reveals the talent that will make her a proficient musician.

Marietta and Farandzem also try to make the home as happy as possible for their two charges. They help with homework while teaching the girls independence and self-reliance. They play games. On winter mornings when their mother gets them up she lets Larisa smell her hands to guess what is for breakfast, pancakes, porridge or eggs, and her younger daughter inevitably gets it right. There is always home-made bread and sweets in the dish on the walnut table. They all dress up for May Day and gather for birthday celebrations as usual, to maintain a sense of normality.

During the school holidays Farandzem takes Zhanna to visit Moscow, a thrilling experience. The young girl feels privileged to be travelling with such an important person on the train. She has her own bunk bed in her grandmother's compartment, where she sleeps on the four-day journey there and back. Her baba serves hot tea in glasses encased in silver-coloured holders, wakes travellers who oversleep, and makes sure they get on and off at the right times. Passengers bring their own hard-boiled eggs, chicken and bread, and replenish their supplies at stops along the way, where they are besieged by peasant vendors. The train passes through cities with evocative names such as Pyatigorsk, Rostov, Ryazan and Voronezh, before pulling into Moscow's Kazansky railway station.

In Moscow grandmother and granddaughter go to Red Square and stand in line for hours to view the embalmed body of Lenin, displayed in a cool chamber inside a red-marble mausoleum. Seeing his wax-like face, with its reddish moustache and small beard, and with his eyes closed as if asleep, is a solemn experience for children taught to regard him as the Father of the Revolution. Stalin's preserved body was removed from the mausoleum in 1961 and placed in the Kremlin wall. To Zhanna's generation, everything good about the Soviet Union stems from Lenin's wisdom and foresight, and they now know he warned before he died that Stalin was crude and not to be trusted.

They queue again to explore the arcades of Glavny Universalny Magazin – the Main Universal Store – known by its initials as GUM, an enormous glass and metal building beside Red Square, with three levels of open walkways illuminated by arched skylights. Every day Muscovites and visitors crowd into its small shops, which contain a cornucopia of items unavailable elsewhere. GUM is intended to symbolize to foreigners the abundance of a Soviet Union attuned to consumer needs. Though a showcase city, Moscow itself suffers from the command economy's inefficiencies, and Muscovites jostle with each other in irritated queues every day to obtain basic essentials such as frozen meat, herring, and even bread. It is said that 'in principle' in Moscow there is everything, leading out-of-town visitors to ask where they can find this wonderful shop called Principle, which they have heard so much about.

Zhanna and Larisa are eventually allowed to accompany their mother to the prison. Laden down with heavy bags, they set off on the tram, then change to a bus and finally onto a special prison bus. It takes two hours. Their grandmother Farandzem comes with them, as well as Sasha Ryzhov and his wife Lisa, bearing vodka for the guards. They are all allowed to crowd into a small room with their father and half a dozen Georgian and Armenian prisoners. Stanislav greets his daughters with hugs and kisses. He makes a great fuss of them, laughing and making jokes, while Marietta serves a meal for everyone, digging deep into her bags to produce bottled preserves, tinned fruits, pastries, biscuits,

Rare smiles inside Grozny's prison camp, 1963.

home-made jam and cigarettes for the cell mates. They pose for an extraordinary group photograph. Sitting in the foreground is Farandzem, beaming. On a bench behind her are Sasha and Lisa on one side, and Stanislav and Marietta on the other. Stanislav, his head shaven, is glancing back fondly at Zhanna and Larisa, who are being held in the arms of prisoners standing in a row by the wall. Everyone looks delighted. In all the years when her father is in prison, it is the only time Zhanna sees her mother happy and smiling.

At home Marietta is often depressed and Lena comes by to keep her spirits up. From the time of Stanislav's arrest the children are aware that everyone is much more serious; the adults whisper things or send the two girls out of the room while they talk. Marietta organizes one or two sumptuous dinners for officials who can make things easier for her husband in prison, but in all the time he is away she never goes out socially, nor does she ever get to wear the Yerevan-made high-heeled shoes with black lacquered toes and suede uppers that she had once bought from a friend in anticipation of an evening out with Stanislav. Zhanna and Larisa take them out of the box and totter around the bedroom when their mother is in the kitchen part of the house.

In October 1964 Khrushchev is ousted as leader of the Soviet Union. He has antagonized the Soviet military and lost international prestige by caving in to US President John F. Kennedy when removing Soviet missiles from Cuba. He has angered people all across the Soviet Union by forcing them to stand in long lines for inferior bread after the failure of his dream to make the Asian steppes into vast, golden corn fields. Most damning of all in the eyes of his comrades in the Politburo, he has ceased to heed them when they object to his 'hare-brained schemes, immature conclusions, hasty decisions, actions divorced from reality, bragging, phrase-mongering, commandism and unwillingness to take into account the achievements of science', as *Pravda* puts it.

A new leader emerges in the Kremlin after a period of jockeying for power. Leonid Brezhnev, a former metallurgical engineer, puts his own people in place. He makes Semyon Apryatkin head of the Grozny communist party in place of the over-zealous Trofimov. Attitudes towards the alternative economy begin to change again, particularly in the case of cars. Brezhnev seeks to end austerity. Over time he takes the attitude that the state should work for its citizens and not the other way around, and that no one should be asked to sacrifice material comforts. Although speculation remains a source of official concern because it smacks of profit or personal gain and can exacerbate shortages, the Brezhnev regime backs away from police pressure and criminal sanctions. Penalties for speculation become less severe, and the mandatory confiscation of property is not enforced. It is Stanislav Suvorov's ill luck

Leonid Brezhnev posing with one of his fleet of luxury automobiles.

to have been a few years ahead of the revised thinking. Under Brezhnev nine out of ten party officials accused of breaking the law will get off with a reprimand, and even non-party citizens will be treated more leniently. Brezhnev himself has a passion for automobiles, and after his installation begins assembling a collection that will include a fleet of ten ZIL limousines, a Lincoln Continental, a Chrysler 300, a Maserati Quatroporte and a Rolls-Royce Silver Shadow. His mother, they say, comes to visit him and, seeing all the cars, asks, 'But Leonid, what if the Bolsheviks come back?'

The 1961–4 anti-speculation campaign is abandoned in part because communist and government officials are increasingly reluctant to enforce it, compromised as they themselves are by their pursuit of their own consumer comforts.

CHAPTER 8

TEARS FOR GROZNY

NOT LONG AFTER Khrushchev's downfall, Stanislav's family petitions the court for his release. They employ the same lawyer. A hearing is set. She argues to the judge that Suvorov the shoemaker has been a model prisoner, something that is confirmed by the prison director. She cites Article 44.2 of the Principles of Criminal Law which provides that prisoners sentenced to more than three years for an 'intentional crime' may be set free after they have served two thirds of their time.

In August 1966 the court makes its ruling. Stanislav Alexandrovich Suvorov's sentence will be reduced for exemplary behaviour. He has served four years and ten months behind bars, just over two thirds of his seven-year sentence, and will be released.

The excitement in the Suvorov household knows no bounds. Marietta offers to come and pick him up, once the necessary papers are signed, but he says no, he will make his own way home.

A few days later Zhanna and Larisa are playing outside the house on Pavel Musorov Street when a crowded No. 7 tram stops on the far side of the road. As it moves away, its bell clanging, a stockily built man wearing a cap and carrying a black suitcase crosses the road towards them. Zhanna's heart gives a great leap. The eight-year-old runs into the house. 'Mama! Mama! Papa is home!' She runs out again. Her father embraces her. 'Zhanna! Zhanna!' He picks up Larisa and carries her past the apricot trees and jasmine in the little front garden and through the wicket door in the double doors of the garage that serves as their front entrance.

Marietta is waiting for him in the yard, tears in her eyes. He sets his younger daughter down and kisses and hugs his wife, then his mother-in-law Farandzem and his mother Sonia, who has hurried in from next door. Bakhshi hears the commotion and rushes over from his shoe workshop to embrace him tightly, laughing and shouting his name. Their Ukrainian neighbours, Alexey, a grumpy pensioner, and Polina, tears streaming down her soft round face, show up. 'Welcome back, Stasik,' says Alexey gravely, kissing him hard on both cheeks. Stanislav's teenage cousin Sasha sprints across the road to catch a tram and fetch Lena and Volodya. Other relatives arrive, including Stanislav's half-sister Nellya and his aunt Anna. Someone is sent out to buy sausage, cheese and vodka to add to the spread of pilaf, *dolma* (vine leaves stuffed with rice and lamb), pickled cucumbers, cabbage salad, bean paté, sautéed aubergine, beetroot, peppers and sweet halva dessert Marietta has already laid out on a long table under the vines in the little courtyard.

Zhanna never sees her mother more excited than that evening. Marietta is glowing with happiness and hardly leaves Stanislav's side. The celebrations continue until late with people coming and going, everyone hugging Stanislav. Zhanna and Larisa, bursting with joy, are allowed to stay up and scurry in and out of the kitchen, clearing plates and keeping an ear to the adult conversation. The evening ends with Armenian songs and much hand-clapping and toasts by Stanislav. 'If we have health and happiness that's all we can hope for, isn't that true?' he says after toasting everyone who has stood by him.

After the celebrations Stanislav has to adjust to life outside, to adapt to the rhythms and demands of the family and to reacquaint himself with his daughters after almost five years' absence. He

Ready for school: Larisa and Zhanna, aged six and eight in 1966.

must face neighbours on the street who see him as an offender. He cannot return to the shoe factory, where everyone knows that he is a jailbird. He is employed instead in a garment enterprise in a different part of town. What a humiliation this must be for him, stitching clothes rather than shoes. He goes to work every morning on the tram, and he and Marietta again do extra jobs together in the evening, cobbling and sewing, making shoes and trousers.

Stanislav refuses to give in to anger over his experience. However, the prison spell has had a devastating effect on his family's prestige. The Armenian community in Grozny is like a village, and as in any village its social cohesion depends on gossip. Everyone knows everyone else's business. The stigma of prison tarnishes his good name and by association that of his wife and mother and mother-in-law and aunt. It could also damage the prospects of Zhanna and Larisa as they grow up.

Marietta and Stanislav are very ambitious for their children. Zhanna is always first in every subject and Larisa is developing impressive musical skills. They plan to send them to university when they are old enough, although having an ex-prisoner for a father might put obstacles in the way of advancement in later life. Though Farandzem and Anna have not had to give up their party cards because of Stanislav's imprisonment, membership of the party, almost a prerequisite for a career in the professions, might be barred to the daughters of a speculator. This thinking is a hangover from Stalin's time, when, as Nadezhda Mandelstam would recall in her 1970 book *Hope Against Hope*, about the effect of the imprisonment of her poet husband Osip Mandelstam: 'Not only ex-prisoners but their families were marked for life ... to cover up such unpleasant facts people were always inventing new life stories for themselves.'

For their own sake and for their children's future, Stanislav and Marietta, aged thirty-eight and twenty-eight, feel they have to invent a new life story for their family, by migrating to some other part of the Soviet Union and starting life afresh. The obvious place to lose one's identity is in a big city like Moscow or Leningrad, but the *propiska* system makes it impossible to get a residence permit without already having a job there and a permanent address. Besides, permits to major cities are refused to convicted persons if the sentence exceeded five years. Stanislav could perhaps choose to take his family to one of the Baltic republics, Estonia, Latvia or Lithuania, which the Kremlin is eager to populate with other nationalities to weaken their ethnic majorities, but that prospect does not attract him. Nagorno-Karabakh is Marietta's homeland, but going to live there is not practical, and there are rumours of ethnic clashes over the imposition of Azeri as the official language and over Azeri police replacing ethnic Armenians.

They contemplate moving to Ukraine after a Jewish friend, a neighbour at their first house in Grozny, suggests that they can have a good life in Cherkassy, fifteen hundred kilometres to the north-west. This city of a quarter of a million people has major industrial and chemical plants, and a large shoe factory. Stanislav and Marietta go to Cherkassy and explore the city on its new trolley-bus system. They are assured of work in the shoe factory and an apartment, and Marietta resigns herself to moving there, but Stanislav is not convinced. Cherkassy feels provincial and is not far enough from Grozny. He wants to go even further, to start life again far over the horizon, in a city where the girls would have good prospects.

One day Zhanna and Larisa come home from school to find their mother looking very serious, and are alarmed to see their grandmother Farandzem in tears. Their father tells them to sit down. A big decision has been made. They are going to live somewhere else. They will be moving to the city of Krasnoyarsk in Siberia. Siberia! They are old enough to know that Siberia is very far away and very cold in winter.

Stanislav tells his daughters that he and their mama will go first. Their baba Farandzem has retired from her railway job, having reached the age of fifty-five, so she can look after them until their parents send for them when they are settled into new jobs and able to provide accommodation. Then Zhanna and Larisa and their grandmother will join them. The girls realize, to their distress, that they are about to lose their father again, for who knows how long, and their mother this time too.

The idea of moving to Siberia originates with a fellow shoe-maker, Misha Avetisyan. He tells Stanislav and Marietta that his brother Sasha, also a shoemaker, lives in Krasnoyarsk and has a reasonably good life. Wages are 20 per cent higher in Siberia than in the rest of Russia, shops are well stocked to encourage people like themselves to move there, and it has hundreds of factories. It is cold in the winter, but the apartments have central heating; the summers are short but hot, and you can get a plot of land to grow fruit and vegetables. There is a constant demand for people with specialist qualifications, not least in shoemaking and sewing. And there are hundreds of Armenians already living there. Misha enthuses so much about life in Siberia that he tells

Stanislav and Marietta that if they decide to take their chances there he and his wife, also called Marietta, will up sticks and go with them.

Two things in the end help Stanislav make up his mind. First, in Krasnoyarsk no one will know he has a prison record, and if they do find out, well, perhaps it will not count for so much there. Many people who go to live in Siberia have reasons of their own for making a new start which they would prefer to keep to themselves. The other is perhaps just as important. His and Marietta's priority as parents is to put Zhanna and Larisa through university to give them every chance in life. Russia's bigger provincial cities have good teachers and education is free, all the way from primary school to university graduation, and Krasnoyarsk, Misha tells them, has fine schools and universities, certainly better than Grozny.

Of course life will be tough compared to their comfortable existence in the balmy climate of Grozny. Conditions are so hard that it is said more people leave Siberia than arrive there, despite government inducements. Stanislav has few worries, however, about coping with the cold. He spent three years in frozen Chukotka doing his military service and survived that.

Stanislav and Marietta break the news to Sonia and Bakhshi and Stanislav's younger half-sister Nellya and stepsister Sveta, following which they take the tram across town to tell Lena and her husband of their decision. It is devastating news for Lena. She came to Grozny to be with her mother and sister. Both are now going to leave for somewhere so far away she might never see them again.

The next day they call in on their Ingush friend Bashir to bid farewell. Bashir's wife Fatima makes a big exception and eats shashlik with them in the green and gold dining room.

Stanislav and Misha prepare to depart first. The two Mariettas will follow when their husbands have found somewhere to stay. There is a great gathering of family and friends the night before the two men leave. Stanislav makes sure that everyone who drinks has a little Armenian brandy in their glass, then stands up and makes the toast: 'God willing, God willing, that we're drinking not for the last time!' Everyone choruses, 'God willing!' This time it has real significance because it may be a long time, if ever, before they are all together again under one roof.

PART TWO

CHAPTER 9

KRASNOYARSK

O N WEDNESDAY, 4 October 1967 the two migrating shoe-makers, Stanislav Suvorov and his companion Misha Avetisyan, each carrying a suitcase heavy with the tools of their trade, arrive by train from Grozny at the city of Mineralnye Vody and board the daily Aeroflot flight to Krasnoyarsk, four time zones to the east. As usual the hundred or so passengers on the Tu-104 twin jet include Russians, Georgians, Azeris, Chechens, even a few Armenians, most of them bearing large hessian sacks of home-grown produce to sell in Krasnoyarsk. Flights are extremely cheap in the Soviet Union and such private commerce is tolerated by the communist authorities to make up for state deficiencies. A peasant can travel across the country with a sack of onions and return with a profit. As the cabin fills with cigarette smoke and the vodka flows, Stanislav is undoubtedly more than a little apprehensive about what life has in store in the frozen wastes of Siberia. He is going to be separated from his children until he finds work and somewhere to live, and when he does, they will have to accept possibly miserable conditions compared to those they enjoy in Grozny. But he is stubborn enough to see it through, whatever the personal cost, for the future of his family. He knows too that Marietta is just as determined as he is. In a family of strong women she has demonstrated resilience and fortitude during his imprisonment.

When Stanislav and Misha disembark from the plane in Krasnoyarsk, Misha's brother Sasha, a tall, handsome, meticulously dressed Armenian with wavy hair, is there to greet them. He escorts his fellow Crispinians to a bus that will take them to his apartment on the eastern side of the city. The new arrivals will stay here until they find their own accommodation.

There is snow on the ground. Winter has already set in, and it will prove to be exceptionally hard, with snow lying for over six months. Arriving at the start of winter will test their resolve. So too will the pollution. It is much worse than in Grozny. There is an acidic smell from chemical plants, and the snow in the streets is flecked with black from coal-fired boilers. Krasnoyarsk is at the heart of the country's military-industrial complex, and houses hundreds of smoke-spewing chemical and armament factories transferred from western Russia to escape the advancing Germans in 1941. It has large-scale metallurgy and mining enterprises, and an immense aluminium plant with no fewer than thirty-seven smokestacks. The city is also a centre for the manufacture of submarine missiles and space technology, and for research into nuclear weapons, though the inhabitants know little about this. For these reasons it is a 'closed' city. Only Soviet citizens can live or visit here. Foreigners on the Trans-Siberian Express, which connects Europe to the Pacific Ocean and stops in Krasnoyarsk, are not allowed to leave the railway station. If they managed to do so, they would be fortunate to detect any secret installations through the toxic fog that, especially in the winter, blocks out the sun for days on end.

As the shoemakers travel across the city they glimpse, amid the factories and concrete-panel apartment buildings, high walls topped with barbed wire and armed guards silhouetted on watch towers. Some local resident inevitably tells them, with a smirk, that there are so many prisons in Krasnoyarsk, it is better to live across the road from a prison than to live across the road from your home.

Krasnoyarsk has a long history as a prison city. Like Grozny it was founded by Cossack soldiers, who in 1628 built a military stockade to defend themselves against hostile nomads. After 1690, when Siberia was joined to Russia, the greater Krasnoyarsk region, a vast expanse a quarter the size of Canada, became a dumping ground for Moscow's undesirables. The first were the Old Believers, expelled after a schism in the Russian Orthodox Church. Then came the Decembrists, Russian officers exiled after a failed revolt for political reform in St Petersburg in December 1825. They were followed by the Polish revolutionaries of 1831 and the Marxists of the 1890s. Vladimir Ilyich Lenin spent three years in exile in Siberia at the end of the nineteenth century, two months in Krasnoyarsk city and the rest in Shushenskoye, a settlement in the wilderness. But common lawbreakers from Moscow were also dispatched to Krasnoyarsk's prisons in such great numbers that at the start of the twentieth century, almost a quarter of its inhabitants were classified as criminals.

After the Revolution the city became the administrative heart of Stalin's complex of prisons and camps, which a former inmate, Alexander Solzhenitsyn, termed the Gulag archipelago, the word Gulag being an acronym for 'Chief Administration of Corrective Labour Camps'. During Stalin's Great Terror of the 1930s people said that the tallest building in Moscow was the secret police headquarters, the Lubyanka, because one could see Siberia from its windows. Camp inmates – some two million at any one time over a quarter of a century – were forced to work as slave labourers, building roads, railways and dams, and constructing facilities to extract coal, diamonds, gas, oil and minerals from some of the coldest tracts of land on earth.

The full story of the Gulag would not become known inside Russia until the fall of the Soviet Union, but Stanislav and Marietta have an idea of its horrors. They have both read Solzhenitsyn's sensational book *One Day in the Life of Ivan Denisovich*, describing the misery of daily life in the camps; Khrushchev briefly allowed its publication in 1962 as part of his de-Stalinization project, and it has been reproduced as *samizdat* – underground literature – and passed from hand to hand ever since, which is how Stanislav got his copy. The new Soviet leader has closed the camps, including the Yenisey laager in Krasnoyarsk city, which housed up to ten thousand inmates, but the infrastructure of the Gulag remains, and the prisons are still used to house the most violent criminals from all over the Soviet Union.

It takes some days before Stanislav comes to appreciate that this city of six hundred thousand people has another side, a more benign character reflecting its history and location. Residents get used to taking their bearings from a small, old Russian Orthodox chapel atop a steep hill in the city centre. With its pointed roof and golden dome, Paraskeva Pyatnitza provides a sense of spirituality and a connection with the historic past in the midst of the urban landscape. The city is bisected by a mighty river, the Yenisey, which flows from the Sayan mountains of northern Mongolia to the Arctic Ocean and forms the border between the grand ravines of western Siberia and the endless taiga of eastern Siberia. The name Krasnoyarsk is derived from *krasny*, meaning both 'red' and 'beautiful', and a native word *yar* – 'steep riverbank'. The lyrical local writer Viktor Astafiev described the river as 'sometimes kind and quiet, broad, sometimes locked in cliffs, sometimes furious, foaming or raging with its white waves in a storm'. On the coldest winter days it envelops both banks in clouds of white vapour.

The east bank is heavily industrialized, but the city centre on the west bank of the river is little changed since pre-revolutionary times, when the playwright Anton Chekhov described it as 'a picturesque, cultured town with clean and paved streets, large houses of stone and elegant churches, compared with which Tomsk is … the acme of *mauvais ton* [vulgarity]'. On the west side is an imposing colonnaded riverboat station built in grandiose, Stalin-era 'wedding-cake' style, with a spire topped by a star. Along a four-kilometre boulevard, Prospect Mira, are found the city's grand party and administrative structures. The tree-lined avenue has several nineteenth-century buildings in varying shades of yellow and orange with ornately decorated windows and tiny minarets, and their ground-floor windows located below pavement level – a novelty to the visitors from the Caucasus. There is an Orthodox cathedral built in Siberian baroque fashion with blue-painted roof and golden domes and a number of small parks and pleasant river walks.

One of Prospect Mira's most handsome buildings is No. 73, the Pushkin Drama Theatre, a grey faux-brick edifice near the river with a set of steps leading up to an entrance flanked by pillars. Stanislav mounts these steps two days after arriving in Krasnoyarsk. Sasha has told him there is an opening here. Soviet theatres sometimes hire their own shoemakers as shoe shops cannot meet their requirements and theatre staff do not have leather-working skills.

Stanislav's home from home: the Pushkin Theatre in Krasnoyarsk, 2017.

The marble-floor foyer opens into a spacious two-hundred-seat auditorium with double balcony, 'royal' boxes lined with red velvet and a large, electric-light-bulb chandelier. In the upper-level corridors are photographs of the grand opening in 1902, and portraits of its most prominent alumni, including the much-loved Russian Hamlet, Innokenty Smoktunovsky, who has also starred in several film comedies. Stanislav has seen his 1966 movie *Watch the Car*, in which he plays a man who steals the cars of the emerging Soviet bourgeoisie and gives the profits to an orphanage.

The manager of the Pushkin Theatre tells Stanislav he needs a shoemaker who can produce, repair and alter footwear for actors, including all sorts of shoes, Cossack boots, military boots, courtiers' slippers, ballet shoes and sandals, while also turning his hand to fashioning sword belts, military helmets and bandoliers. The person hired would work flexible hours, leaving free time for another job, and he would be eligible to apply for accommodation in the theatre's official residence for actors and staff when it becomes available, though there is a long waiting list.

At such interviews the employer normally asks to see an applicant's *trudovaya knizhka*, or work record. This has a section in which is recorded a person's qualifications, recommendations, honorary titles, orders and medals. Stanislav has a war commendation as a replacement worker when he was in his teens and a service record from the army. He has earned high praise for his skills from the Grozny shoe factory. But he is also identified as an ex-convict. The director must see this. Perhaps he asks for an explanation. Perhaps he doesn't care, as decent shoemakers are very *deficit* in Siberia. Whatever transpires, he offers the Russian-Armenian shoemaker the job of the theatre's first leather worker. The new employee is shown to a vacant storeroom beneath the theatre. He sets about converting it into a temporary workshop, laying out the tools of his trade on an array of shelves – anvil, scissors, pliers, hammer, awl, rasp, skewers, ruler, needles, thread, tacks, wax and nails. In time he will be given a proper atelier in a courtyard behind the playhouse.

Sasha also tells Stanislav of vacancies in the city's two foot-wear factories. One is Spartak, which is automated and produces typical Soviet-quality shoes in bulk. The other is the Krasno-yarsk shoe factory, which uses traditional methods to produce customized footwear. The director of the latter recruits Stanislav immediately and finds him a place on the shop floor. Again the issue of time served in prison is glossed over.

Situated on Svobodny Prospect at the western end of the city centre, the shoe factory is a medium-sized enterprise with eight hundred workers, most in the main building but with others at repair shops and four outlet shops around the city. It possesses a fleet of vehicles comprising a Volga for the director, two Moskvich cars and twenty-two vans. The shoemakers are mostly Russian, but include Tatars, Baltic nationals and four Armenians. They produce fur-lined boots for hunters, men's high boots for winter wear, men's walking shoes, women's semi-high boots, women's high boots, slippers for the home, cork-heeled shoes and sandals. There is a particular demand for fur-lined leather and suede boots, ideal for the dry snows of Siberia. The factory has three specialized work departments. In the cutting department pieces of leather are stamped using lasts and presses, and individual tools and devices are employed to cut patterns and eyes in the leather. In the sewing department the pieces composing the uppers are sewn together. The fin-ishing department is where the shoes are assembled. Stanislav starts work in the finishing department, removing the lasts, then paring, smoothing and burnishing the edges of the soles and heels.

The Grozny shoemaker has, so to speak, landed on his feet, securing two jobs in a matter of days. Neither is well paid but between them he has a decent wage.

Misha also finds work in the shoe factory, and he and Stanislav rent a tiny apartment on the east bank of the Yenisey. As newcomers they are put at the bottom of the housing list for allocated accommodation, but they can now obtain permits and make their living in Krasnoyarsk as accredited residents.

Three weeks after leaving Grozny they are able to invite the two Mariettas to join them. On the day they arrive, the temperature does not rise above minus ten degrees Celsius. The two young women feel terribly cold after they descend from the plane as they are not wearing proper Siberian winter clothing.

One can imagine the dismay they feel in those first few days, having left behind comfortable homes with modern conveniences and a warm climate with abundant produce. Here they have to face the humiliation of huddling together in a small room, suffering the indignity of sharing with strangers a toilet, a bathroom and a kitchen, and all that goes with the misery of communal living in Russian cities, not to mention enduring the metallic cold outside, the depressing landscape of factories and prisons and the polluted air.

Misha's wife finds it impossible to bear. She complains incessantly about the dirt, the pollution, the food and the cold, 'all worse than in Grozny'. She yearns to go home. After less than a month, the very one who helped persuade them all to come to Krasnoyarsk decides it is not for him and his wife after all. Misha and Marietta Avetisyan say their goodbyes and return to Grozny, where Misha resumes work at the shoe factory.

How lonely and miserable Stanislav and Marietta must feel now, abandoned by their two friends and missing their family. Those early days are also overshadowed by the knowledge that when they left Grozny Stanislav's aunt Anna was dying of skin cancer. Because of her standing as a member of the Supreme Soviet she is cared for in the main oncological centre in Moscow. However no treatment can save her, and she passes away that November, two years short of her fiftieth birthday.

To cope with the loneliness, Marietta begins to keep Stanislav company in the evenings at the Pushkin Theatre. She does some stitching and sewing work. When he learns of her skills, the director hires Marietta too.

Before the winter is out, Marietta has become the wardrobe mistress of the Pushkin Theatre and a regular presence behind the scenes during performances. She accompanies the production crew and cast when they go on tour to Omsk and Barnaul, a round trip of almost three thousand kilometres, with a repertoire that includes *The Old Man* by Maxim Gorky, about the escapades of a group of revolutionaries in tsarist Russia, and a comedy, *The Millionairess*, by Bernard Shaw.

Like any husband, Stanislav is not happy about his attractive wife going off with a fun-loving theatrical troupe and he doesn't want her to accept any further such assignments. In any case, having acquired confidence and a sense of independence that work gives, and aware of her lack of education, Marietta becomes more ambitious for herself. She applies for and is accepted as an apprentice in the patterns workshop of the same shoe factory where her husband works, and takes evening classes in economics in the city technical college.

Within a year Stanislav and Marietta have established themselves in good employment, and as the winter finally gives way to spring and the trees on Prospect Mira burst into leaf they can better appreciate the positive aspects of their new surroundings. The benefits about which Misha's brother, Sasha, enthused turn out to be real: corruption is less prevalent than in the Caucasus and the shops are well stocked compared to the state stores in the Chechen capital. But they sorely miss their children and cannot bring them to live in the tiny apartment. They fret about their school work and friendships and how Marietta's mother is coping. Telephone calls are a major hassle, as they must be made through telegraph offices and both parties need to be there and agree the timing in advance. They write letters and send parcels with presents as often as they can. Their work distracts them from their misery. They console themselves with the knowledge that they are making this sacrifice for their children in the long run.

Zhanna and Larisa too yearn for their parents. But they have their beloved baba Farandzem to look after them. She makes their meals, gets them ready for school, takes them to music lessons, ballet and gymnastics, knits them garments and comforts them in their loneliness. They sometimes sleep overnight at the house of their aunt Lena who makes them everyday clothes. They eagerly anticipate letters and parcels from their papa and mama, which contain scarce items they have managed to find in Krasnoyarsk such as tangerines and blocks of chocolate, and once two pairs of tights which are the envy of their school friends. They treasure most the letters in which their parents express their longing to be together with sentiments such as that expressed by Marietta, 'I would fly to see you all if I had wings.'

Their parents have to endure a second winter in Siberia, living in the tiny apartment and working day and night, but in the spring of 1969, a year and a half after leaving Grozny, Stanislav and Marietta are at last provided with better accommodation. They are allocated a family space in the Pushkin Theatre's House of Actors at No. 72 Markovsky Street, close to the theatre. This tree-shaded road is named after a Bolshevik hacked to death by Cossacks in the civil war of 1918, and was once known as Windmill Street. In its pre-revolutionary heyday the district housed hotels, baths and drinking dens. Most of the nineteenth-century dwellings which line the street are built of logs and have decorated window shutters. Lenin lived at No. 27 for two months when exiled to Siberia, and it is now a museum to his memory.

The House of Actors is a long two-storey wooden structure with thirteen apartments on each level. The entrance leads to a central staircase with creaking corridors running off to the left and right. All the lodgings are single rooms occupied by actors and retired players of the Pushkin Theatre, with the exception of the apartments at the end of the corridors, which have two rooms and are reserved for families. Stanislav and Marietta are allocated one of these on the upper floor.

Their delight knows no bounds as they inspect the apartment. They can now bring their daughters and Marietta's mother to live with them. They can say goodbye to the cramped little space in a concrete block on the east side which has been their home for almost two years. They really like the idea of living in a pre-revolutionary building with an interesting cast of characters as neighbours, some of whom they already know from their association with the theatre. It is as if they are emerging from the darkness into the sunlight. There is not much room for three adults and two children but they will cope. Millions of people are worse off. They move in their belongings and Stanislav heads for the airport.

A day later, back in Grozny, Zhanna is called out from her grade four class by the headmistress, who tells her with a twinkle in her eye, 'Suvorova, there is somebody here to see you who looks very important.' She finds her father, dressed in a fine coat and cap, waiting at the school office with a big smile. She and Larisa are allowed to take the rest of the day off school, and when walking to the house, their father tells them the news that will change their lives for ever. They are at last going to Krasnoyarsk, to live together there with their papa and mama and their baba Farandzem. Stanislav cautions them not to get too excited about their new accommodation but that they will manage, and he asks them to be patient for a little longer as he must help their grandmother Farandzem sell the house first and then go back to Krasnoyarsk before sending for them when they have finished the school term. In the next few days Stanislav and Farandzem, whom he addresses fondly as 'mother', go through their belongings and sell off the furniture other than two beds, the sewing machine, china, carpets, books and linen, for which he arranges shipment to their new home. The truck will also take the shiny black Rostov-Don piano, so the girls can continue with their musical education. He returns to Siberia after making arrangements for Farandzem and the children to follow by train with their luggage when the school breaks for the summer holidays in a few weeks' time. To Zhanna it seems like an eternity.

For the retired Armenian woman from Nagorno-Karabakh it is a time of very mixed emotions, joy at the prospect of being reunited with Marietta after being parted for the best part of two years, but heartbreak that she will be living far from Lena and Lena's children Misha and Yura. Farandzem cannot escape a sense of once more leaving Lena behind, and the parting from her and her other grandchildren is very painful. They will be in the same country but at such a distance from each other that travel will involve a major expedition. Also, she is going down in the world for a second time. In her thirties she quit the fine house her husband owned in Martakert, and her work there as a party official, to live in a single room in the Oil Workers' Block in Grozny. Now in her late fifties, she is leaving behind the spacious two-section house and garden in Grozny, where she has enjoyed a certain status as a party stalwart and conductress on the Moscow train, to move to a cramped space in an industrial city, in Siberia of all places.

She must accept what fate, and her son-in-law and younger daughter, have decided for her. Farandzem notifies the Grozny party branch that she is moving on, says goodbye to her comrades and friends, and sets out with Zhanna and Larisa for the railway station, where Lena and her family gather to see them off, amid tears and embraces, on the long journey to Siberia, not knowing if they will ever meet again.

CHAPTER 10

BECOMING SIBERIANS

THE TRAIN JOURNEY from Grozny to Krasnoyarsk takes almost a week, two and a half days to Moscow and three and a half more from the capital to their destination. Farandzem spends most of the time reading while the children play in the corridors or gaze out from the top bunk of their compartment at the towns and villages they pass. They have supplies of chicken and sausage, and their grandmother occasionally gets off the train to buy fruit, smoked fish and home-made pies from the hawkers who appear at every station. There is a great hustle and bustle when other passengers get on and off at the big cities between Moscow and Krasnoyarsk, Gorky (today Nizhny Novgorod) on the first day, Sverdlovsk (Yekaterinburg) on the next, and Novosibirsk. The scenery gradually changes from the greenery of western Russia to a landscape of rockfaces and trees, then endless expanses of wheat, followed by forests of silver birch and meadows of wild flowers. Finally, after crossing red-shaded hills silhouetted against the rising sun, the train steams into Krasnoyarsk, where they see Stanislav and Marietta waiting for them on the platform.

Over the following days the joy of being together again as a family is tempered by the living conditions in the House of Actors. The children and their grandmother, accustomed to separate bedrooms in Grozny, now have to share one room, with a bucket in the corner for toilet emergencies at night, while their parents sleep on an extending couch in the tiny room which serves as the living and dining area. They have a little kitchenette with a gas burner so they do not have to make meals in the common kitchen, but they must use a communal bathroom and toilet on the upper corridor, which all the residents are responsible for cleaning. Zhanna is considered old enough to take her turn at mopping and scrubbing. It is nevertheless a novelty to the eleven-year-old and her nine-year-old sister to live in such an unusual and interesting place and they are just so happy to be reunited with their parents.

Living in the House of Actors exposes the Suvorov family to the cultural elite of the city. The shoemaker and his wife do not regard themselves as intellectuals but they are well read and enjoy lively interactions with the actors, writers, musicians, stage managers and other theatre folk with whom they share the log house. It is a world where conversation centres on books, plays and films, and where *samizdat* copies of the latest literary works circulate among the residents.

The family settles into a routine. The parents work every day at the shoe factory, and Stanislav spends the evenings in his studio at the theatre. Baba Farandzem looks after the girls while both parents are absent. In September Zhanna and Larisa begin classes in Krasnoyarsk School No. 11, a four-storey brick and concrete building on Prospect Karl Marx, four blocks from the apartment. The weather was pleasantly warm when they arrived, but by mid-October the permanent winter snow already covers the ground. It is another exceptionally hard winter with temperatures sometimes dipping below minus forty Celsius. The school stays open even in such intense cold, though it does close one mid-January day when the temperature drops to minus fifty-one. Even walking the short distance to and from school swaddled from head to foot, Zhanna and Larisa sometimes feel frozen to the bone. At a minimum, three layers of clothing are said to be necessary for the Siberian winter, the first to keep dry, the second to be insulated and the third to be windproof. They find that they never have enough layers on the coldest days. People in the street warn each other of the first sign of frostbite by pointing to their face if they see a white patch on the nose or cheek.

There are other new and more pleasant experiences. They all became regular visitors to the public *banya*. The bathhouse is not so much a luxury as a necessity, because of the grime of the streets and the often-sooty air, and the inadequacy of their shared washroom. On entering the male or female section, a customer is given a sheet for use as a toga and a bundle of leafy birch branches known as a *venik* with which they gleefully smack each other's bare backs in the sauna to open the pores and tone the skin.

The girls are also introduced to the winter sports of ice skating and skiing, and get used to asking not if it is cold enough but warm enough to ski, as outdoor sports are not possible in extreme cold. After the first frosts of winter, a large area just off Prospect Mira is flooded to become an ice rink, and they are soon able to circle round and round on skates with their father and hundreds of others at weekends. As part of their school sports curriculum the girls go on bus trips to the forest, where they are given cross-country skis and sent off round the forest trails.

Few cities in the world have as great a range in temperature between summer and winter as Krasnoyarsk. When the snows melt the seasons are like those of southern Europe, if one excludes the occasional snowfall in May or September. On warm days there are opportunities to explore the taiga, the subarctic forest of larch, pine, spruce and fir which covers most of Siberia. On clear days they can see the 'smoke-coloured and dreamy mountains' which Chekhov said reminded him of the Caucasus and prompted the playwright to describe Krasnoyarsk as the best and most beautiful of all Siberian cities.

One day in the taiga, according to Astafiev, is worth a whole season in Crimea, and Stanislav takes the family for picnics to a spot where Scots pines provide shelter from the hot summer sun, and they can roast fresh lamb and aubergines, Caucasian fare, over a campfire. However, Astafiev's rhapsodic one day in the taiga is often shortened as the air begins to hum with clouds of biting mosquitoes, especially on sultry late-summer afternoons.

In the autumn they join the weekend exodus out of Krasnoyarsk to hunt for mushrooms at the edge of the forests. Zhanna and Larisa are taught in school how to recognize the forty or so most popular types, and those to avoid, especially the attractive little white mushrooms with red dots known as death caps. They are told that the pink *russula* can be nibbled raw or eaten fried, and that the thin-capped *Boletus lutens* must be pickled for six weeks before eating. They hunt in the shade for a delicious fungus known as round-the-tree-trunks, they scrabble among the leaves for saucer-shaped milk mushrooms, which they take home in buckets to dry and store for the winter, and best of all they delight in locating clusters of golden chanterelles in mossy glades. Mushrooms form a big part of Siberian cuisine. They are fried with potatoes, folded into omelettes, made into soup to eat with sour cream, and pickled and transformed into *zakuski* (tasters) to accompany a glass of vodka in the long winter evenings. The Armenian family soon gets used to Russian cuisine, as they cannot always get the herbs, spices and greens of their healthy Caucasian diet, and they begin to enjoy the frequent mushroom dishes and new favourites like salmon fish pie.

One thing casts a shadow over their lives: the secret. Like all children, Zhanna and Larisa make new friends in the neighbourhood. They chat away with them about everything under the sun. However, the girls never, ever speak about the reason the family has moved from the Caucasus to Siberia. If asked, they say it is because of their parents' work. They love their father and are fiercely protective of him, and his spell in prison is never mentioned even at home, not even in passing. It is as if it never happened. It becomes a blank page in the history of the Suvorov family. It is a secret that helps bind the family together during all the triumphs, tragedies and hardships they will experience in Siberia.

They are not the only ones who have come to Krasnoyarsk for reasons that are best left unspoken. Some residents have served prison sentences in Siberia for crimes committed elsewhere or have been incarcerated in the Gulag for political reasons and after their release have stayed to make a new life for themselves. It is not difficult to assimilate: here, besides Russians, there are pockets of Latvians, Lithuanians, Estonians, Ukrainians, Byelorussians, Tatars, Jews and Germans, the latter descendants of the settlers who lived along the Volga until Stalin uprooted them as potential collaborators. The city market stalls are serviced by Uzbeks, Turkmens and Tajiks, who bring great sacks of produce on cheap-ticket flights from their home republics. And there is a small Armenian community, to which the Suvorovs become attached, though Marietta now speaks and thinks in Russian, except when conversing with her mother. Stanislav uses less and less Armenian. The two girls speak Russian as their native language.

It is a friendly city, its population drawn together by shared hardship and distance from Moscow. Siberians are less afraid to speak out about the irritants of Soviet life than inhabitants of the capital. A group from the Siberian School of Economists even sends a proposal for a free market to the Kremlin, a daring act in the 1970s. What can Moscow do? Send them to Siberia? People live more freely here than in western Russia. Despite being associated with isolation, cold and deprivation, Siberia never experienced serfdom, and it is synonymous with independence and self-sufficiency, notions attractive to the shoemaker.

After their first winter in Krasnoyarsk, Zhanna and Larisa are sent to spend a long summer holiday in Grozny, partly to bond with their aunt and cousins, but also to have access to the fresh fruit and vegetables that are deficient in Krasnoyarsk stores. Their parents put them on a flight to Mineralnye Vody, where Lena picks them up. While staying with her they play with their cousins and help with stitching, cooking, painting and gardening. Aunt Lena spoils them in return, giving them treats and taking them on outings. Every year from then on they spend summers back in Grozny.

Their grandmother, Farandzem, celebrates her sixtieth birthday on 1 May 1972, not long before Zhanna and Larisa leave Krasnoyarsk for their annual vacation in Grozny. As she gets ready for a festive dinner she asks Zhanna, who is doing her homework, to help put rollers in her silver-grey hair. Zhanna says she needs to finish her work, and baba Farandzem says, 'Never mind.'

Farandzem on her last birthday, 1972.

That summer it transpires that Farandzem is fighting stomach cancer, but she is expected to live for at least another year. However on 2 August 1972, while the girls are still in Grozny, she collapses in the communal bathroom in the House of Actors and never recovers consciousness. A distraught Lena breaks the news to the girls that their grandmother has died. The grief of the children is compounded by the fact that they are five thousand kilometres away. Failing to help her beloved grandmother fix her hair on her last birthday adds to Zhanna's grief and makes her feel guilty for many years afterwards.

Lena and Volodya fly to Krasnoyarsk for the funeral, though the girls stay behind with their cousins. A quarter of a century has elapsed since Farandzem Gukasyan left Nagorno-Karabakh and moved to Grozny, never imagining she would end up in Siberia. She is buried in Krasnoyarsk cemetery, thousands of kilometres from where her husband lies in an unknown grave on a remote wartime battlefield.

In October 1972 the domestic life of the Suvorovs, and of the other members of the close-knit theatrical community in the House of Actors, is disrupted: the old wooden building is to be demolished to make way for a multi-storey block of apartments. The shoe factory has an allocation of living space for its employees, and assigns the family a two-room flat with separate bathroom and toilet. It is on the third floor of a new concrete building on Zheleznodorozhnikov Ulitza, or Railway Street, three kilometres from the theatre. Outside is a grass strip which doubles as a children's playground. Space is constricted but the experience of living in a communal building has made them appreciate the benefits of a private bathroom and kitchen, however small, and of the central heating and permanent hot running water, which is piped to all city apartments from water-heating plants. Nevertheless, Stanislav and Marietta are unhappy at leaving the

House of Actors and the break-up of the intellectually stimulating community it housed, among whom they have many friends such as the retired piano-player and her actor husband along the corridor, and all of whom, like themselves, are forced to relocate to the bleak concrete stairwells and indifferent neighbours of Soviet-era apartment blocks. Marietta is depressed for months.

Their new building is one of tens of thousands of similar blocks being constructed in cities across the Soviet Union, from Riga to Vladivostok, as first Nikita Khrushchev and now Leonid Brezhnev seek to improve conditions for the millions of Soviet citizens living in communal flats, inhabiting damp former mansions with dividing walls of hardboard, or stuck in rural *izbas* with no running water or toilet.

Central planning under the socialist system does not allow for individual architectural expression and results in almost identical cities and towns. All residential blocks look the same. Each city has its statue of Lenin, its streets named for Lenin and Marx, its gable-end art of heroic workers brandishing scythes and bushels of wheat, and roof-top slogans urging 'Forward with the Communist Party of the Soviet Union'. The shops are all the same, with numbers rather than names. There is also uniformity in fixtures and fittings, and in the furniture, linoleum, books, pictures and utensils found in every household. Life becomes so indistinguishable from one city to another that in a popular film of the time, *The Irony of Fate*, an intoxicated Moscow resident who arrives in Leningrad by mistake finds himself in a street and in an apartment so identical to his own that he is convinced he has arrived home.

One unforeseen result of the provision of private space for the masses is that people can now voice their opinions without fear of being reported by a communal neighbour, and the private Soviet kitchen becomes a place where opinions and anecdotes critical of the communist system can be freely expressed and

Krasnoyarsk apartment block. Home of the Suvorov family since 1973.

dissidence can take root. State control of the people is impercep-
tibly but significantly loosened.

A year later, in recognition of their growing prominence
in the shoe factory, the Suvorovs are allocated a bigger apartment, on the eighth floor of the block across the way on the
same street. By Soviet standards it is quite spacious, with a corridor, three bedrooms and a living room, though the kitchen
is the same cramped, centrally planned nine square metres,
and is next to the toilet and bathroom. They are so delighted
that Zhanna makes pretend cocktails to celebrate their 'posh'
surroundings. At the back is a long balcony which they enclose
in glass and which acts as a giant refrigerator in the winter.
They qualify for a telephone, and a handset is mounted in
the hallway. They have room to display a multi-volume set of
the World Classics Library which they buy for themselves

Reunited in Siberia: the Suvorov family in Krasnoyarsk in 1970, after Zhanna and Larisa arrive from Grozny.

as much as for their children. Their intellectual space now is inhabited not just by the great Russian writers, but by H. G. Wells, Charles Dickens, Mark Twain and Stanislav's favourite, Victor Hugo, the nineteenth-century French writer and critic, whose quotes appeal to him, for example, 'He who opens a school door, closes a prison,' and 'To learn to read is to light a fire; every syllable that is spelled out is a spark.' Both Stanislav and Marietta missed out on higher education and they are determined that their daughters should strive for the highest academic achievements to make a success of their lives.

The road outside is often muddy and the entrance is dingy, and the four-person (at a squeeze) lift with its metal concertina doors is sometimes out of service, but the apartment is an oasis of silence, order and cleanliness. Shoes are always left at the door, and slippers worn inside – all made by Stanislav of course. This shoemaker's children do not go barefoot.

Chapter 11

PRISONERS OF SUCCESS

Now in his forties, Stanislav is recognized as a master shoe-maker and a prized asset of the shoe factory. He attends a two-month course at a professional development centre in Tarasovka, a small town thirty kilometres north of Moscow, and begins travelling to footwear shows in Moscow and Leningrad and other cities. He is expert at taking measurements for the lasts around which the shoes are built, simulating the shape of the foot with accuracy, and taking into account the way the foot rolls during walking and how it varies subject to heel height. These are rare skills and his reputation grows in his adopted city, not just as a shoemaker but also as a shoe designer.

His work ethic is matched by Marietta's. The eighteen-year-old whom he married in Grozny is now a self-assured woman in her early thirties. Having completed her economics course, she graduates in the shoe factory from being apprentice pattern-maker to an administrative role in the dispatch department, where she displays exceptional managerial abilities.

As in politics, however, the more one succeeds, the greater the risk of one's secrets being exposed. In 1972 the new factory director, Pyotr Baloban, invites Marietta to apply for membership of the communist party. A 'primary party organization' exists in every factory, office, educational institute, collective farm and military unit in the Soviet Union. With eight hundred employees in the factory, its communist cell is a significant element in the city party structures.

Marietta at thirty-five, shortly after becoming a senior official in the Krasnoyarsk shoe factory, 1974.

Special order for sports shoes: Stanislav at work in 1973.

This is an awkward moment for her. How can she not follow the family history of service to the party? Her mother was a second secretary in Martakert. Her father was a judge of the people's court who gave his life in defence of the Motherland. Her husband's aunt was a member of the Supreme Soviet of the Soviet Union. It is natural for Marietta to follow in their ideological footsteps. But there is a danger that her husband's prison record might emerge in the process of form-filling and interview. On the other hand, declining the invitation would not only be embarrassing, it might raise questions that could result in the disclosure of the very thing she wishes to hide. Besides, it could also impede her advancement and Marietta is ambitious. There are two kinds of communists in Russia: party members who see it as their duty to administer, and talented administrators who become party members. Marietta, it is clear, belongs to the latter grouping.

She submits the application form, and confronts the issue of family history head-on by telling the party third secretary of her husband's prison term. To her enormous relief she is informed that it will have no bearing on her request. Her application is approved by the various committees up to the office of Pavel Fedirko, the head of the party committee for Krasnoyarsk city since 1970.

Their enormous gamble in starting a new life in Krasnoyarsk is paying off. No one here in a position of authority seems to care what happened in their previous life. Nevertheless the prison episode, the cause of so much personal pain and shame, is still never, ever mentioned in the family, or made known to their new friends, acquaintances and workmates in the Siberian city.

A year after Marietta's acceptance into the party she becomes chairperson of the factory trade union branch. The shoe factory is formally owned by the Services Trade Union of Russia, an

A rainy day in Krasnoyarsk: Marietta with co-workers, 1973.

adjunct of the party. Membership of the union is compulsory for employees and strikes are forbidden, but the union officials have a voice regarding production plans, workers' rights, accommodation, welfare benefits and cultural and sporting activities. The trade union issues passes to holiday resorts and awards prepaid holidays. As head of the branch, Marietta assumes considerable responsibility for the welfare of the workers, and she is often frustrated in seeking new housing and childcare facilities for her members.

One day in October 1974, when Marietta shows up at work at the shoe factory after a short holiday, a colleague tells her, 'You have got a car. Your name has come up on the list.'

As in other enterprises, the employees of the Krasnoyarsk shoe factory have an allocation for automobiles. The Suvorovs have had their names down for many months and the

Trade union leader: Marietta addressing workers at the shoe factory in 1975.

combination of Stanislav's high-quality work and Marietta's increasingly prominent role in factory life has brought their turn earlier than expected.

Despite the Kremlin's efforts to make the Soviet Union a consumer paradise, the choice of cars for its citizens remains very limited. At the top end is the ZIL 114 limousine modelled on the Cadillac Fleetwood, with a monstrous V8 seven-litre engine. It is manufactured for the sole use of top party leaders. Below that is the Chaika (Seagull), a limousine based on a 1950s American Packard, which is favoured by the KGB and Soviet ambassadors and can only be hired by citizens for weddings. The Volga saloon, like the one Stanislav drove in Grozny, is a favourite of lesser party officials and the state taxi company, and is available for purchase, but there is a very lengthy waiting list for this car and it is too expensive for most people. At the bottom end of the scale is the VAZ-2103, a version of the Fiat 124, built under licence for the Soviet market and known as a Zhiguli in Russia and a Lada in the West.

Stanislav had put their names down for a Zhiguli. To acquire even a Zhiguli has demanded much planning and hoarding of money, as bank credit and hire purchase are not available in the USSR. Marietta gathers up their cash and goes to the car shop to pay. They wait another two months before a card arrives by post on a frigid day in December instructing the Suvorovs to take delivery of their car at the railway yard. Stanislav goes to collect it.

Anyone buying a new car in Russia is aware that parts might be missing, and this problem has become more acute since Stanislav bought his first car in Grozny. Automobiles quite often arrive at their destination without tool kits, windscreen wipers, batteries, spare tyres, or even essential components, these having been pilfered on the rail journey from the manufacturer. Such accessories are in short supply everywhere, as Soviet-made cars age faster than spare parts are produced. However, typical of Stanislav, the stock controller at the yard, Boris Arutyunyan, is a family friend.

A thin, moustachioed Armenian with twinkling eyes and a penchant for kissing acquaintances full on the lips in true Caucasian style, Boris often visits the Suvorov apartment as a guest. He takes Stanislav past lines of parked vehicles to the back of the yard, where a number of fully equipped and intact Zhigulis are parked. 'Take your pick,' he says. The shoemaker selects a chocolate-coloured model with a seventy-five-horsepower engine, vacuum brake booster, self-adjusting rear brakes and a dashboard clock, and drives it home through the snowy streets. He is back behind the wheel of his own car again thirteen years after the Chechnya police seized his Volga GAZ-M21 in Grozny.

He buys a lock-up garage for the car two blocks from his home in a row of little storehouses beside the railway embankment which carries the Trans-Siberian line. If he is outside when the long express train rumbles past, international passengers might glimpse from the carriage windows a sturdy middle-aged man with lank hair and a broad grin exposing two gold teeth, waving his joined hands over his head in a gesture of peace and solidarity. He enjoys doing that, and getting them to wave back and make signs of peace.

Thanks to her organizational skills and dedicated adherence to party discipline, Marietta becomes head of human resources in the shoe factory, with an office in a single-storey red-brick building by the entrance gates, and subsequent to that is elected secretary of the party cell. The latter is a voluntary position requiring her to spend much of her free time on paperwork and in meetings, but the post ensures she earns a management salary for her work in the factory: the party leadership in Moscow insists that senior party personnel in Soviet enterprises should not be seen as the poor relations of managers or that their work does not really count. She becomes one of the most important figures in the factory after the manager himself.

Stanislav never applies to join the party; his collision with the law in Grozny makes him ineligible, while his witnessing of the Chechen genocide opened his eyes to the excesses committed in its name. Remaining *bez partinyi* does not make him any less of a patriot, if patriotism is defined by hard work, decency and pride in the Soviet Union's achievements. In any case, it is not in his nature to attend meetings or proclaim ideological positions, though his choice of reading indicates a strong social conscience. For relaxation after dinner he puts on his outsize spectacles and buries himself in the writings of Victor Hugo, or in the essays of Vissarion Belinsky, another nineteenth-century champion of the dignity and rights of the individual, for whom 'to think, to feel, to understand and to suffer are one and the same thing'.

As in Grozny, his life is dedicated to providing for his family. He makes things for which there is a great demand – good shoes and boots, and even leather jackets and sheepskin coats known as *dublyonkas*, which are all the rage. He does not smoke and is a light drinker, he gives his earnings to Marietta to put aside, and he always has an eye out for good connections.

His and Marietta's circle of contacts extend to include a couple of like-minded entrepreneurs whom the girls refer to as Aunt Valya and Uncle Gena. The former teaches apprentices how to make clothes to order, and the latter is Krasnoyarsk's master tailor. They barter materials and finished goods with each other, so Zhanna and Larisa are always able to wear the most fashionable dresses and coats, as well as good shoes.

Ironically the road to renewed prosperity for the entrepreneur who served jail time for the crime of speculation is made smoother by Krasnoyarsk's top communist. Pavel Fedirko, first secretary of the Krasnoyarsk City Communist Party, a powerfully built round-faced Russian, is a cultured, dynamic leader, the antithesis of the stereotypical communist boss who puts subservience to party dogma above the needs of the people. He is an avid theatregoer and rarely misses a first-night performance at the Pushkin Theatre, unlike his predecessor, a technocrat who in his time as Krasnoyarsk party boss came to an opening night only once. When Fedirko is elevated to party boss for the whole Krasnoyarsk Region in 1972 at the age of thirty-nine he promotes the slogan 'Let's make Siberia a region of culture'.

As leader now of one of Russia's eighty-three regions, Fedirko is answerable only to the Central Committee in Moscow and cannot be touched or contradicted by anyone other than the general secretary – not even the KGB – which gives him the powers of a provincial tsar. He announces plans to build in Krasnoyarsk an opera house and a concert hall despite growing evidence of stagnation in the economy. He orders the erection of a five-storey Dom Byta – House of Everyday Life – at No. 60 Prospect Mira, three blocks from the Pushkin Theatre. With its metal and glass frontage, the modern style of the services centre clashes with that of the elegant old buildings along the street, but it is convenient for those living and working in the city centre, including members of the city and regional administration. They can drop in to avail themselves of hairdressers, barbers, tailors, milliners, watch repairers, dry-cleaners and other services all under one roof. Because of shortages in the Soviet Union, a lot of things are made and repaired in such places.

The fourth floor of the House of Everyday Life is allocated to the Krasnoyarsk shoe factory to promote its products. Stanislav is put in charge of a team of the best shoe fitters, pattern designers and craftsmen capable of creating bespoke footwear. He is given access to premium and patent leather, the most important prerequisite for making quality shoes. He is now the person to see for those in the city prepared to pay for good-quality boots, shoes and slippers.

Pavel Fedirko becomes a client. He and his second wife Lydia, a lecturer at the pedagogical institute, take a liking to the shoemaker and find the footwear they order comfortable and elegant. Sometimes Fedirko asks Stanislav to come to his apartment on Prospect Lenina, to take measurements for shoes and boots according to the latest fashion, both for himself and his spouse.

Stanislav is now one of a protected species in the Soviet Union, the providers of footwear to party bosses. At the exhibitions he attends in Moscow and Leningrad he meets other shoemakers to Soviet dignitaries, talented Crispinians like himself such as Alexander Heimbichner, from the southern Stavropol region, who is so well known to top communists there that he is commissioned by local party leader Mikhail Gorbachev to make a pair of boots for his mother Maria Gorbacheva in the village of Privolnoye.

Suvorov and Heimbichner, who in later life runs a custom shoe and orthotic store in Alberta, Canada, are successful because of the system's failure to shoe the people adequately and comfortably. The quality of mass-produced footwear is so poor that one in ten shoes sent to retail outlets is returned as unsaleable.

More often than not, gratitude for good shoes is accompanied by favours. Fedirko has access to a special warehouse, known as the *baza*, or base, which provides top officials and other privileged or favoured citizens with imported goods and scarce items. Stanislav gets access to the *baza* and acquires the coupons with which purchases are made. In time he is able to buy a suite of lacquered furniture for the new apartment. He loves to arrive home from this Aladdin's cave and surprise Marietta with something special, like a foreign brand of soap or skin cream. Once he calls her to say, 'I'm at the *baza*. What size bra do you take?'

His success does not come without sacrifice. Stanislav subjects himself to a punishing daily regime. He gets up at six o'clock in the morning, does his exercises in the living room, has a breakfast of tea and a slice of bread and cheese, goes to the Dom Byta, comes home for dinner, reads the papers, then leaves for the theatre atelier, where he has installed a miniature television. He wears a hairnet at work, as his heavy locks, parted in the middle, tend to fall forward as he bends over his shoemaking. Somehow he finds time to shop for provisions, using a bulky briefcase he has made for himself shaped like a doctor's medical bag. In a country where a woman almost never goes out without a string shopping bag in case she comes across something scarce being 'given out', Marietta is an exception. Her husband always comes home with provisions in his case – bread, sausages, confectionery, Armenian brandy, a new book or a toy. The children call it the magic briefcase because of what he might produce from it. There is always excitement when their papa comes home between his two jobs, and they make sure to see to his every need, especially if Marietta is at work, before he heads off again. They love the weekend when there are family gatherings around the dining table and their papa is not rushing off somewhere.

Stanislav and Marietta are doing well. They have not given up the prospect of one day returning to live in gentler climes, and the long winters wear them down. However, they have become prisoners of their success in Krasnoyarsk. Stanislav has even become something of a star at the theatre, with his portrait, labelled 'Suvorov, S.A. Master of Footwear', displayed alongside pin-ups of nationally known actors and production staff in the upper foyer. It is hard for them to imagine repeating their extraordinary achievements anywhere else, or guaranteeing their daughters the same educational benefits.

The shoemaker reads Chekhov extensively and he surely identifies with Vasily Sergeich, the fictional gentleman in the playwright's short story *In Exile* who finds himself banished to the east. Sergeich tells the old-timer Semyon, 'I want to live by my own labour, in the sweat of my brow ... Yes, Semyon, even in Siberia people can live. Even in Siberia there is happiness.'

In 1975, Bakhshi dies in Grozny, aged eighty-six. Stanislav and Marietta fly there for the funeral and to comfort Stanislav's mother Sonia and Bakhshi's children. Despite the family crisis several years before when Bakhshi took up temporarily with a much younger woman, the old cobbler and Sonia continued to occupy the same house in Pavel Musorov Street, and had seen out their declining years in each other's company. Stanislav never knew his own father, and he grieves for Bakhshi, whom he called 'papa', and who gave him his first lessons in shoemaking. He and Marietta take care of the funeral arrangements. Bakhshi is buried in the Russian graveyard; the Armenian cemetery is not available as it has been abandoned since the closure and destruction of

Male pin-up: photograph of Stanislav on display with cast and staff in the Pushkin Theatre in the 1970s.

the old Armenian church in the anti-religion campaigns. The day of the funeral brings further tragedy. Sonia herself suddenly dies. Stanislav now finds himself grieving for his mother too. His half-sister Nellya, the only child of Bakhshi and Sonia, has lost both her parents within days. A second funeral is arranged. Sonia's remains are laid in a plot next to Bakhshi's resting place. Stanislav orders separate headstones for the graves.

He makes no claim on the estate of either, and the house goes to Nellya. It is the end of the Suvorov name in the city of Grozny.

CHAPTER 12

THE SHOEMAKER'S DAUGHTER

Pavel Fedirko once told a reporter how individuals advanced through the ranks in the Soviet system. 'We watch people constantly,' the Krasnoyarsk party boss told Anthony Austin of the *New York Times* who came across him on the fringes of a party conference in Moscow in March 1981, and anyone 'who is especially conscientious and talented' is selected for advancement.

The name Zhanna Suvorova is likely mentioned among party officials in the Siberian city as an 'especially conscientious and talented' person, suitable for advancement, as she attracts attention as a natural leader and a role model for young Soviet citizens.

The character of the Suvorovs' elder daughter is shaped by her life experience. As a child she is aware of how her parents have always been determined to create for her and her sister a home atmosphere of culture and learning, which they themselves did not have, so that they can progress academically, and Zhanna determines to do her best to meet their expectations. As an outsider, a recently arrived Armenian in a mostly Russian city, she feels that she has to work and study harder than anyone else to get on in life. If anything needs to be done, she happily volunteers.

She first comes to the notice of the party as a Young Pioneer. Children in the Soviet Union are enrolled at the age of ten in the Vladimir Lenin All-Union Pioneer Organization, a body

Zhanna, left, first row, as senior leader with other supervisors at Pioneer Camp, 1979.

similar to the Scouts and Girl Guides of the West. Pioneers are 'Always ready!' Zhanna was made a Pioneer in her last year in Grozny, her hair in ringlets, wearing the regulation white shirt and bright red scarf, which has to measure exactly one metre by three hundred millimetres. She made the same solemn promise her mother did on joining the Pioneers as a child in Nagorno-Karabakh: 'to passionately love my Motherland and to cherish it as I can, to live, study and fight as the great Lenin has instructed, as the Communist Party teaches me'. All newcomers are taught to take their inspiration from Pavlik Morozov, whose statues and busts are a feature of Soviet schools. This thirteen-year-old Russian Pioneer became a revolutionary symbol during the collectivization of farms in the 1920s, when, it is said, he was beaten to death by his relatives for informing the secret police that his father was resisting collectivization and helping enemies of the state.

New Pioneers are solemnly enrolled in stages during third grade, with the best students in the first batch and the worst in the last. They are given a Pioneer notebook, in which they are encouraged to paste Pioneer symbols and memorabilia, and a Pioneer handbook with recommendations for activities, such as the active promotion of atheism. The Pioneer organization is designed to provide an opportunity for adults to assess the abilities and skills of new generations of Soviet citizens. Grown-up supervisors organize social activities and parades on festival and commemorative days, accompany the children to summer camps and take their measure. Zhanna shows a natural enthusiasm and displays organizational abilities and is made leader of her class in Krasnoyarsk. She is eventually selected by the teachers as the top Pioneer for the whole school, and is chosen to lead Young Pioneer parades on festival days.

Such volunteerism comes with rewards. In the summer of 1973 her mother secures a place for her, through the shoe factory trade union branch, at the Artek Pioneer Camp on the Crimean peninsula, a playground spread over an area the size of Monaco with seven miles of shoreline reserved for high-achieving or well-connected Young Pioneers. When her sister Larisa's turn comes, for she too is an exemplary Young Pioneer, she is sent to the equally prestigious Orlyonok – Little Eagle – Camp on the Russian Black Sea coast.

At the age of fourteen Zhanna is automatically enrolled into the next level of party apprenticeship, the Komsomol, the Leninist Young Communist League. As with the Pioneers, the Komsomol commands almost universal membership among Soviet youth. No one is required to join, but it is a rite of passage so widely accepted as part of Soviet growing up that those who do not become members are stigmatized as recalcitrant, and are excluded from state-funded holiday camps and often from higher education. It is a source of potential candidates for the communist party and a vehicle for teaching young people about its values and achievements.

Zhanna accepts this as a natural progression. The Soviet Union is her world. She has no reason to question it. She is a perfect expression of her time. The violence and repression of the Revolution and the Stalin era belong to the older generation. The Soviet Union won the war and is now a superpower. The system is entrenched and will go on for ever. Her generation has no way of knowing whether communism gives people a better life than capitalism, but they are constantly informed that it does. No one of her or of her parents' generation has ever seen a private shop in the USSR. The last one in Russia closed in 1928, the year before her father was born, when Stalin ordered the Great Turn away from Lenin's New Economic Policy, which had allowed individuals to operate small businesses like cafés and follow private pursuits such as shoemaking for a profit. She has no reason to doubt or question the way of life to which she is exposed, nor do she or any of her family feel the urge to become dissidents or to aspire to life outside the Soviet Union. It is in Zhanna's nature to be loyal, dedicated to her family and the people to whom she becomes close, and, like her father and mother, to be proud of her country. She believes the party leadership is doing its best for the people, that the ideals it espouses are achievable, that there is nothing wrong with thinking they are all equal.

Her world view is shaped by her reading and school instruction, especially concerning the Great Patriotic War. In one early school project she learns about the horrors of Buchenwald, a Nazi forced-labour concentration camp, whose commandant was prosecuted by Roman Rudenko, the same party official who turned down an appeal by Zhanna's great-aunt and her grandmother against her father's prison sentence. Like other children she is inspired by stories of Soviet heroes such as Zoya Kosmodemyanskaya, executed by the Germans for partisan activities against Hitler's armies on the outskirts of Moscow.

Not long after pinning the red Komsomol badge with its profile of Lenin onto her school uniform, Zhanna is selected as school *komsorg*, organizer of Komsomol events and meetings and of *subbotniks*, special days when citizens voluntarily clean up the streets and parks and do useful things like collecting scrap metal. Her tasks include motivating students to make banners and attend the May Day and October Revolution demonstrations and other red-letter-day celebrations. As *komsorg* she is also put in charge of the student groups taken by bus every October to harvest crops such as potatoes, carrots and beetroot at state farms outside the city. It is tough work for the teenagers. Some days they are soaked by rain and wet snow, and occasionally early frosts harden the ground.

One week of the year Zhanna stands guard duty at the eternal flame for the casualties of the Great Patriotic War, which burns brightly on a low concrete dais on Prospect Karl Marx beside a larger-than-life sculpture of two soldiers, one male and one female, holding aloft the sword of victory. This is considered a great honour, and the duty is rotated around the schools. The uniformed teenagers march in military fashion towards the flame, stiff-legged and swinging rigid arms back and forth

Zhanna, second from the left, on a school trip to Moscow in 1974.

across the body, where they stand to attention for thirty minutes, though this is cut to fifteen minutes when the temperature gets dangerously low.

Senior Komsomol leaders are also expected to give motivational talks, and are issued with guidelines on how to write political speeches, such as never to put the word 'and' before the last item in a catalogue of Soviet achievements, so as to give the impression that the list can go on and on. While tedious, such activities are accepted as part of the life trajectory of an idealistic young Soviet citizen, though in Zhanna's case accepting the duties of Komsomol leader is less a career thing than simply what goes with being a natural leader. At school Larisa is also a top-class student but she is a bit of a tomboy and misses some classes to watch football, and has the misfortune to be constantly measured against her always-perfect elder sister. Once, after Zhanna completes for her a mechanical-drawing project, the teacher says, 'It is very good, but Zhanna's was better!'

Though she never imagines living outside the Soviet Union, like many of her school friends Zhanna has a great curiosity about the outside world, and she loves the English-language classes given by her teacher Emma Weber.

When she graduates, aged seventeen, Zhanna is one of only four pupils in her class year of one hundred to get straight As. For this she is awarded a gold medal depicting the hammer and

No more uniforms: Zhanna (with flower) on her last day at school, aged seventeen in 1975.

sickle of the Russian Soviet Federative Socialist Republic and a citation for 'excellent progress in study, hard work and exemplary behaviour'. As the holder of such an honour Zhanna is excused three of the four entry examinations for university. She is admitted to Krasnoyarsk State Pedagogical University on Prospect Mira and, encouraged by Emma Weber, enrols in the foreign languages faculty to specialize in English and German. It is a rather exotic choice for a student in a closed city and surprises some friends who have been expecting her to rise high in the party, in which case history would be a more usual choice. She dreams of being a diplomat but fears that this occupation is reserved for well-connected Moscow families. She will advance in life and travel far, however, according to her high-school maths teacher Uliya Vasilyevna, who acknowledges Zhanna's prospects by quoting the Russian proverb 'Big ships will go into the high seas', words that she will recall in later life when far from home.

For the first two years of Zhanna's five-year course, all students are required to study the history of the CPSU, which they mostly find extremely boring, and Zhanna is no exception. They have to absorb long passages of Lenin's writings and make copious notes on the decisions of the party congresses, from the first in 1898 to the twenty-fifth in 1976. With the Cold War requiring military preparedness, all undergraduates also have to take nursing classes, and Zhanna earns a military card that qualifies her as a medical reservist. Stanislav wanted his daughter to become a doctor but she has no stomach for medicine, as becomes evident when she is required to attend the dissection of an old man's body in the city morgue and almost passes out.

She also has to study atheism for a year, which entails comparing religions and understanding how their influence can be subversive in a communist society. The lecturer in atheism, a charismatic man in his fifties, believes in exposing his students to the reality of religious practice, and takes them to see Baptist meetings and Russian Orthodox services. Baptists have been active in Russia since the 1860s, and they have a small congregation in Krasnoyarsk, kept under surveillance by the secret police and sometimes persecuted. The teacher also takes his students to the Intercession Cathedral at the junction of Prospect Mira and Surikova Street to see the congregation, mostly old women in headscarves, singing, chanting and blessing themselves before richly decorated icons. Founded in the nineteenth century, the cathedral is the only church in Krasnoyarsk allowed to remain open out of eighteen Orthodox churches and a Lutheran and Roman Catholic church that existed before the Revolution and which were either demolished or used as warehouses. Zhanna has never ventured inside the cathedral before. It belongs to another world, disapproved of by the system, a place for those few people, protected by age, whose belief is strong enough for them to defy official orthodoxy. Bureaucrats or teachers going to church would definitely lose their jobs. Priests are allowed only to conduct services; they are forbidden to proselytize, do charitable work or comment on the state of society from the pulpit.

Inevitably the always-helpful shoemaker's daughter is made *komsorg* of her faculty at university. She is popular and always remembers faces and names. Aged eighteen, her name is put forward by her class, and she is 'elected' by the class leaders. In typical Soviet style there is no opposing candidate. She is given responsibilities akin to that of a leader of a students' union, but with little autonomy. She is also made a *starosta*, an 'elder' chosen by the dean to act as a spokesperson for her academic group in interactions with professors, to look out for students with personal problems, and to monitor attendance, in the manner of a super-prefect. The lighter side of her student role is representing her class in KVN – the Club of the Merry and Inventive People – competitions, in which university students compete to give humorous answers to questions and perform sketches. A pro-gramme featuring the finalists was shown live on the First Soviet Channel until 1972, when it was banned as anti-Soviet because of the students' impromptu jokes.

In common with her fellow students, Zhanna receives free tuition and also a stipend equivalent to the minimum wage, which she dutifully hands over each month to her mother to put in a savings account.

Her dedication to voluntary work and party organizations again yields benefits. In her second year as an undergraduate Zhanna is sent to the most prestigious summer camp for Kom-somol youth, Sputnik. This is her second trip to the Crimean peninsula. Before she leaves, Marietta stays up nights to sew special summer clothes for her. At Sputnik Zhanna spends two weeks with the young men and women who are expected to lead Soviet society in years to come. She is billeted with five Musco-vite girls who at first shun the provincial, but better-dressed, non-Russian in their midst. The teenager from Krasnoyarsk also incurs their envy when she has a short romance with an exceptionally handsome Tatar boy who turns out to be the rather arrogant son of a top official. The young people ride boats, swim, go on excursions, tidy up the beach and sing Komsomol songs around campfires. Zhanna also meets foreign students for the first time, exotic creatures from the capitalist world, which most assume they will never get to visit. Exit permits are hard to obtain and the ruble is not convertible. People joke about yearn-ing to go abroad. One says, 'I want to go to Paris again.' The sec-ond exclaims, 'What? Have you been to Paris before?' to which the first replies, 'No, but I have wanted to go before.' Zhanna longs to know more about the outside world and to travel, though she and her family aspire only to make the best of life in Russia, where they have the skills to survive and thrive within the constraints of the imposed ideology. In this respect Zhanna is very influenced by the attitude of her parents. Stanislav is fond of saying, 'No matter where you are in the world, you have to work hard.' He takes life as it comes. He suffered under the system but he never blames it or wants to escape by emigrating. The idea of going to live abroad as part of the Armenian diaspora is never brought up, nor does it enter the minds of family members, even the ever-curious Zhanna.

CHAPTER 13

FULL HOUSE

IN STARK CONTRAST to Krasnoyarsk, with its queues, surly shop assistants, chronic shortages and ill-kept streets, there is a city situated a mere sixty kilometres to the south with pleasant cafés, well-stocked shops, smiling assistants and tidy avenues of white stone houses with neat gardens. It has an artificial lake with bathing beaches, several sports centres, a cinema and a manicured park with a large statue of Lenin. Here everything is brought in from Moscow for the pampered inhabitants, who are known as chocolate-eaters because they have everything required for the good life.

The city has no name but is referred to as Krasnoyarsk-26, after the number of its post office box for mail. Krasnoyarsk-26 does not appear on Soviet maps, and its one hundred thousand residents are not included in the Soviet census. There are no telephone lines connecting it to neighbouring towns as all communications go directly to Moscow. The only clue to an outsider of what goes on behind its razor-wire perimeter fence is a statue at the entrance of a bear tearing open the nucleus of an atom with its claws.

Krasnoyarsk-26 is the Soviet Union's nuclear research and manufacturing centre, with three reactors producing plutonium, the essential ingredient for nuclear weapons. It has a small railway station, patrolled by armed KGB personnel, from where trains run into a fortified mountain. At the other end of a five-kilometre tunnel is a complex of nuclear reactors, plutonium laboratories and a radio-chemistry laboratory for separating plutonium from nuclear waste. After the fall of the Soviet Union it will emerge that, from the time of its construction under Stalin in 1950, the scientific and engineering community here produced a total of forty tons of plutonium, sufficient to make up to ten thousand nuclear bombs. The complex is capable of withstanding nuclear attack, thanks to the slave labour of the seventy thousand Gulag prisoners who excavated the mountain and created a honeycomb of corridors and rooms. The ledgers show that they came mostly from Eastern Europe and included 'one Negro'. When they died on site they were buried in an untended mass grave on the edge of the secret city.

Everyone knows there is a closed military installation at Krasnoyarsk-26, but few citizens of Krasnoyarsk guess at the utopian conditions inside. However, Stanislav and Marietta manage to get day passes and find stores with eye-opening items such as fine coats from Yugoslavia and patent-leather shoes from East Germany, and they stock up on what they can afford from a choice of such things as bananas, salami, caviar and pairs of tights. The Suvorovs also manage to visit Krasnoyarsk-45, a secret community of more than sixty thousand people attached to the city of Zheleznogorsk, seventy kilometres east of Krasno-yarsk, where uranium is enriched for the nuclear programme. Zheleznogorsk also manufactures satellites, as well as audio and video tapes, and is known as the best place to purchase elec-tronic goods.

Few people would begrudge the nuclear scientists and other employees of these cities their comforts if they knew the per-sonal cost. Residents are required to stay confined in these hide-away communities for years at a time, separated from friends and relatives, their very existence denied. In their golden cages they are watched by resident KGB agents for any deviation from good behaviour. Anyone who gets drunk, misses work, abuses a spouse, commits a crime, tunes in to the Voice of America or allows their children to listen to the Rolling Stones could well be featured in a monthly KGB report to the regional communist party committee and be forced to return to the harsh conditions of a society still bogged down on the road to socialism.

In the ten years since arriving in Siberia, the now forty-eight-year-old shoemaker and his thirty-eight-year-old wife have done very well for themselves. Their standard of living again would be the envy of many city dwellers in Western Europe. They have good jobs, a centrally heated apartment and a car. They can take holidays and send their daughters to the best youth camps. Their refrigerator is always full. They have good contacts to help cope with shortages. They have savings from their work and Stanislav's private enterprise, and from the sale of their Grozny house and furniture.

Now at last they can make their life complete, and acquire what is the ultimate accessory of the Siberian family. They can get a dacha.

There is no counterpart in English for the Russian word *dacha*. It is so much more than 'a country house or cottage in Russia, typically used as a second or summer home', as it is defined in the *Oxford Dictionary of English*. The word originally meant the grant of a small country estate by the tsar. It can refer to a party leader's country mansion, the fine residence of a writer or artist, the summer home, with vegetable garden, of a city dweller or the lean-to shack of the poorest urban worker, the common denominator being that a dacha is always situated in the countryside. In principle a city dweller cannot use a dacha as a family home, or install permanent heating, or build an upper storey, or have more than sixty square metres of living space. One of the advantages of communism, however, is that the land is free. It belongs to the people and is in the gift of the people's representative, whether a collective farm manager or a village

Communist turned capitalist: Pyotr Baloban, director of the Krasnoyarsk shoe factory, which he takes over and closes down after Russia's capitalization, 1980.

committee. But the plot on which the dacha stands must not exceed four hundred square metres.

Pyotr Baloban, a short-tempered overweight man with a florid face, has a country retreat in a colony of dachas at Pugachovo village just outside town. The shoe factory director and his tall frizzy-haired wife keep very much to themselves but they have taken a liking to the Suvorovs, who are helping to make a success of the enterprise. He persuades them to apply to the Pugachovo village chairman for land and they are allotted a regulation-size plot. It is five stops from their home on the *electrichka*, the electric commuter train, and a walk of less than a kilometre from the station.

Wanting plenty of floor space, Stanislav decides that if he cannot build out, he will build up. Somehow he is able to get around the single-storey regulation and in six months he erects a three-storey dacha with a ground-floor garage, a large first-floor room with a marble fireplace – which proves of little use in very cold weather – and three bedrooms upstairs. Perhaps he is attempting to recreate on the little plot of land something resembling the spaciousness of their home in Grozny. For the first time since leaving the Caucasus the family can enjoy living in a house again at weekends and working to produce their own fruit and vegetables in the short but hot summers.

One day Pyotr Baloban invites the Suvorovs to visit his dacha. They are rather shocked by the opulence of the summer home of the factory boss, who has clearly done well under communism (and will do even better under capitalism). He startles the then eighteen-year-old Zhanna by saying to her, 'All this will be yours, if you marry my son.' He seems to be serious, but neither of the two parties, who hardly know each other, is in the slightest bit interested in the proposition.

Stanislav and Marietta have a good reason to make their dacha roomier than the norm. When an 'emigrant' prospers, others follow. A trickle of relatives and friends seeking, like themselves, a better life begin arriving in Krasnoyarsk from the Caucasus, and at first they stay with the Suvorovs. Their apartment becomes a little crowded at times, but the dacha relieves the pressure in summertime. The couple encourage members of their extended family to come to Siberia and explore new opportunities, and in keeping with Armenian custom and their innate generosity no one is ever expected to pay towards their upkeep, however long they stay. Whatever is on the table, they share. It is a matter of family honour.

The first to arrive is a teenager called Bogdan, son of Stanislav's Ingush friend Bashir. He enrols in Krasnoyarsk University and

Stanislav's multi-storey dacha on the Krasnoyarsk outskirts, 1982.

stays with them for a few months until he gets a place in a campus dormitory. Aunt Lena's son Misha also comes from Grozny, and they help him secure admission to the Technological University. Zhanna and Larisa are happy to have their cousin to stay, but Misha pines so much for his Armenian sweetheart Tamara, whom he has left behind, that he returns to Chechnya after three months. Marietta feels he is throwing away a chance to get on in life. Back in Grozny, Misha marries Tamara and is immediately called up to the army. A few years later he comes back to Krasnoyarsk, now with Tamara and their two children, and again the family provide them with accommodation, but after a year Misha, with his family, returns once more to southern Russia.

Elvira is next. The thirty-year-old daughter of Aram, an elder brother of Farandzem who also moved to Grozny, has a typically aquiline Armenian nose and keeps her hair tied in a bun on the side of her head. Elvira has hopes of finding a husband and works for a few months in a Krasnoyarsk shop, but she also returns home, disappointed, to Chechnya.

In November 1977, just as the winter is taking hold in Krasnoyarsk, Zhanna's cousin Ararat Gukasyan arrives at their apartment with his father Alyosha, much to the joy of Marietta. Alyosha is her half-brother who spoiled her when they lived at their father's house in Nagorno-Karabakh. Ararat has just turned twenty. He has a broad cheerful face, close-cut dark hair, brown eyes and hairy arms, and is bright and ambitious. His father has brought him to Siberia in the hope that Stanislav and Marietta will put him up while he prepares to enter university to study law. Admission to higher-level education in the Caucasus is out of the question because of the outrageous bribes demanded for what should be free. Krasnoyarsk, for all its faults, does not suffer from the blatant corruption that distorts life in the mountain republics, where it has become so bad that money and favours now regularly triumph over merit and diligence, and even communist party posts are sometimes bought and sold. As Marietta puts it, corruption in Krasnoyarsk amounts to a bottle of vodka. She and Stanislav readily agree to take in Ararat.

With his easy-going disposition, the young man becomes a popular member of the family. He is the son the couple never had, and a big brother to Zhanna and Larisa. He and Marietta

Stanislav relaxing after a sauna at the dacha, with brother-in-law Alyosha (with towel on head) and Alyosha's wife Zhenya at far right, visiting from Nagorno-Karabakh in 1982.

have a special affinity, as they both speak the Armenian dialect of Nagorno-Karabakh which includes many words of Turkic and Iranian origin unintelligible to other Armenian speakers. Having just completed two years' national service in East Germany, he is already quite proficient in Russian but does not have university entry qualifications, although as an ex-serviceman he is able to get prompt admission to the *rabfak* attached to Krasnoyarsk State University. This is a preparatory course created after the Revolution to enable promising young workers from country towns and villages to achieve a higher level of education and thus gain access to professions previously reserved for children of privileged parents. Khrushchev, like many party grandees, is a product of a *rabfak* – short for *rabochiy fakultyet* or workers' faculty.

As so often in the life of this family, connections play a role in getting Ararat a part-time job while he is a student. Stanislav has a friend whose uncle is deputy head of the regional ministry of internal affairs. With his assistance, and with the status that goes with Ararat's army service, the young Armenian is able to get a desk job at a regional *militsia* station while he studies. The following year he qualifies to enter the university law faculty as an evening student, while continuing to work in the police office.

After two years with the Suvorovs, during which time they look after his every need without complaint, the moment comes when his adoptive parents feel Ararat is accomplished enough to live on his own. Now twenty-two, he moves to a workers' dormitory. There he meets a pretty young Russian woman called Galya, and they marry – despite his parents' reservations that she is not Armenian – and move into a small apartment. After finishing his law studies he becomes a full-time police officer. He has by this time put down roots and is a settled member of the Armenian diaspora and a promising policeman. He treats the Suvorovs' apartment as a second home.

Ararat's younger brother Araik also comes from Nagorno-Karabakh, after finishing school there. He aspires to enter higher education in Krasnoyarsk but his Russian language skills are inadequate and the seventeen-year-old leaves soon afterwards to do his national service. He serves in the marines for three years and returns to Krasnoyarsk and this time is accepted into the university law faculty and goes to live with Ararat and Galya.

With guests and lodgers coming and going, Stanislav and Marietta frequently have to put food for six to eight people on the dinner table. Meanwhile the economy is stagnating under Brezhnev and shortages are worsening. However they have a regular supply of preserved food from the dacha and some important friends. They establish special relationships with two key people in the city's economic hierarchy: Lyudmila Nikolaevna, administrator of the vegetable warehouse, and Ivan Kasyanovich, director of the meat factory, both of whom benefit from Stanislav's shoemaking skills. Lyudmila knows when special consignments of produce come in, and Ivan even calls sometimes at the apartment with special cuts of meat. Years later, Larisa's then three-year-old son Valera overhears someone comment about a lack of meat, 'Don't worry, Ivan Kasyanovich will fix that,' and the little boy remarks innocently next day, when his parents complain about potholes in the road, 'Don't worry, Ivan Kasyanovich will fix that.'

In the Soviet system administrators wield extraordinary power to fix things, either through knowledge of supplies about to be delivered or through control of something only the state can provide, such as travel tickets. Stanislav becomes good at recognizing when a *nyet* is not a no, but rather an invitation to offer a bribe. On one occasion when he and Marietta make a last-minute decision to go to the wedding of Stanislav's cousin in Grozny and are told in Moscow that the connecting flight is full, he hands over his passport with banknotes inside. They are immediately assigned seats on a half-empty plane.

CHAPTER 14

PEOPLE'S DEPUTY

As Zhanna grows to adulthood, she becomes increasingly interested in the outside world. At the age of nineteen she gets the first opportunity to satisfy her curiosity. Her papa receives a phone call from the father of her best friend, Lena Weinbaum. He tells Stanislav that Lena wants to join a group of Krasnoyarsk citizens who are going on a two-week holiday to Bulgaria and Romania, socialist countries within the Eastern Bloc and more accessible to Soviet tourists than countries on the other side of the Iron Curtain. He will only let her go if Zhanna goes as well. Both sets of parents are strict with their daughters, insisting on them being home at a certain time in the evenings and forbidding them to go to parties in empty dachas. Stanislav agrees. He pays for a travel voucher covering her air ticket and accommodation.

Fairly bursting with excitement, Zhanna goes to the foreign travel office on Prospect Mira to apply for an exit visa, without which no Soviet citizen can leave the country. An official gives her an application form to fill out at home and tells her to take it next day, with her passport, to a building on Prospect Karl Marx where it joins Dzerzhinsky Street, a short walk away.

The brass plate at the door of this building reveals its occupant to be the KOMITET GOSUDARSTVENNOY BEZOPASNOSTI, the Committee of State Security, known by its initials as the KGB. Formed in 1954 as the successor to Stalin's notorious secret police and headed by future Soviet leader Yury Andropov, the

KGB is responsible for intelligence, counter-intelligence, internal security and espionage abroad. It has offices in every Soviet city, from where it conducts surveillance of suspected dissidents, especially among the clergy and intelligentsia. This 'sword and shield' of the communist party has a directorate responsible for the Soviet Union's borders, and its officers have wide discretion to deny exit visas to anyone whose family record has been tarnished with the broad brush of anti-Soviet activities.

Having to enter the KGB building is a cause of nervousness for even the most conscientious Soviet citizen, and especially now for Zhanna. In the apartment the evening before her visit she begins to fill out the form for the KGB at the dinner table. It is headed 'Application to Travel Outside the USSR'. It has twenty-two questions. One requires the applicant to list all family members living in the USSR or abroad. As she fills this in she wonders if they will check into her father's past. Her heart misses a beat when she is confronted with the final question: 'What else do you want to add about yourself or your close relatives?' If they know about her papa and she does not mention his prison sentence here, they could accuse her of dissembling and refuse the application. She says nothing to her parents. She spends a sleepless night wondering how to respond. In the end the prospect of seeing the world beyond the horizons of the Soviet Union proves too alluring for the young Armenian. The risk is worth it. In the morning she writes 'Nothing' and leaves the form with the receptionist at the KGB office.

The world does not come to an end. Her exit visa is granted. The KGB's filing and cross-referencing system on family histories has its limitations. The travel office sends her passport to the Bulgarian and Romanian embassies in Moscow and it comes back stamped with the appropriate entry visas. She is now officially trusted to make contact with foreigners in a socialist country on the 'right side' of the Iron Curtain, which is considered by

Russians to be the 'real abroad', as distinct from Soviet republics like Latvia and Armenia which are sometimes called the 'near abroad'. The holiday is everything she expects. There is exposure to Eastern European architecture and arts, glimpses of quality goods in the shops and glorious days of sunshine and flirting on the Black Sea coast.

In a way the holiday is yet another reward, this time for putting up with the tedium of the Komsomol meetings which Zhanna is required to chair at the university. It is difficult for a *komsorg* to round up apathetic fellow students and hold their attention while expounding on political-ideological education and promoting 'a non-conciliatory attitude towards bourgeois ideology and morality'. Komsomol leaders are encouraged to speak out against decadent Western phenomena such as jazz and rock and roll, which have huge appeal to elements of Soviet youth, and to disapprove of the swinging refrains of jazz musicians like Duke Ellington and such pop artists as Elvis Presley and the Rolling Stones. But while these issues agitate party officials in Moscow and Leningrad, they do not impinge much on provincial life in faraway Krasnoyarsk.

Despite her prominence in the Komsomol, Zhanna does not contemplate taking the next step, that of applying for membership of the Communist Party of the Soviet Union. She does not feel any pressure to do so. Undergraduates who study foreign languages are regarded as a little bit politically unreliable – except for those singled out and trusted enough to contemplate careers as diplomats or spies – and few of her fellow students are party members. Many of the faculty's lecturers and professors are also *bez partinyi*, so she is not the only 'white crow' outside party ranks.

She knows nevertheless that one day she will be approached, and she resolves to decline the invitation for as long as possible. She is a leader and a proud citizen but she is not ideologically committed. She is not opposed to membership because of the crimes of the party in the past and its present suppression of dissent, because she is hardly aware of them. Beneath her conventional, obedient, patriotic exterior, however, she harbours resentment about how her father suffered at the hands of communist officialdom. Stanislav's imprisonment has tainted her perception of the whole system and planted a seed of subversion in her conformist character. He is a hard worker but also a wheeler-dealer. He takes risks, but only for his family – to enable them to eat well, to be well dressed, to travel and to have opportunities not open to Marietta and himself when they were younger. He sees party membership as something of a joke and that rubs off on her.

There is also a concern that by applying to join the party she will invite scrutiny which will reveal her father's prison record to her tutors and fellow students. Her mother managed to get through the induction process at the shoe factory without any problem, but Zhanna has complicated her personal situation by not being fully upfront with the KGB on her exit visa application.

The approach comes in a casual fashion shortly after her foreign trip. One afternoon in the autumn of 1977, when walking along a corridor between classes, the dean of her faculty, Professor Yulia Khudonogova, asks Zhanna to drop into her office. There, the plump, pleasant, middle-aged academic, who specializes in the methodology of teaching foreign languages and is a leading party figure in the university, asks the young Armenian, 'Are you thinking of joining the party?' Zhanna replies that she has not considered it. 'You should,' says the dean. Three months later the dean asks her if she has had any thoughts on the matter. 'I am thinking about it,' she replies. 'Good.' Shortly afterwards the dean confronts her again. 'I would really like to recommend you to the party committee.' Zhanna can no longer be seen to play hard to get. 'I would be honoured,' she replies. To refuse a third invitation might mean that in future she would be seen, not as a citizen who is simply 'non-party', but as someone who has spurned an invitation to become a member of Lenin's great political family, and therefore is not to be fully trusted by higher-ups in the party ranks who could determine her future career prospects.

She informs her parents about the step she is about to take. Marietta tells her that she will be asked why she is applying to join the party and that she should reply that she wants to offer her services 'to make sure the country prospers'. The dean sets the process in motion. She recommends Zhanna to the university party committee, and three communists on the staff vouch for her, as required under the rules. Zhanna is then invited to a full meeting of party members in a seminar room. The institute's party secretary, French lecturer Yevgenia Steberg, asks her why she has applied. 'Because I want to make sure our country prospers,' she answers. She is asked to leave and is brought back almost immediately to be told she has been approved as a candidate member. Everyone congratulates her.

Her acceptance into the Soviet Union's ruling party as a candidate member turns out to be as much a formality as her mother's was. There is no inquiry into her family background, no referral to the KGB. After completing the required twelve months as a candidate, Zhanna is called before the committee again and her full party membership is confirmed. She goes to the head office on Prospect Mira, where the Krasnoyarsk party secretary issues her with a red membership card embellished with an engraving of Lenin and the slogan 'Workers of the world unite', which the official takes back and files in a cabinet. The twenty-year-old becomes one of almost sixteen million members of the Communist Party of the Soviet Union, out of a population of two hundred and sixty million. Under Stalin the membership was a quarter of that. In the 1970s one in three Soviet citizens with higher education is a party member, and joining is becoming more of a career than an ideological choice. A relatively small proportion of communists hold full-time administrative posts as members of the *nomenklatura*; the majority do little more than attend meetings of the party branch.

At home that evening the family has a small celebration. Her father makes a toast with a tiny glass of vodka: 'Long live the Communist Party of the Soviet Union.' He laughs good-naturedly. They think it amusing.

Being officially a communist does not change Zhanna's life. There are no special shops open to her or special privileges. It does, however, qualify her for another, more exalted, role. A short time later the university rector calls Zhanna into his office. He informs her that a vacancy has arisen for a candidate to represent the city's central district in the Krasnoyarsk Regional Soviet. The pedagogical institute has been tasked with filling the vacancy. He tells her that she has been chosen at a meeting of department heads.

The university student has little say in the matter. There is no competition for the position; she will not be doing any campaigning or submitting a policy statement or debating with a rival candidate for a role akin to that of a member of parliament. The meeting to approve her candidacy is a formality. Zhanna Stanislavovna Suvorova becomes the youngest of two hundred deputies of the Krasnoyarsk Regional Soviet, nominally responsible for the governance of a land mass stretching from Mongolia to the Arctic Circle and containing the greatest world reserves of oil and gas, and the largest arsenal of weapons of mass destruction.

The Krasnoyarsk Soviet assembles twice a year. When she turns up at her first meeting, held in the city's musical theatre, Zhanna is ushered to a seat in the auditorium along with

Final year student: Zhanna at twenty-one, 1979.

scores of fellow deputies from settlements across the region such as Achinsk, Divnogorsk, Nazarovo, Snezhnogorsk and Zheleznogorsk. They are separated from the party leaders on the stage by the orchestra pit, reflecting the chasm between the deputies in the stalls and the decision-makers facing them. The role of the deputies is to endorse the decisions of the hierarchy, and as a rule discussion is minimal and endorsements unanimous. Despite the Bolshevik slogan 'All power to the soviets', all power rests with the Krasnoyarsk Communist Party and its first secretary, Pavel Fedirko.

The meetings last for two days, during which time the function of the deputies is to pass resolutions presented to them, which they duly do with a show of hands. Every time a vote is required a voice calls out, 'Those for?' All hands go up. 'Those against?' No reaction. 'Those abstaining?' No reaction. 'Motion passed.' Zhanna's hand goes up and down with the others.

The system has evolved little from the 'democratic central-ism' espoused by Lenin in his 1902 text *What Is to Be Done?* The insistence on strict adherence to party discipline contributed to the split between Lenin's Bolsheviks and the Mensheviks, who favoured looser decision-making. In 1921 Lenin banned fac-tions in the party on the grounds that they caused animosity among members and provided their enemies with opportunities to exploit internal differences. Under Stalin the Supreme Soviet in Moscow and regional soviets like that in Krasnoyarsk became vehicles for approving decisions made by the party leadership and giving them the force of law.

Elevation to the regional parliament is nevertheless a high honour and Zhanna's parents are proud, but she has to take some teasing. Her father's friend Boris, the stock controller at the rail-way yard, likes to cry out when he calls at their apartment, 'So, how is the deputy today?'

Deputies do have some responsibilities other than rubber-stamping party decisions. During the two-day sessions Zhanna attends group seminars on student affairs where she is able to voice some of the concerns of her peers. Complaints and sug-gestions are noted and channelled upwards. Also, between meet-ings deputies are expected to ascertain the needs of the *narod*, the people. Zhanna finds herself accompanying an older man and woman to knock on doors in a run-down district of Krasno-yarsk called Pokrovka. She is shocked at the primitive conditions endured by some citizens, many showing the ravages of alcohol. More than once doors are slammed in their faces. Conscien-tiously she writes reports of complaints for party consideration.

The young deputy is also required to patrol the streets one day a month as a *druzhinnik*, a member of the People's Volun-teer Squads. Wearing red armbands with the hammer and sickle insignia under a star, the *druzhinniks* go out in pairs, usually under the protective eye of a uniformed *militsia* man. The system of civilian support for the police was formalized in 1959 for 'the participation of the workers in the maintenance of public order'. Patrol duties are also assigned by trade unions and party and Komsomol branches, and Stanislav and Marietta have to take their turns. They can perform citizens' arrests for petty offences but rarely ever do. Little happens on Zhanna's watch. She feels only embarrassment, especially walking past people drinking in the street or queueing outside vodka shops.

It is the custom in Russia for those fond of a drink to share a bottle of vodka *na troikh* – among three – in the open air, or to cluster around kiosks selling weak beer. Western-style bars and pubs do not exist in the Soviet Union where formal drinking is confined to restaurants or the home. In Krasnoyarsk, despite its fearsome reputation as the capital of Russia's prison world, the streets are reasonably safe, even in the darkness. People are rarely mugged or shops robbed, partly because there is nothing much worth stealing. This time in the late 1970s will become known as the era of stagnation as the Soviet Union goes into decline under the sclerotic leadership of the ailing general secretary Leonid Brezhnev, and vodka drinking becomes a national epidemic and law and order begin to break down.

CHAPTER 15

MOSCOW AND MARRIAGE

ARLY IN 1979 Zhanna meets a slender, bespectacled Russian-Latvian student engineer at the birthday party of his cousin, Zhanna's fellow student. She likes him from the start. He is smart, good fun and loves reading. Viktor Naumov, two months older than her, is an undergraduate at the Institute of Technology, where he is studying to become an engineer in the wood and pulp industry. They begin going to the cinema and for walks with another couple, Viktor's best pal and his girlfriend.

Viktor is not her first love. When she was fourteen she had a crush on a high-school boy who played drums. Her father found them kissing and sent him off with such a vigorous handshake he broke the musician's finger. After leaving school they drifted apart. Stanislav first meets Viktor when he comes home late from work, and the couple are saying goodnight at the entrance to the apartment after a date. He takes to the young trainee engineer. The handshake is gentle this time. Viktor is impressed at how respectably dressed Stanislav is, attired in a leather coat he has made for himself. However, her father is not happy that Zhanna might be contemplating marriage before graduating. The shoemaker has great hopes for his daughter's career and he takes steps to further it.

In early September, in the week before she begins her fifth and final year in university, Stanislav takes his daughter to Moscow. He wants Zhanna to complete her final university year in the Soviet capital. Her academic future, he believes, lies not in

Krasnoyarsk but at a prestigious institute of learning in a major city. The Moscow State Pedagogical Institute in Komsomolskaya Square is the most important teaching university in the whole of the Soviet Union. Its alumni include another Siberian, Raisa Gorbacheva, born in the Altai region and wife of Mikhail Gorbachev. It takes some days to arrange an appointment at the faculty so they can submit a formal application for Zhanna's admission.

In the meantime Stanislav tries to organize lodgings for her in Moscow. They call at the apartment of a family contact, Yevgeniya Liholatova, the Armenian stepmother of Russia's famous ballad singer and actor Vladimir Vysotsky, who lived with her for many years and calls her 'Aunt Zhenya'. Zhanna is a big fan, and she feels a sense of pride that she has a connection to Vysotsky, albeit somewhat remote – Zhenya is a cousin of Zhanna's uncle Volodya through his adoptive parents. Vysotsky is especially popular in Krasnoyarsk, where he gave several concerts in the 1960s. At the apartment they discuss Vysotsky's health. They learn that the singer collapsed two months before when touring central Asia and almost died.

In the distinctive gravelly voice of a heavy smoker, Vysotsky satirizes the more ridiculous aspects of Soviet life and articulates the distress of ordinary people who fall foul of the system. He breaks taboos about official hypocrisy, sex and violence. Only a tiny, sanitized portion of his work is released by the state record company, Melodiya, but everyone, even Brezhnev it is said, possesses shelves of his songs on tape – and it will become known years later that KGB chief Yury Andropov sings Vysotsky ballads when on holiday in the Caucasus. In one celebrated composition, 'After Ten Years', Vysotsky sympathizes with a friend who is 'delighted' to be stranded by a cancelled flight at Krasnoyarsk airport because he is afraid of flying, the real point being to expose the unreliability of Soviet airlines, something akin to a state secret. In Krasnoyarsk Zhanna often spends evenings hanging out with a multi-ethnic group of friends – Lena, a Jew, Natasha, a Russian, and Ramil, a Tatar – listening to Vysotsky's songs. This is hardly seditious when his voice is coming from almost every open window in the neighbourhood.

Zhenya arranges for Zhanna to lodge with another Armenian woman living in Moscow should she be accepted to do her final year there, but it is not to be. In her interview at the university, a professor gives her an oral examination in English conversation. The dialogue, in Zhanna's recollection, goes quite smoothly, despite her having learned the language in a closed city without any exposure to native speakers. The professor says she will be happy to accept her as a transfer student, but only if she repeats her fourth year in Krasnoyarsk, as her spoken English skills need a little refining.

Zhanna declines the offer, not being willing to add a year to her academic life, especially as she is contemplating marriage to Viktor. Deflated, she and her father return home. It was an extraordinarily bold thing to turn up unannounced from Siberia to request a place in the final-year language course at a top institute of learning in Moscow, but they almost pulled it off.

Zhanna's father has never stood in her way in making major life decisions, but she wonders if he was not really trying to get her away from Krasnoyarsk in the hope that she would put off marriage in favour of achieving academic distinction first. She reflects too, though much later, that her own willingness to move to Moscow is an indication that, while she believes she is in love with Viktor, she is subconsciously worried about taking the next step.

On returning from Moscow however she and Viktor continue their courtship which inevitably leads to thoughts of marriage. They are both twenty-one and it is normal for couples to marry young. Some of Zhanna's university friends are already

Zhanna and Viktor on their wedding day, 1980.

starting families. Living together without marrying is out of the question; it is not part of Russian, let alone Armenian, culture, and securing accommodation and other benefits without a marriage certificate is well-nigh impossible. Before they know it they fix a date.

The wedding ceremony takes place on 26 January 1980 in the local register office, with Zhanna wearing a dusty pink outfit and off-white shoes made by her father. The event is celebrated with eighty guests at a restaurant. It is more of a Russian than an Armenian occasion, with none of the flourishes of a traditional Caucasian wedding. Zhanna's cousin Ararat makes a heartfelt speech wishing them well. Both in their last term as university students, the young couple do not have a honeymoon.

Viktor moves into the apartment with Zhanna and her parents. He is content there: he did not have a happy home life and is relieved to find himself in a peaceful domestic environment where there is no shouting or heavy drinking. Stanislav and Marietta never argue or raise their voices in front of anyone. Viktor and Zhanna's father take to playing chess together. They have something else in common: they love reading anything they can get their hands on – newspapers, journals and books of all kinds. Viktor is keen on science fiction, particularly the works of Jules Verne, H. G. Wells and the Russian writer Alexander Belyaev. He amuses Zhanna by relating Belyaev's most popular stories, such as the tale of a megalomaniac Russian, backed by evil Western imperialists, who steals and freezes the earth's atmosphere and sells it back to become master of the world.

Zhanna believes that her husband, an only child, had a very sad upbringing, with constant rows over his father's drinking, and that he escaped into another world by burying himself in books. She feels little connection with Viktor's parents. When he asks her if they should follow the common practice and call each other's in-laws mama and papa, she cannot bring herself to agree.

Upon graduation from university in the early summer, Zhanna gains a red diploma, the equivalent of a first-class honours degree. Blue diplomas are awarded to most students who successfully complete their courses, while red diplomas are reserved for the very few whose marks are all 'good' or above, and whose total number of 'excellent' scores is not less than 75 per cent. She achieves 90 per cent 'excellent' in nineteen subjects, including English and German, and the history of the Soviet Union and Marxist-Leninist philosophy.

It is routine for graduates to be sent to a village to teach for three years, but this is not required of someone married and expecting a baby. Zhanna is pregnant by the time she graduates. The baby is due in December. This does not stop her from attending the 1980 Summer Olympics in Moscow, after Marietta manages to get tickets through the shoe factory trade union.

Zhanna, second from left, at her university graduation, 1980.

Winning the right to stage the Games of the XXII Olympiad has been a major international achievement for the Soviet Union and its leader Leonid Brezhnev, especially as things are going downhill at home. The Kremlin spares no expense to make the competitions a showpiece of Soviet achievement. They are the first Olympic Games to be staged in Eastern Europe, and the first in a socialist country. The games are, however, the subject of an international boycott. Eight months earlier the Politburo sent thirty thousand troops into Afghanistan to prop up a communist regime under attack from tribal and urban groups opposed to its land and social reforms. Sixty-five countries, led by the United States, pull out of the games in protest against the Soviet occupation of Afghanistan. Eighty others take part, as do individual athletes from absent nations, and the games take place as scheduled, from 19 July to 3 August.

Zhanna and Larisa fly to Moscow the day before the opening ceremony, which is choreographed by a noted ballet master from Krasnoyarsk, Mikhail Godenko. They are allocated a room in a dormitory for ticket-holders. Viktor, now ensconced as an engineer in the Krasnoyarsk Pulp and Paper Mill, joins them later when he gets leave from work. Cousin Ararat also travels to Moscow for the Olympics, as part of a *militsia* contingent to help police the great event. It is a proud occasion for the twenty-three-year-old Armenian, who less than ten years previously was a village lad in a remote Caucasian town who could not speak Russian. This is what the Soviet Union means to him: education and a decent career.

Early on Monday, 28 July, the day of the cycling and diving finals, word spreads among spectators that Vladimir Vysotsky died the previous Friday. It is a great shock. The singer is only forty-two. No official announcement is made, other than a brief obituary in the evening newspaper *Vechernyaya Moskva*; people learn by word of mouth that his body is being brought to the Taganka Theatre.

Vladimir Vysotsky, beloved folk singer and actor and distant relative, pictured in 1979, a year before his death.

Zhanna and Larisa join scores of Russian spectators who abandon their seats in the Lenin Stadium and take the Koltsevaya metro line to Taganskaya Square, where the theatre is located. When they arrive, thousands of fans have already assembled in front of the red-painted two-storey theatre, mostly young people in jeans and leather jackets. Police on large brown horses help white-shirted Moscow *militsia* to keep them from spilling onto the main thoroughfare. (Ararat, on duty at the stadium, is not among them.) A picture of Vysotsky is displayed in an upper window. The singer's body lies in an open casket on the stage where he performed his classic Hamlet for the last time a week earlier. The queue to file past it stretches for over a kilometre. Flowers and wreaths with verses attached cover the pavements outside.

After four hours the body is carried out and the cortège sets off for Vagankovskoye cemetery across the city centre, where a service is conducted by a remarkable priest of Jewish origin, Father Alexander Men, unofficial chaplain to Moscow intellectuals. (He will be murdered ten years later, possibly by anti-Semitic nationalists.) The crowd outside the theatre refuses to disperse despite orders from the police, who are faced with an unauthorized assembly, something strictly forbidden in Soviet Russia. When the picture of Vysotsky is taken down from the upstairs window on police orders, there is a crescendo of whistling. It does not stop until an even larger portrait of their idol is displayed, and people eventually drift away of their own accord.*

Zhanna always felt irritation at the way the state marginalized Vysotsky during his lifetime. Now she feels something else: anger

---

* I can describe this event in some detail as I was there, reporting on assignment for the *Irish Times* on the Olympics. I might have been standing right next to Zhanna and Larisa for all I know; but it will be some years yet before we meet.

that the same state is not showing respect to those who want to mourn him. That day the conscientious party member and people's deputy from Krasnoyarsk feels somewhat estranged from the political society of which she has been so integral a part. She has just been a willing participant in an unsanctioned and defiant street demonstration and it feels somehow exhilarating.

More disillusion follows. Some months after Vysotsky's death the founder and director of the Taganka Theatre, Yury Lyubimov, is stripped of his Soviet citizenship and forced to work abroad. Lyubimov made the Taganka the most popular playhouse in Moscow and frequently challenged the stifling orthodoxy of the Soviet ministry of culture with daring works such as the dramatization of Mikhail Bulgakov's *The Master and Margarita*, about a visit by the devil to a godless Russia.

The Vysotsky family suffers another tragedy eight years later, in December 1988, when his Armenian stepmother, his beloved 'Aunt Zhenya', is killed in a freak accident: a heavy icicle falls onto her head as she is walking along the pavement in a Moscow street and strikes her dead.

Four months after the Olympics, on 29 December 1980, Zhanna gives birth to a daughter, Yulia. Viktor is beside himself with joy. Like all new grandparents, Stanislav and Marietta are overwhelmed with happiness. Stanislav comes home from work every day and says mock seriously, 'I looked at every infant in the streets and I can say without any doubt that Yulia is the most beautiful of all.' Marietta replies, 'Because she is ours!'

Zhanna has no plans to work while nursing Yulia but an unexpected part-time vacancy arises in the pedagogical institute and the dean asks her to undertake the position of assistant professor of English philology, teaching conversational English and grammar, as soon as possible. It is the opportunity of a lifetime to get such a start. She takes up the post in February. Everyone rallies round to help the young mother. Marietta leaves work to mind Yulia at lunchtime. Larisa, in the final stages of a degree course in music specializing in the piano, is often at home and helps out too. Viktor works night shifts at the paper factory, which means that he can be at home looking after Yulia during the day, and Maya, Viktor's mother, comes when nobody else is available.

Barely out of university, Zhanna is embarking on an academic career which creates a new dynamic in her life. She cannot hope to advance to a full professorship or higher without at some point gaining a PhD, which will involve full-time study over a period of three years. No professor at the Krasnoyarsk Pedagogical Institute is sufficiently qualified to supervise a PhD student in Germanic languages, her specialized subject. To achieve a doctorate she will have to live and study in Moscow or Leningrad, and this will mean uprooting the young family for the sake of her advancement. Before this arises however, she must obtain work experience and professional development, and undergo special examinations. It will take years and the practicalities are too distant in the future to be discussed. They will cross that bridge when they come to it.

CHAPTER 16

HOME AND ABROAD

O NE DISADVANTAGE OF being the youngest member of staff in any organization is that the old hands like to pass on the most unpleasant tasks to the newcomer. When in September 1982 the Krasnoyarsk party headquarters 'invites' the pedagogical institute to provide its annual quota of 'volunteers' to help with the harvest on a state farm, naturally the staff look to Zhanna to be brigade leader. As *komsorg* at school she led pupils on day trips to pick potatoes. This will be different – two weeks on a distant stretch of muddy fields with no facilities and primitive sleeping arrangements.

Her mother has already grappled with the problem of sending shoe-factory workers to the countryside every year to harvest the factory's allocation of five hectares of potatoes, five of beetroot and five of cucumbers. As trade union leader at the enterprise, Marietta has more than once spoken out against the practice, not only on behalf of the cutters, machinists, last-makers, stitchers, finishers and all those whose hands are their livelihood and who hate such work, but also on behalf of the management. During the harvest machines lie idle and the factory loses production. She has suggested that the money which the enterprise allocates for buses, petrol and food would be better spent paying the farm workers to do the work themselves. But logic cannot argue with ideology; the principle of factory workers volunteering on state and collective farms is always upheld.

Zhanna is given charge of one hundred students from the institute. Three buses take them to a state farm where they will work for two weeks. Her daughter, Yulia, is not yet two years old and Zhanna is still finding her feet as a lecturer, but she has no choice. All across Russia similar arrangements are being made to bring in the harvest with the aid of millions of students and urban workers.

Equipped with food packages, tape recorders and a few guitars, they pile onto the buses for the six-hour journey to their destination. The further they get from the city the more they become aware of what the Russians call *bezdorozhnost*, meaning literally 'without roadness' – vast stretches where the highways marked on the map turn out to be muddy tracks. They arrive late in the day to find that nothing has been made ready for them by the farm management. They clean out a barn that has housed animals for use as a dormitory. There is no canteen and no running water. One of Zhanna's first tasks is to locate a well and some buckets. The city arrivals have to make do with a tiny electric stove and one big cooking pot for a hundred hungry mouths. The farm manager appears the following day to show them where to gather the potatoes. It is back-breaking work in which Zhanna also participates. That evening and every evening they have to beg villagers to allow them the use of their primitive *banyas* to wash off the glutinous mud that sticks to everything.

Zhanna tries to make conditions as bearable as possible and keeps up morale by organizing guitar sessions and dancing in the evenings to the music of Abba and Pink Floyd in the village's basic civic club. The lorry drivers who come to collect the potatoes and beet regularly harass the female students. Meanwhile the farm workers do little or nothing; it is a holiday time for them. The manager repeats to Zhanna a common saying among the peasants: 'We sow, God sends rain, then people come from town to get the harvest in.'

The allocation of harvesting to city dwellers stems from Stalin's decision to appropriate all agricultural land to the state. For
the first ten years after the Revolution almost all Russian farmland continued to be tended by small-scale landowners, some of
whom became quite wealthy through the sale of grain to the cities. These well-off peasants, known as kulaks, were brutally eliminated when Stalin introduced mass collectivization in 1929–30.
He fanned class conflict in the villages and encouraged poor
workers to steal from richer families. Many kulaks were shot or
sent to concentration camps. The chaos and upheaval resulted in
a famine in Ukraine in 1932–3, in which millions died, though
nothing of this is known to Zhanna or her colleagues. In his
secret speech in 1956 cataloguing Stalin's crimes Khrushchev
did not mention the man-made famine or the liquidation of the
kulaks, and under Brezhnev criticism of Stalin has been stifled.

Practically all Russian farmland has by now been reconfigured into collective or state farms. The collectives were initially
formed by up to one hundred households pooling their livestock
and implements on state-commandeered land, on which the
individual families were allowed to cultivate a small plot and
keep a cow, a pig, four sheep and several hens, whereas the bigger state farms are run by administrators and the work is done
by wage-earning peasants. In practice the difference is only in
size. On both types of farm the work is now done by employees who are paid a pittance and find it impossible to leave. Until
1976 collective farm labourers were denied internal passports,
thus tying them to the land as securely as the serfs of old, and
since then their passports have been stamped with secret marks
which reveal to the police their origins. Any worker who leaves
is turned away from hotels and has to sleep rough, and if appre-
hended by the police, is taken back to their farm.

Fifty years of collectivization and state farming has wiped
out centuries of knowledge of animal husbandry and crop

rotation. The connection of people to the land has largely been lost. Tillage policy is left to bureaucrats in distant cities with little expertise in agriculture. Tractor drivers are paid according to the acreage they plough and the fuel they conserve, and their wages are reduced if there are any machinery breakages, so they plough furrows that are too shallow. There is a chronic shortage of spare parts for farm machinery, and immobilized tractors, threshers and trucks are left to rust. The system of food distribution is also chaotic. The potatoes picked, the grain gathered and the milk extracted at Krasnoyarsk farms might be shipped thousands of kilometres away, before being returned to local stores. Pressure from the top to produce more meat has on occasions led to over-slaughtering on cattle farms. Much grain is lost because of a lack of storage elevators and spillage from open trucks on potholed roads. Fresh milk is often sour and diluted by the time it reaches the breakfast table, even in the village next to the dairy farm. On 17 November 1979 the novelist Fyodor Abramov writes in *Pravda*, 'The old pride in the well-ploughed field, in a well-sown crop, in well-looked-after livestock is vanishing. Love for the land, for work, even self-respect, is disappearing. Is all this not the cause of absenteeism, lateness, drunkenness?'*

---

* This is not the image the Kremlin shows to the world. In May 1980, when on assignment in Russia, I asked to visit a collective farm and was taken by an escort from the foreign ministry to a two-thousand-hectare cotton and tobacco farm in Uzbekistan. In the farm clubhouse I was fed pilaf, vodka and endless statistics by the manager, a squat Uzbek in a blue suit and brown homburg, who then took me to meet a 'typical' worker, a well-dressed comrade who graciously showed off his spotless cottage with carpets and modern appliances and perfect children. Only later did I learn that every foreign visitor was taken to the same model farm to witness the success of collectivization.

Because of such waste and inefficiency, the shelves in food shops are increasingly bare, making it necessary for people to grow their own food. The real farm work in Russia is done by peasants and urban workers on their private plots, which they tend with the care of the despised kulaks.

The students from Zhanna's university work hard to bring in the potatoes from their allocated fields in two weeks, otherwise their rural idyll will be extended. They succeed, and the buses reappear and take them back to Krasnoyarsk, exhausted and with sore backs. Zhanna's reputation as a responsible leader is enhanced.

Her next assignment as a model Soviet citizen is less onerous.

It comes about by default. One Thursday afternoon in October 1983 a representative of the official youth travel organization, Sputnik, calls in to see Marietta at the shoe factory to discuss workers' holiday arrangements. He says he cannot stay long as he has an emergency on his hands. A tour group of thirty people from Krasnoyarsk is setting off for a Mediterranean cruise on Monday, and his arrangement for an interpreter to travel with them has fallen through. He has to find a Russian–English interpreter, quickly, who would be acceptable to the 'competent authorities'.

Marietta tells him that her daughter Zhanna might meet his requirements. She is a party member, a graduate with qualifications in the English language and a lecturer at the pedagogical institute. Perfect! He arranges to meet her right away and start the process of documentation.

Travel outside the Soviet Bloc is a relatively new phenomenon in Russia. Less than five thousand Soviet citizens were permitted to visit capitalist countries the year Zhanna was born. The numbers have grown to three and a half million a year, thanks to Brezhnev's support for détente between the

USSR and the United States. Still, foreign travel remains a state-controlled privilege and only certain categories of citizens are approved. According to a resolution of the CPSU Central Committee, these include 'advanced workers and employees, engineers and technicians, agronomists, doctors, teachers, workers of science and culture, being politically proved and stable'. The resolution does not mention good connections in the party and state apparatus, but everyone understands that these help enormously. The leader of the Krasnoyarsk Region party committee, Pavel Fedirko, has already been to Italy, Cuba and the German Democratic Republic to 'learn more about the world'.

Zhanna hesitates. Yulia is still a little child. But her mother tells her it is the chance of a lifetime to experience the outside world and that she will take time off work to look after Yulia while she is away.

Getting approval to travel abroad is normally a tedious process, taking months, but when the system wants something done quickly, bureaucracy can move with astonishing speed. The next day Zhanna gets permission from her dean to act as an interpreter on the trip, readily given as it reflects well on the institution. She obtains a character testimonial from the university rector, a certificate declaring her to be a responsible person from the university party committee, and tickets and vouchers from the man at Sputnik. She is also able to change some rubles for *valuta* – hard currency. Normally Soviet citizens are forbidden Western money, but everyone on the cruise is allowed to take fifty US dollars for spending ashore. All sleeping accommodation, meals and entertainment will be provided aboard the cruise liner. The passengers have paid for everything in advance. Because she will be their interpreter, Zhanna does not have to pay, but nor will she be paid for her services.

Sputnik also issues Zhanna with an application form to apply to the KGB for a foreign passport and exit visa. All other members of the group have already gone through this procedure, listing their personal and work histories and character references. As she completes it, Zhanna encounters again the trick question: 'What else do you want to add about yourself or your close relatives?' She answered 'Nothing' before and got away with it. She once again enters the word 'Nothing'. An official from the Sputnik travel agency takes the form and her passport photographs to the KGB offices on Dzerzhinsky Street.

To her consternation Zhanna is summoned shortly afterwards to the KGB offices, where she is ushered into the presence of a tall man in his forties wearing a grey suit. Behind him the cold eyes of the bearded Felix Dzerzhinsky, founder of the Soviet secret police, stare at her from a portrait above his desk.

The KGB agent checks everything on her visa application, running his finger down the entries. 'I have just one question about your family,' he says.

It is as if the clock on the wall stops ticking as she waits for him to continue.

'Do you have any relatives living abroad?'

'No,' she replies, trying not to show that she is overwhelmed with relief.

She understands the reason for his question. A Mediterranean cruise would provide an ideal opportunity for a potential defector to slip away into the arms of a waiting contact. Such an incident would be a serious embarrassment to the authorities, especially if the person has knowledge of some of Krasnoyarsk's industrial secrets.

Then he looks at her directly and says that, as the interpreter, she must realize she has special responsibilities. The state expects her to keep an eye on the members of her group and take note of any negative behaviour or criticisms of the Soviet system voiced to foreigners. 'Let us know if you pick something up' is how he puts it.

This she has not expected. But she is too swept up in the excitement of a first visit to the West to question the notion of 'picking something up' thrust upon her by the KGB. She nods her assent. 'Of course.'

On Sunday the tour group assembles in the Sputnik office for a briefing on how to behave. They shall only go ashore in groups. They shall not walk around any city on their own, especially at night. They shall not give information about Krasnoyarsk to foreigners. They shall not give any foreigner their home address. They shall not engage in black-market transactions. They shall remember that at all times they are responsible for the image of the Soviet Union in the eyes of Westerners.

The party travels by air to Moscow and on to Odessa, where they join other Soviet tour groups boarding the MS *Shota Rustaveli*, an East German cruise ship named after a revered medieval Georgian poet. Passengers are assigned two to a cabin. They are mostly young and middle-aged people with responsible jobs, and include engineers, managers, favoured authors and party apparatchiks. Most of them, like Zhanna, were brought up far from the sea.

Over the next ten days they sail across the Black Sea and around the Mediterranean. They dock in Athens and Thessaloníki in Greece. The local guides speak English and Zhanna interprets. It is a demanding task requiring quick responses which she does not always get right. When a Greek tourist official says, 'There is our marina,' Zhanna translates, 'There are our submarines.' This produces considerable merriment and an embarrassing memory. From Nicosia in Cyprus they are bussed to Famagusta, divided between Greeks and Turks since the Turkish invasion in 1974 and still bearing the scars of war. Zhanna finds the sight of the Turkish troops disconcerting, remembering that their forerunners carried out the genocide against Armenians in 1915.

During the trip the Krasnoyarsk travellers keep apart from the other groups of passengers. They dine together on board, and onshore they travel as a group to see selected sights, such as the Colosseum in Rome. There is little opportunity for shopping and in any case they have little to spend. Zhanna is able to afford only a few trinkets as souvenirs and a set of Sony earphones for Viktor. The MS *Shota Rustaveli* makes a brief stop in Barcelona, just enough time for them to marvel at Gaudí's unfinished cathedral, before turning back along the Mediterranean and across the Black Sea to Odessa. She is enraptured at seeing sights she has read about and is in a constant daze. She absorbs all she can, hoping to capture this unique experience so she can share her memories in detail when home. She knows that people are hungry for information on life in foreign countries and will be showering her with questions. It is the same for everyone else in her group. Though envious of the seeming abundance and prosperity of these exotic countries, their life is back in Krasnoyarsk, for good or ill.

On returning to Krasnoyarsk Zhanna is again summoned to see the KGB agent. Sitting in his office under Dzerzhinsky's accusing gaze, she tells him she has not 'picked anything up' and that everyone conducted themselves properly. She does not mention that as the days went by and the travellers got to know and trust each other, they chatted idly among themselves about who might be the KGB agent on board, as they were sure that at least one of the passengers was a member of the security services posing as a tourist. At one time such talk would have been dangerous, but they are children of Khrushchev's thaw and Brezhnev's consumer society, and they are less afraid to speak openly than the previous generation, which remembers too vividly Stalin's arbitrary and cruel punishments for even a hint of dissidence.

Zhanna is sure her fellow passengers also assumed that the interpreter assigned to each group had special responsibilities, but this did not prevent her from making several friendships with individual voyagers on the ship. Years later she learns that the Soviet liners were seen as spy ships by Western governments and that it wasn't just the KGB agents on board who were scrutinizing the passengers for any hints of defection, but Western agents on the quays watching them closely for the same reason.

Once people hear about her amazing odyssey Zhanna finds herself giving talks at the university and in schools to groups of people who want to hear a first-hand account of visiting tourist attractions and exotic destinations most will only experience through magazines or tourist brochures.

Zhanna's mother too gets a chance to experience a foreign culture when she travels to East Germany as part of a fifty-strong tour group which includes one KGB man and Pyotr Baloban and his wife. On a personal level she is very impressed to find a well-organized society which puts great store on cleanliness and order and she is especially taken with the fact that they recycle used goods and rubbish for the sake of the environment. In East Berlin Marietta and the Balobans take off on their own to visit the Soviet War Memorial in Treptower Park, a twelve-metre-tall statue of a Soviet soldier holding a German child while standing over a broken swastika. It is a kind of pilgrimage for her, a way of commemorating her father, who died as the Red Army advanced through Eastern Europe to claim victory in the German capital, and whose last resting place is still unknown.

CHAPTER 17

DEATH ON THE STREET

IN AUGUST 1982 the Suvorov family had expanded again. Larisa married an Armenian, Vladimir Airiev – whom everyone calls Vova for short – a wiry, cheerful truck driver with a moustache. Vova is a brother of cousin Misha's wife Tamara. He met Larisa in Grozny during a summer holiday and followed her to Krasnoyarsk. The newly married couple moved into the Zheleznodorozhnikov Street flat, and Zhanna and Viktor moved out. They bought a one-bedroom apartment nearby with some financial help from both sets of parents. Stanislav provided furniture, and Viktor, who is good with his hands, put everything in working order and made the apartment comfortable for his wife and little daughter.

This move, though exciting at first, has unintended consequences for Zhanna and Viktor. For the first time they begin to have marital problems. Viktor becomes somewhat jealous of Vova, as he imagines that as a Russian-Latvian he is less favoured than the Armenian son-in-law, though he got on well with everyone when living with Zhanna's parents. He liked being part of a household where people talked to each other and had meals together, which wasn't the case in the home in which he grew up, and he now acts as if he has been evicted from the Suvorov family circle. With just the two of them living together with their little daughter, his personality changes. He begins drinking with friends from the pulp and paper mill where he works shifts. During their courtship he got tipsy once and she found it amusing, but there has never been a culture of drinking in her family and Zhanna dislikes the mood changes that alcohol brings out in Viktor. Two or three times he stays out all night, making her sick with worry. Baba Farandzem once told Zhanna that she would have to come and live with her if ever she married because, while Zhanna might be a strong presence outside, in the home she was a different, more vulnerable person, as a child even allowing herself to be bossed around by her younger sister, kind and gentle Larisa, and she would need someone to speak up for her.

The marriage also comes under strain over Zhanna's ambition to study for a doctorate in Moscow, a necessary step towards obtaining a professorship at the Krasnoyarsk Pedagogical Institute, but one which will take her away from home during term times for three years. An opportunity to begin the process arises in early 1984 when her faculty dean sends her to the Soviet capital on a professional development course. One of the lecturers on the course is Yelena Borisovna Cherkasskaya, a professor at the Lenin Pedagogical Institute in Moscow and a compiler of the standard *Müller English–Russian Dictionary*. Zhanna manages to get a private interview with her and expresses her wish to do a PhD on the lexicology of the English language under her guidance. Impressed by the academic qualifications and determination of the young lecturer from Siberia, the professor asks her to undertake some research so she can make a decision about taking her on. Zhanna does so and, pleased with the result, Yelena Borisovna, as she is always respectfully known, agrees to supervise her studies for a doctorate in the Department of Germanic Languages, Literature and Linguistics. It is the beginning of a friendship between Zhanna and the elderly Jewish professor that will endure for many years. Having been accepted for the course on the basis of her examination results and research project evaluation, Zhanna automatically qualifies for a Moscow *propiska*, a residency permit that allows her to live in the Soviet capital as a student. She begins making arrangements to move there in the autumn of 1985.

At this point Zhanna has to face up to the crisis in her personal life. She is going to Moscow – in her thinking she has no alternative – but the question is whether Viktor will accompany her. He has his own work as an engineer in the paper factory for which he has been specially trained, and it might be difficult to find suitable work in the Soviet capital. He takes some time to make up his mind, but in the end, partly at the urging of his mother, he decides to stay in Krasnoyarsk, which means Zhanna will be on her own in Moscow without her husband or daughter.

By now Zhanna's relationship with her in-laws has also deteriorated. Viktor's father drinks and abuses his wife, who in turn disapproves of Zhanna going to Moscow. She tells Viktor that when his spouse gets her doctorate she will have no time for him. She complains to Zhanna that her son could easily have found a more beautiful wife and forecasts that her absence in Moscow will have consequences: 'What do you expect, that he is going to be sitting here waiting for you?' Viktor has little patience for such talk and more than once tells his mother to leave their apartment and go home.

Zhanna worries about being away from Yulia, by now four years old, but Stanislav and Marietta strongly encourage her to take this opportunity and stress that Yulia will be with a loving family. They, along with Larisa and Vova, who now have their own first baby, Valera, will look after Yulia, a good-natured child who gives no trouble. Viktor will take Yulia off their hands at weekends and spend time with his daughter. Life dictated that, when young, both Zhanna's grandmother and her mother were separated temporarily from their daughters – Farandzem from Lena when she married Nerses, and Marietta from Zhanna and Larisa when she first went to Siberia. Now the same wrench of separation faces Zhanna, as it is not possible for a PhD student to bring a child to temporary student accommodation in Moscow. However, because of the cracks in her relationship with Viktor, she is less inclined to sacrifice a chance to fulfil her ambition for a career in higher education, and after some agonizing she decides she will go on her own.

Zhanna leaves for Moscow at the end of September 1985 to begin her first year of study. She reports to the office of postgraduate students at the Lenin Pedagogical Institute on Kropotkinskaya Street. The location is convenient for Red Square and for the city's theatres, art galleries and libraries. She also registers as an out-of-town member with the communist party branch in the university and moves into accommodation provided by the institute, a ninth-floor room in a multi-storey suburban block of student apartments on Vernandsky Prospect, a thirty-minute metro ride south-west of the city centre. She shares the room with a young Russian widow, Ira Zakharova, whose little daughter, like Zhanna's, is being looked after at home, in a village near the Russian city of Yaroslavl. They become soul mates, sharing a yearning for their little girls whose framed photographs they put side by side on the table. Twice a week Zhanna goes to the telegraph office in Gorky Street to call home and talk to Yulia on the telephone.

From the start, feeling the need to prove herself as a provincial in a big city, the daughter of the Krasnoyarsk shoemaker applies herself assiduously to her academic work. She spends long hours studying in the State Library of Foreign Literature in Tagansky district, which is open to scholars and contains many books and publications unavailable elsewhere, including translations of foreign books with political themes, known as white books, which have a very restricted readership.

Now twenty-seven years old and passionate about English, she is for the first time able to enjoy the company of native English speakers and other foreigners. The occupants of the institute's dormitory include students from lands as diverse as Scotland, England, Wales, Vietnam, China, Cuba and Bulgaria. She takes some of them under her wing, helping them to cope with the idiosyncrasies of life in the Soviet Union and to learn Russian. She finds it exciting to be at the intersection of two spheres, the enclosed USSR and the anything-goes outside world. The inhabitants of each view the others with some suspicion, as such a melting-pot of well-educated and curious young people is fertile ground for intelligence gathering. When they become more familiar with each other they gossip about the possibility of so-and-so being connected with the KGB or its British equivalent, MI6. They explore Moscow together in multinational groups, visiting theatres, museums and art galleries. One day, curious to see how foreign tourists are treated, Zhanna and a Bulgarian friend nip into the Intourist Hotel on Gorky Street, but leave quickly when they realize they might be mistaken for prostitutes hanging about in search of clients.

Zhanna's arrival in Moscow coincides with the start of an exciting new era in Soviet politics. Leonid Brezhnev died in 1982, leaving a legacy of social and economic stagnation, while his successors Yury Andropov and Konstantin Chernenko expired in such quick succession that it was said foreign diplomats were getting season tickets for state funerals. Mikhail Gorbachev has just become general secretary of the CPSU. He calls for *glasnost* (openness) in literature, speech and the media, in the belief that only by exposing the wretched state of the Soviet economy can a cure be found. He also declares that there should be no blank pages in Soviet history.

There is much to be written on those blank pages. For seven decades it was the practice of Soviet writers and editors, with the exception of a few courageous dissidents, to promote party ideology in their works and to ignore inconvenient historical truths. For this they were rewarded with good salaries, pleasant dachas and plenty of coupons for special treats. *Glasnost* exposes how shallow their belief in socialist orthodoxy has been. Most 'approved' writers begin reflecting reality in their literature, publishing information that challenges the state's version of events and voicing complaints about its shortcomings.

Like her father an avid reader of contemporary journals, Zhanna cannot get enough of *glasnost*. She becomes a regular customer at the newspaper kiosk on the street adjoining her Moscow student residence. As its content becomes more outspoken and revealing, the clamour for contemporary reading material grows, and copies of the most daring publications are sold out within minutes. On days when the avant-garde magazines *Ogonyok* (*Little Flame*), *Novy Mir* (*New World*) and *Literaturnaya Gazeta* (*Literary Gazette*) are published, Zhanna can be found at the kiosk at six in the morning, fully an hour before it opens, to make sure she gets her copies. *Ogonyok*, under a new editor, Vitaly Korotich, breaks the taboo on criticism of Stalin, which was reinstated by Brezhnev. He prints pieces depicting the former dictator as a traitor to socialism who wiped out talented writers and army generals and courted flattery like an Eastern despot. Zhanna manages to get a copy of *White Clothing*, a new book by Vladimir Dudintsev, whose work has been suppressed since the publication of his anti-bureaucracy book *Not by Bread Alone*, which so excited her parents in Grozny during Khrushchev's thaw thirty years earlier. *White Clothing* reveals how Stalin repressed gifted scientists in favour of crackpot genetic theories.

More shockingly, *Novy Mir* publishes an article arguing that Stalinism was merely an extension of Leninism. Vladimir Ilyich Lenin is the great untouchable of Soviet mythology. Zhanna's estimation, shaped by years of exposure to party doctrine, is that he was a great visionary. Everything that went wrong in Russia was the result of non-adherence to Leninist principles. If Lenin himself was fundamentally wrong and as ruthless as Stalin, the whole edifice of Soviet communism is hollow. She finds this difficult to assimilate. She welcomes *glasnost* as a means to improve, not demonize, the system.

Zhanna becomes part of a small group of Soviet students who discuss the latest developments in the privacy of their rooms with a mixture of excitement, disbelief and cynicism. They pass journals and books from hand to hand. They crowd into the cinemas to see previously banned movies such as Gleb Panfilov's *Theme*, made seven years earlier but kept from the public, about a Jewish artist torn between his work as a favoured Soviet intellectual basking in official approval and his true creative energy, which can only find expression abroad. When a film censor instructs director Mikhail Ptashuk to take harrowing scenes out of another movie, *A Sign of Disaster*, about the killing of innocent villagers in the war against the kulaks, word comes back from the Kremlin that there should be no cuts. Zhanna emerges from the cinema quite shocked.

One day the student from Krasnoyarsk joins a small crowd attracted to an official exhibition staged by the Soviet Academy of Arts at a gallery near the Old Arbat pedestrian precinct. A painting by artist Dimitry Zhilinsky – who will one day design postage stamps for an independent Russia – depicts his father being dragged from his bed by Stalin's secret police, before being liquidated. Moscow police close the exhibition down when the painting becomes a focus for people with similar family histories who want full exposure of Stalin's crimes. There are still limits on artistic freedom, imposed by officials who do not quite know how to cope with the growing intellectual counter-insurgency supported by the general secretary himself. Zhanna also witnesses dozens of people staging ad-hoc demonstrations for greater artistic freedom. Some are detained by men in leather jackets with clunky radio telephones.

The young woman from Krasnoyarsk is fascinated. She feels she is experiencing something which she can only compare to a springtime of the mind. The new freedoms are like oxygen: once you breathe them in you want more.

During her first term Viktor comes to visit her in Moscow and suggests that on completing her doctorate they might consider moving to his father's home republic, Latvia, on the Baltic coast. They take the overnight train from Moscow to Riga and spend three days based at his grandmother's apartment in the Latvian capital exploring the city and looking into career opportunities. They decide, however, against making their lives there.

For the first two years of her three-year course, Zhanna returns to Krasnoyarsk each December for Yulia's birthday and to see in the new year, and again for the spring break. She and Yulia spend the long summer vacations either at the apartment with Viktor or at the dacha with the family. Viktor commutes by electric train to the dacha when she is there, but sometimes he stays away because of his shifts.

The state of their marriage does not improve. Viktor resents her long absences in Moscow. Sometimes when she is in the apartment in Krasnoyarsk, her husband does not come home after his night shift and says he was drinking with friends. She tries not to think there may be someone else in his life. Viktor reassures her that when her time in Moscow is finished everything will be all right, but in her heart she feels the marriage might not survive. While she partly blames herself for the distance that is growing between them because of her absences, she instinctively feels that he is not investing in the marriage any more and is not supporting her in something that is for the ultimate good of the family. She has excelled in everything, and now she faces failure in the most important exam of her life, that of sustaining a loving relationship.

In mid-September 1987 Zhanna returns to Moscow after three months at home to begin the last year of her PhD studies. Her father drives her to the airport. Viktor comes along to bid her farewell. Once again he reassures her that when she comes back to Krasnoyarsk permanently, everything will be all right. Encouraged by his words she departs in good spirits. It is the last time she sees him alive.

Three weeks later, on Saturday, 10 October Zhanna spends part of the day working in the Library of Foreign Literature in downtown Moscow. It is six in the evening when she returns to the student dormitory. As soon as she opens the glass door to the foyer, the security woman on duty rises from her table beside the lift with a serious expression. 'There was a phone call for you,' she says. 'You must return home immediately.' The caller left no details.

The instruction to come home can only mean very bad news. The telephone at the reception is not equipped for outgoing long-distance calls, so she cannot ring home to find out the nature of the emergency, and there is no inter-city call centre in the vicinity. She rushes to her room, packs her bag and runs out to the main road. She knows there is an evening flight to Krasnoyarsk from Domodedovo Airport, and the terminal has long-distance telephones. She puts out her hand and explains to the first driver who stops that she has to get to the airport without delay. It is common practice for private-car owners to double as taxis. He takes her along the southern ring road and onto the seemingly endless highway through the forests of south-east Moscow that brings them to the airport. She is able to get a ticket on the overnight Aeroflot flight to Krasnoyarsk, leaving at 10.25 p.m. Then she finds an inter-city telephone and calls Krasnoyarsk.

Her mother answers. There is a long silence before Marietta speaks. 'Viktor is dead,' she says.

Zhanna has to endure a nightmare four-and-a-half-hour flight, fighting back her tears for Viktor. She cannot bear to think that he has gone, despite everything. She loved him and he was her husband and Yulia's father. They were going through a tough time but she had hoped they could weather their personal crisis. She agonizes that somehow she is to blame for their failings as a couple. Her father is waiting for her at the airport and they embrace for a long time. 'My poor Zhannochka,' he says, as she sobs on his shoulder. During the thirty-minute drive to the family apartment he tells her what has happened. On Friday Marietta got a telephone call from a lawyer in the procurator's office, who knows Zhanna through a mutual friend. He told her that Viktor had been assaulted in the street and was in intensive care in Krasnoyarsk's main hospital. Marietta called the hospital immediately and was informed he was still alive. On Saturday Viktor was pronounced dead due to a 'closed fracture of [the] skull'. He never regained consciousness. The doctor had said it was better that he died as his brain was badly damaged and he would never be able to function normally. Stanislav tells Zhanna that they do not know the names of his assailants.

The funeral is held on 12 October at the vast Badalyg city cemetery, a maze of paths and stone effigies covering three square kilometres of gentle hills north of the city. On the way to the cemetery Marietta quietly tells her daughter without any explanation, 'I forbid you to cry.' Zhanna dares not ask why, but her heart sinks at the realization there is something untoward connected with her husband's death.

After the funeral Zhanna comes to appreciate why her mother says this. She gets a call next day to report to the October District police headquarters. A woman investigator discusses the killing with her and suddenly remarks, 'You are so beautiful, why would he go off with another woman?'

It is so humiliating for the young widow to hear such a comment in a public space from a tactless official who thinks she is being smart. Her mother did not have the heart to tell her that, in Zhanna's absence, Viktor had stopped coming to take Yulia out at weekends, and her parents guessed that he had found someone else. Zhanna knew her marriage was in trouble and she is tortured by the thought that she had been asking a lot of Viktor, leaving him to cope by himself in the little apartment for months at a time.

Zhanna is comforted by Ararat. Her thirty-year-old cousin from Martakert has excelled in the police and has recently been promoted to the regional criminal investigation department of Krasnoyarsk Region, which excludes Krasnoyarsk city. Investigation into Viktor's killing is the responsibility of the Krasnoyarsk city CID. Nevertheless, through his contacts there, Ararat helps them piece together an account of what happened the night her husband was killed.

It seems Viktor and his female friend spent the evening drinking with several acquaintances in a café in the Kopylovo area, a ten-minute drive from Viktor and Zhanna's apartment. After the café closed at eleven o'clock they decided to continue partying at the apartment and piled into two cars. On the way, Viktor objected when one of the group put an arm around his girlfriend's shoulder. An altercation began which turned violent. When the car stopped, two men seized Viktor, who was of slight build, and dragged him out of sight behind an electricity substation where they beat and kicked him senseless. The men scattered. The woman called an ambulance. Viktor was rushed to hospital with a broken skull and jaw. His girlfriend told the police the names of the two men involved but next morning withdrew her evidence and made herself scarce. So too did the culprits.

Ararat finds out that one of the two assailants is a veteran of the war in Afghanistan, while the other has connections with highly placed officials. The woman has refused to testify against them and the case is closed. Zhanna is angry and despondent. The system has failed her. Her husband, the father of her daughter, has been killed, and his murderers have got away with it.

As a police officer Ararat sees from the inside how things are changing for the worse in Krasnoyarsk. Young men are returning from Afghanistan brutalized by the war and dependent on illegal drugs. There is growing disillusionment with the Soviet system after years of stagnation. There is nothing to do and little to buy in the shops. Corruption is becoming rife. Viktor's death comes at a time when instability is replacing certainty and violence is increasing on the streets. In a country that historically has been associated with heavy drinking, Russian consumption of hard liquor has reached such proportions that Gorbachev has launched an anti-alcohol campaign. In consequence, some drinkers have turned to making a fiery, grain-based concoction called *samogon*, the Russian equivalent of moonshine, and this has made the streets even more dangerous.

Zhanna's misery is worsened when Viktor's parents, who live on the east bank of the Yenisey River, take up residence without her agreement in the apartment she shared with Viktor. They say it should be theirs as they helped pay for it. His father, Albert, whom she never did call papa, wanders around the confined space in his boxer shorts and a vest. Zhanna is outraged to find one day that they have read all the letters which she sent once a week to Viktor while she was in Moscow, evidently looking for mention of tensions so as to deny her the apartment, but they find only routine news and some terms of endearment.

Her in-laws file a motion in court to establish their claim to the property. Their case is heard and rejected on the basis that Albert, a Latvian, is officially registered in Riga and therefore has no basis for a claim in the Russian republic. Moreover, as Zhanna has a Moscow *propiska*, the only person registered to live in the apartment is Yulia, whose temporary guardian is Marietta. The apartment is locked up by the authorities.

A few days later a neighbour calls Marietta to inform her that Viktor's father has broken into the premises and moved in again. Zhanna's mother calls the court. Officials evict him and seal the doors.

Humiliated and grieving, Zhanna comes close to despair. She shuts herself off from her friends. She does not want anyone's sympathy. Her family is her refuge and source of strength. Stanislav and Marietta urge her to continue with her life and not let the tragedy derail her education. She must get away from Krasnoyarsk, for her own sake and to finish her studies. It will be best for both herself and Yulia.

At the end of October she takes her parents' advice and pulls herself together. She returns to Moscow to complete her doctorate and, after some difficulty, resumes her routine of lectures and study. She is no longer the happy person her fellow students knew, but they rally round to boost her spirits and encourage her not to bury herself in her studies. When asked what happened to her husband she tells people only that Viktor died in an accident. Ira, her room mate at the hostel for the last two years, and her closest friend among the students, lost her husband not long ago to a muscular disease, and the two young widows, each with a daughter at home for whom they pine, draw closer through their shared heartache.

After a few days she makes a call from a public telephone to a downtown number. 'We can proceed with the Russian lessons if you still want to,' she says.

CHAPTER 18

THE NUKE NEXT DOOR

IN SEPTEMBER 1987 Pavel Fedirko is contacted by Mikhail Gorbachev. The Soviet leader wants the Krasnoyarsk Region Communist Party boss to help implement his policy of *perestroika* – reconstruction – designed to revive the moribund economy by introducing market-style reforms. Could he please come to Moscow and join the Central Committee of the CPSU as chairman of the USSR Union of Consumer Societies?

Since taking office as general secretary of the Communist Party of the Soviet Union two years earlier, Gorbachev has sought fresh blood for his Kremlin team from around the country, especially comrades who are not stuck in the past and can get things done. Fedirko's record of energy and achievement makes him an obvious candidate. In his fifteen years as regional party secretary he has made good on his promise of a cultural renaissance in Krasnoyarsk. One of his foremost achievements was the establishment of the Krasnoyarsk Opera and Ballet Theatre on Perenson Street, two blocks from the Pushkin Theatre.

Stanislav obtained tickets for the opening-night performance of *Prince Igor*, by Borodin, an opera based on an ancient epic recounting a Russian campaign against outsiders. Marietta, Zhanna and Larisa attended the gala occasion dressed to the nines. Fedirko, beaming, was there with his wife Lydia, herself a pianist, and they were all present again at the debut performance of the up-and-coming local baritone Dmitri Hvorostovsky, singing Marullo in *Rigoletto* long before he became an international opera star.

Fedirko has also provided Krasnoyarsk with a magnificent concert-hall complex at the river end of Prospect Mira. When told that the venue would not attract top performers if it had only a standard Red Moscow grand piano, he authorized the expenditure of eighty thousand dollars on an imported Steinway. Svyatoslav Richter, one of the greatest pianists of the twentieth century, and a succession of other world-class performers subsequently came to play in Krasnoyarsk. The party boss also recruited a top-class conductor, Ivan Shpiller, from the Soviet capital, to create the Krasnoyarsk Symphony Orchestra and secured funding for its one hundred and twenty musicians, along with forty apartments for them and the best imported instruments.

The Dance Company of Siberia, which captivates audiences worldwide with its energy and innovative footwork, has thrived during Fedirko's time in office. No big event takes place in Russia without a performance by these Krasnoyarsk dancers, especially when foreign delegations need to be impressed at the Kremlin. Their leader, Mikhail Godenko, was chosen to choreograph the opening and closing ceremonies of the 1980 Olympics.

Fedirko is credited too with the restoration of Paraskeva Pyatnitza, the Russian Orthodox chapel on the hill near the centre of Krasnoyarsk, a gesture to believers and a recognition of its importance as an architectural focus in an open city space. Close to the Suvorovs' apartment building, it is a place of respite from the traffic and noise all around and has sweeping views of the city.

While enhancing the city's cultural life, Fedirko has also secured his ideological credentials by overseeing the construction of the most modern, expensive and extravagant building in all of Siberia, a state-of-the-art museum on the banks of the Yenisey dedicated to the life of Lenin. Situated at the end of

Prospect Mira, on the former site of an Orthodox cathedral torn down during the Revolution, it comprises three floors of marble and glass, and is equipped with the latest electronic and video guides, plus cushions for patrons to lean on while studying old photographs of the Bolshevik leader.

The investment in culture and ideology comes at a cost. Krasnoyarsk is badly run down. Metal signs bearing slogans extolling communism rust on the roofs of the buildings on the main avenues. Roads are rutted and pavements cracked and broken. Stores are shabby and dust gathers on empty shelves. Suburban apartment buildings are in poor external condition and badly serviced. It is a time of contrasts. In the Siberia of the 1980s a city dweller can spend the day in a mad search for sausage and the evening listening to a sublime piano recital by Svyatoslav Richter.

The condition of Krasnoyarsk is little different from that of other provincial cities in the Soviet Union of the time. Badly needed investment has been diverted to the military budget in a hopeless competition with Ronald Reagan's Star Wars initiatives, and to the ill-judged military venture in Afghanistan, not to mention world-class Lenin museums.

After getting his summons to Moscow, Fedirko contacts his friend Stanislav. He tells him that while he and Lydia are in the capital they want to continue being shod by the best shoemaker in Siberia. Good shoes and boots are hard to get, even in Moscow. In fact Soviet footwear manufacturing is in deep crisis. *Glasnost* reveals how the idiocies of central planning make it almost impossible to find a decent pair of shoes or boots. In one case a shoe factory is ordered to produce one hundred thousand pairs of shoes, but faced with a shortage of leather, fulfils the quota by making only children's shoes. At the same time retailers are flooded with an over-supply of women's woollen boots that they cannot possibly sell.

So, grateful to Stanislav and knowing that the shoemaker is on a waiting list for a new car, Fedirko tells him that he has instructed the chairman of the regional executive committee, Viktor Plisov, to attend to the matter. Shortly after Fedirko departs for Moscow on 3 October 1987, Stanislav is notified that he may take delivery of a silver-grey GAZ-24–10 Volga sedan, the very latest model from the Gorky Automobile Plant. It has a ninety-eight-horsepower engine, flush door handles, aerodynamic plastic hubcaps, superior headlights and several other innovations.

It is more than a quarter of a century since the shoemaker's Volga was confiscated by the authorities in Grozny. It is poetic justice that the authorities in Krasnoyarsk should help him get a new one, at long last. Now reasonably prosperous, Stanislav is well enough established to be seen driving the status car of the Soviet Union without fear of negative consequences. Also, the anti-speculation fever of Khrushchev's time has well and truly abated.

Stanislav has been careful with his car dealings since the affair in Grozny. Four years after acquiring the chocolate-coloured Zhiguli, he sold it, taking every precaution to ensure that the transaction was conducted through official channels: he took the car to an appraiser, had the value notarized, and went with the buyer to the state commission shop to register the change of ownership. This accomplished, he took possession of a version of the Zhiguli nicknamed the *kopeyka*, after the smallest Russian coin, the kopeck, which he now trades in, through the proper channels, for the new Volga.

The magnitude of the party boss's gesture can be measured against the fact that there are a million people on the waiting list for a car in the Soviet Union because of an acute country-wide shortage of automobiles, a statistic revealed by the government newspaper *Izvestia*. In the whole of the Soviet Union there are just forty-five cars for every one thousand people, four times less than in other socialist countries like East Germany and Czechoslovakia.

The timing is good. Stanislav unexpectedly needs to do a lot of driving, and in a bigger car than the *kopeyka*.

Just after acquiring the Volga, Stanislav and Marietta sell their dacha outside town, having got an offer from an enthusiastic buyer they can't refuse, and decide to build a new dacha further out. They have several compelling reasons to do this. Crime in Krasnoyarsk is making everyone nervous. Their dacha has been broken into twice and ransacked; a house in a village is considered much safer for a summer home. Because of *glasnost*, everyone is now aware from radio bulletins just how bad the pollution is in the city. 'Black-air days' caused by cancerous particles in the fumes and smoke emanating from industrial enterprises are common. They need to breathe fresh country air for the sake of their mental and physical wellbeing, and they want a garden much bigger than the one they have at Pugachovo. Stanislav is due to retire in 1989 and Marietta in 1994, and they will have time to cultivate more fruit and vegetables. One of the last acts of Leonid Brezhnev before he died was to increase the size of private plots to half a hectare so people could grow more produce and peasants take more to the markets, a recognition that amateur market gardeners and dacha owners are feeding the nation.

The shoe factory director, Pyotr Baloban, has already sold his dacha in Pugachovo and built a new one on a much bigger plot in the village of Bulanovka, seventy kilometres north of the city among undulating hills carpeted with conifer woods and meadows. He wants neighbours there he knows, and he cajoles the Suvorovs to follow his example. Stanislav is not enthusiastic; he prefers to keep a distance from his boss. Also it will mean round trips of one hundred and forty kilometres every weekend, more than they have bargained for. However, Marietta, who works directly under Baloban, finds it more difficult to ignore her director's urging.

One day in the spring of 1988 the family piles into the new Volga and sets off to Bulanovka to have a look. The last ten kilometres of road are unpaved. An occasional car or motorbike with sidecar kicks up dust on the rutted village street, where cows wander between weed-covered footpaths. There is hardly any sign of life among the ancient, sagging *izbas*, the traditional Russian cottages made from split pine trunks with decorative carving around the windows.

Like most Russian villages, Bulanovka is characterized by what it does not have: it has no square, no post office, no café or bar, and no stores other than a tiny shop with a sign above the door saying *produkti*. The 'produce' rarely amounts here to more than a few loaves of black bread and jars of fruit compote. The once-lively Russian villages romanticized by the classic nineteenth-century writers Tolstoy, Chekhov and Turgenev are no more. As recently as the 1950s, the writer Efim Dorosh was able to describe a typical Russian village shop in his *Rural Diary* in almost lyrical terms: 'It was semi-dark in the shop and smelled of all kinds of groceries. Two sales girls were busy at the counter. One was selling salted herrings, butter, salt and sausages; the other, wine, sugar, sweets and gingerbread.' Bulanovka's almost-empty village store epitomizes the decline of Russian rural life and the snuffing-out of individual enterprise among country folk. Any dacha owners moving here for the summer will have to bring soap, cooking oil, flour and electric light bulbs from far-away Krasnoyarsk – if they can find electric bulbs that is, as they are currently *deficit* in the city.

The Suvorovs seek out the local collective farm director, who is responsible for allocating plots for dachas. 'Take as much as you want,' he says, casually indicating where a few dachas have been built on the fringes of the forest. The Suvorovs are able to secure a large plot just off a new dirt road leading into the trees, and next to where Pyotr Baloban has built himself a grand brick house.

For the next year the shoemaker and family helpers organize the clearing of the site and the construction of a new dacha. When everything is finished the family have a roomy red-brick and wood summer home nestling beside the spire-shaped pines of the forest, with kitchen, living room and four bedrooms. There is a well for fresh water and a separate wooden *banya* with dressing room and a stove to heat stones for producing steam, and nearby a wooden hut over a dry toilet. At the bottom of the garden are three large greenhouses. Within little more than a year Stanislav and Marietta have planted blackcurrants, redcurrants, white currants, strawberries, raspberries, gooseberries, potatoes, lettuce, cabbage, cauliflower, onions, peas, beans, radishes, garlic and herbs. In the greenhouses they raise tomatoes, cucumbers, peppers, aubergines and even watermelons, which remind them of the Caucasus, and, being Armenians, more herbs of every type. For the next quarter of a century they will spend the short but hot Siberian summers here, labouring happily to cultivate a cornucopia of produce.

They do not worry about thieves, as they have inadvertently chosen a site close to a small high-security military installation, hidden behind the first rows of trees. There are always army personnel around to guard it, not conscripts but disciplined professional soldiers. The site is encircled by three compact perimeter fences, two of barbed wire and the third humming with electricity. Metal signs warn of mines. Others, painted red, command: STOP. GO BACK. FIRE WILL BE OPENED WITHOUT WARNING.

The new dacha owners know better than to ask too many questions about the nature of this heavily guarded installation,

Siberian country living: the Suvorovs' second dacha, with nuclear missile hidden in the trees at the rear.

but they learn soon enough that it contains a nuclear missile. The Suvorovs have built their rural retreat beside a silo enclosing a solid-fuel, nuclear-tipped RDS-10 Pioneer medium-range missile, known to NATO as an SS-20, with a range of five thousand kilometres, capable of reaching cities in Western Europe. The soldiers guarding it are from the Omsk-based 33rd Guards Rocket Army – twice awarded the Red Banner Order of Suvorov, a tribute to Stanislav's famous namesake. The military personnel who come and go in new army vehicles rotate each week. They occasionally call at the dacha to ask for water and herbs, and, as the garden flourishes, Marietta makes sure to let them take what they want.

At weekends the electricity on the perimeter fencing is turned off for testing. When it is turned back on it makes a very loud sound and the dacha residents are informed via a loudspeaker, 'Please do not touch the electric fence; it has been activated.'

As they tend their raspberry bushes and potato drills in the hot summer sunshine Stanislav and Marietta do not give a thought to the likelihood that in the event of a nuclear war and the missile site being targeted, they and their dacha and the village of Bulanovka would be incinerated. They are more concerned about the ticks from the forest, carried into the garden by field mice. Each evening in the *banya* all who have spent time outside inspect themselves for tick bites, particularly under the armpits. Several times Marietta has to remove ticks from her skin and once she has to have hospital treatment. Mosquitoes are also more than a nuisance, though over time the Suvorovs seem to build up immunity to the stinging saliva from the insect as it penetrates their skin for its evening meal.

Mikhail Gorbachev and Ronald Reagan decide the fate of the Suvorovs' nuke on 8 December 1987, at a summit meeting in Washington which signals the beginning of the end of the Cold War. The Soviet leader and the US president sign the Intermediate-Range Nuclear Forces Treaty. Under its terms over a period of three years all six hundred and fifty Soviet intermediate-range missiles of the type deployed in Bulanovka are to be dismantled under the watchful eye of teams of US inspectors, while all American Pershing II missiles in Western Europe will be removed.

One April morning, before the snows have melted and before the dacha families have begun their seasonal migration from Krasnoyarsk, specialists arrive from Omsk to deactivate the warhead. This delicate task completed, an immense green-painted twelve-wheeled flatbed truck with crane drives up the dirt road past the dacha. The transporter crane raises the sixteen-metre-high missile from its silo, lays it on the flatbed, and the vehicle lumbers slowly away.* The electric fence is switched off for good. An explosives unit arrives and digs up the mines. With that the military are gone.

The forest is quiet that summer apart from the faint whine of mosquitoes. No longer do the Suvorov family hear the sound of engines and soldiers' voices or the hum of the electric fence in the adjacent trees. The dacha owners and the villagers come to have a look at the site. Everyone knows that a nuclear weapon was deployed there and a neighbour brings a Geiger counter to test for radioactivity. It registers normal levels. They find waist-high barbed-wire fencing still in place around the silo. The soldiers have not bothered to remove the MINES notices dangling from the strands, though they have assured everyone that all explosive ordnance has been dug up and removed. The shoot-on-sight warnings lie discarded on the ground.

The abandoned concrete silo has a thick metal cover mounted on rails, which is left open. Steps in the concrete walls lead down to short underground tunnels and a command room two storeys below. Children come to play in the chilly underground passages. Villagers and farm workers wander into the forest and take wire and fence posts when they need them. They also help themselves to an unexpected gift left behind by the soldiers. In late spring, when the forest undergrowth comes to life, strange plants flourish all around the silo. They are soon identified as *Cannabis sativa*. The locals contemplate how a weapon capable of levelling a small city may have occasionally been in the charge of soldiers high on marijuana.

Some time later an officer notifies the dacha owners that a demolition crew is coming to blow up the silo and that they

* Several of these specially designed launcher trucks are used in future to transport piping; others will be sold to North Korea.

should tape up their windows. The explosives have to be set in such a way that the destruction of the silo will leave a large hole; under the nuclear disarmament agreement with the Americans, the resulting wreckage must be visible to satellite verification cameras.

Pyotr Baloban manages to talk the officer in charge into using less dynamite than originally intended. The explosion still shreds some fir trees and shakes the village. One large chunk of concrete flies over the roof of the Suvorovs' dacha and lands in their potato patch, but the military has made sure no one is close. The glass in their windows, criss-crossed with masking tape, remains intact. All that is left of the silo is a big rubble-filled depression for the benefit of the eyes in the sky.

With the soldiers gone, there is little to deter thieves, who have begun roaming further afield as the economy worsens. Stanislav, Ararat and Vova drive out one winter's day to check that everything is secure. They wade through thigh-deep snow with the texture of white sugar and find to their dismay that a window has been broken. Burglars have got in and taken the television, refrigerator, kitchen table, chairs, dishes, cutlery, bed-clothes and wall shelving. At least the intruders did not find the underground cellar, which is stacked with jars of fruit and sacks of potatoes and carrots. All the summer homes in Bulanovka suffer a similar fate. It is a blow to their sense of rural security. The Suvorovs had come to regard the village as a sanctuary from the city. Nowhere is now safe, it seems.

Ararat lights the wood-burning stove to warm up the dacha. Outside in the crystal-clear air they cook pork shashlik on a metal barbecue over a hole filled with hot embers. They light another stove in the sauna for a steam bath and rub-down with soft snow, and reflect as they relax afterwards on the prevalence of crime and on how *perestroika* is bringing only chaos, and maybe the old times weren't so bad after all.

CHAPTER 19

THROUGH OTHER EYES

THE TELEPHONE CALL Zhanna makes on her return to Moscow in November 1987 is to me.

I arrived in the Russian capital eight months earlier, in March of the same year, to establish a bureau for the *Irish Times*. I had been to the Soviet Union a number of times on assignment since 1979 and it had become evident that a political thaw was taking place in Russia and a full-time correspondent was desirable. People in the West were seized with curiosity about this vast secretive and hostile superpower that had failed to keep up with the modern world's technological and consumer advances.

One of the stories that interests me, not long after I arrive, is the opening of the Blue Bird Jazz Club on Moscow's Chekhov Street. Jazz was banned as decadent in the Brezhnev era and has re-emerged as a popular music form under *glasnost*. I have an official interpreter provided by the Soviet foreign ministry, but I need an out-of-hours translator to accompany me to an evening event. A Scottish exchange student, Alison Henderson, who speaks good Russian, agrees to help. When I learn that Alison shares her dormitory with Soviet students, I mention that I wish to circumvent the restrictions imposed on foreign correspondents and get to know a Soviet citizen who might act occasionally as an informal interpreter and help me improve my Russian.

Since tsarist times it has been Russian policy to isolate foreigners in the capital. All Western correspondents in Moscow exist in an official bubble designed to prevent contact with ordinary people. Our apartments are mostly located in designated compounds where all comings and goings are noted by *militsia* in sentry boxes. I have no choice but to accept the accommodation offered by the foreign ministry, a tiny flat and adjoining office on the top floor of a new concrete one-stairway sixteen-storey apartment block on the edge of Moscow's Taganskaya Square where my neighbours are other new arrivals – journalists from the London *Independent*, ITN and *Newsday*, and diplomats from developing countries.

The building is badly finished. Door handles come off, television sockets are cemented over, windows do not shut properly, light fittings fall from the ceiling, and pipes rumble like ships' engines. We suffer blackouts because of circuit overloading, which is inconvenient when halfway through sending a dispatch by telex, the only means of instant communication. We are supplied with official interpreters, drivers and cleaners by a foreign ministry department known as UPKD – the Administration of Diplomatic Personnel. Our cars carry distinctive yellow licence plates identifying the owner's occupation and nationality: K037 signifies a *korrespondent* from Ireland. We have special hard-currency stores to meet our lifestyle needs, and there are separate departure terminals for foreigners at the country's airports. The result of all this is that diplomats and correspondents tend to form strong bonds within the foreign community and rarely get to make the acquaintance of non-official Soviet citizens.

Alison tells me she has a friend from Siberia in her residence who might enjoy the opportunity to practise her English, but that if I offer her money for helping me with my Russian I will never see her again. She knows Zhanna is married with a daughter. The next day she tells her about this Irish journalist who is divorced and has five children and is looking for help with his Russian conversation skills. The upshot is that they both call to see me one evening in June 1987 when the water pipes in my office are rumbling like continuous thunder. The young woman from Krasnoyarsk insists on telephoning the building supervisor, demanding that something be done, and, amazingly, the noise stops. She tells me she is returning to Siberia for the summer and promises to contact me when she comes back to Moscow in the autumn.

The summer passes. In mid-September I get a note from Zhanna saying, 'I do not know if you still need help in Russian. I will ring you up very soon.' It turns out that she studies most days at the Library of Foreign Literature close to my office – we use the same metro station – and she is willing to meet when convenient for both of us. The library opens at 10 a.m. She starts coming to my office at nine three mornings a week. We have barely got into a routine when Zhanna telephones one Saturday evening to say she is at the airport. She is returning to Siberia and is sorry she will have to cancel the lesson scheduled for Monday as her husband has died suddenly. I express my shock and condolences.

I assume that in the circumstances it is unlikely she will come back to Moscow, but that day in November after she returns she calls me, and we agree to resume the lessons. She does not talk about what has happened other than to say that her husband was assaulted in the street and received fatal head injuries. Our meetings seem to spark inordinate curiosity in the stout woman assigned by UPKD to clean the offices in the building. Valya makes sure to fuss around when Zhanna is arriving and leaving.

I find our exchanges tough going as Zhanna insists on communicating in Russian and sometimes I wish she would just speak English. She seems more concerned about helping her student than improving her own foreign language skills. We conduct some of our lessons walking around Moscow streets so we can get away from the boredom of grammar books. I guess that this makes it easier for her to distract herself from her grief.

It so happens that the early winter of 1987 is when political momentum in Russia is moving out of the Kremlin and onto those same streets. The first demonstration we come across is on the Old Arbat, the popular pedestrian walkway in the centre of Moscow. An early snowfall has coated the tiled surface, and a group has unfolded posters outside the Vakhtangov Theatre. These call on people to sign a petition for a memorial to victims of the Stalin era. A crowd gathers. Men in parka jackets and ski hats begin to take pictures with zoom lenses. At a signal from one of them, a snow plough appears and scatters the demonstrators, some of whom are detained and led away.

This is one of the last times the KGB is permitted to interfere with public gatherings. Shortly afterwards small groups begin marching on party headquarters, brandishing placards critical of the treatment of Boris Yeltsin, the popular Moscow Communist Party first secretary. Yeltsin was subjected to a dressing-down by Mikhail Gorbachev at a party meeting for daring to criticize the slow pace of reform. The KGB can hardly start detaining citizens supporting a member of the party elite.

Seeing that nothing happens to them, the people lose their fear of speaking out in public. Impromptu street debates take place. Passers-by join in for a while and move on. In one place we hear that in Canada a man, his wife and a dog can manage a farm better than a hundred collective farm workers in Russia, and in another a bearded fanatic calls for the return of the tsars. Everyone it seems has an opinion and wants to be heard.

Moscow is a city of contradictory moods. For most people *perestroika* is not working. With the footpaths deep in slush, Muscovites cannot find decent winter boots. There are crush barriers and endless lines outside vodka shops. Shoppers queue all night for a kilo of sugar as supplies have been depleted by the manufacture of home-brewed liquor. In a country where everyone drinks endless cups of *chai*, the Politburo devotes a whole session to finding a solution to the scarcity of tea leaves. Toothpaste is in short supply. Kettles are impossible to buy because kitchenware factories find them less profitable to make than saucepans. Windscreen wipers are such a rare commodity that it is common to see drivers pull into the side of the road in the event of a sudden downpour to attach the wipers they keep hidden inside the car.

But despite all this it is an exhilarating time. As the winter gives way to spring in 1988 reassessments of historical figures and events, and revelations about the past, become ever more frank. Gorbachev grants Soviet writers unprecedented licence. He needs the intelligentsia on his side to discomfit the hardline conservatives who are obstructing his reforms. Every day brings a new sensation. A discredited author is recognized as a saviour of the nation's conscience or a vilified comrade is hailed as a martyr to Stalin's executioners. In Catholicism, it is said, there is life after death; in communism there is posthumous rehabilitation. The whole country is obsessed with its past. People wonder not just what the future will look like in a year's time but what their past will look like.

Though citizens have been deceived and lied to for decades, at this stage the disclosures produce a degree of optimism that the Soviet Union will become a better country where there will be no repeat of the horrors of the past. We find out, for example, courtesy of a performance of *The Peace of Brest-Litovsk* at the Vakhtangov Theatre in the Old Arbat, that Nikolai Bukharin, a reforming communist who opposed collectivization and was executed by Stalin in 1938, did not plot to murder Lenin. It is a surreal experience to meet the participants backstage still dressed as Stalin, Trotsky and Bukharin, having a smoke together and laughing. The play lay on the censor's shelf for a decade and is staged now because Gorbachev signals that Bukharin can be absolved of anti-party crimes after half a century of calumny. The author Mikhail Shatrov stages *Onward, Onward*, a play featuring other ghosts of Soviet history in which Trotsky rises from the dead and accuses Stalin of having him murdered, and Stalin confesses he is indeed responsible. Such an allegation has never been made publicly before in the Soviet Union, even in Khrushchev's speech denouncing the former dictator.

Just as yesterday's communist villains become modern-day heroes, so too revolutionary icons are consigned to the dustbin of history, or even denounced and rehabilitated in the space of a few weeks, and then discredited again.

This happens in the case of Pavlik Morozov, whose virtues Zhanna once had to uphold as an example for Soviet youth because as a thirteen-year-old he was murdered by kulaks for allegedly informing the NKVD of his parents' disloyalty. Morozov's role as a martyr to communism is scrutinized anew in the spirit of *glasnost*. The official youth magazine *Yunost* publishes the view of historian Vladimir Amlinsky that the boy is 'a symbol of legalized and romanticized treachery'. Komsomol officials rush out a rebuttal, and Morozov enjoys a brief respite, but his statues disappear from Soviet schools and the Pavlik Morozov museum in the city of Sverdlovsk is closed, coincidentally just about the time that city decides no longer to honour Yakov Sverdlov, the Bolshevik assassin of Tsar Nicholas II and his family, and reverts to its pre-revolutionary name of Yekaterinburg, after Peter the Great's wife Yekaterina.

If museums to controversial figures are a touchstone of a society's values, then the fate of the Pasternak museum reflects the changes taking place in Russia. It is located in Peredelkino, a village south of the capital with writers' dachas half hidden among elm, oak, sycamore and fir trees and a tiny Orthodox church with gold-and-blue domes. Like most Soviet citizens,

Zhanna, who comes with me to explore the village one Saturday afternoon, regards Boris Pasternak as a gifted poet who was discredited through unauthorized publication abroad of his critical novel *Doctor Zhivago*, which of course she and her parents read many years ago in *samizdat* form. Pasternak was vilified by the Soviet authorities for the 'anti-revolutionary' sentiments in his novel, and the book is still not officially available in Moscow. Since his death in 1960 his rambling two-storey dacha had been kept by his family as an informal museum, but in 1985 its owner, the Soviet Writers' Union, had the family evicted. However, no other writer could be found to move into such a sacred place, and by 1988 it has become a museum again. Every weekend lovers of Pasternak's poetry gather around his simple white tombstone among the caged graves of the village cemetery, taking turns to recite his poetry aloud – a common tradition among Russia's lovers of classic verse.

A second dacha deep in the Peredelkino trees contains an informal museum to children's writer Korney Chukovsky, who died in 1969. Zhanna knows many of Chukovsky's verses by heart from school. His daughter Lydia incurred the Kremlin's disfavour by giving Alexander Solzhenitsyn shelter before his expulsion from the Soviet Union, and she tells us when we call by that until recently she kept a pitchfork in the dacha's main room to deter official intruders. It is also allowed to stay open after an outcry from prominent poets, authors and academicians.

At long last Vladimir Vysotsky gets his due. On 25 January 1988, when he would have turned fifty, we join hundreds gathered around his grave in Vagankovskoye cemetery, where Zhanna tells me about the distant family connection with the people's favourite protest singer. His songs are played over loudspeakers in sunshine so bright that tiny frost particles glitter and twinkle in the cold air. Vysotsky was a tough-talking, heavy-smoking detective in movies and a brilliant Hamlet on the stage of the Taganka Theatre, but most of all he was the poet and balladeer of the ordinary people during the years of stagnation and neo-Stalinism under Brezhnev. People resent the fact that, as he expressed it in one of his songs, Soviet organizations and individuals had declared war on him because 'I disturb the peace, and croak out my words across the land.' Mourners recall how he sang about the misery of prisoners so movingly that people asked him when he had been in prison, though he was never in fact arrested. In the new Soviet Union of *glasnost*, Vysotsky is eulogized as a voice that spoke out when others would only whisper, and he is posthumously awarded the State Prize, second only to the Lenin Prize, a gesture which many of his fans, including Zhanna, dismiss as a travesty, seeing it as the appropriation of a folk hero by a party scrambling to save itself.

The impact of films in undermining the communist ideal, for Zhanna and countless millions across the Soviet Union, cannot be overestimated. We experience together one of the most electrifying moments of *glasnost* in the Star Cinema on Leninsky Prospect at the end of a screening of *The Cold Summer of 1953*, directed by Alexander Proshkin. This is the story of a gang of criminals who take over a coastal village and terrorize the inhabitants, a metaphor for Stalin's seizure of power in the Soviet Union. The hero is a dumb woman who waves frantically for help to revellers drinking and dancing on the decks of a passing steamer but is ignored. The criminals are ultimately killed by two exiled political prisoners, one of whom declares, 'I just want to live the life of an ordinary person. I just want to work because I have a lot to do.' An announcement as the lights come on that these are the last words spoken in his final role by the popular actor Anatoly Papanov, who died after the film was completed, produces wild applause and tears in many eyes, including ours.

Another movie to shock audiences is *Little Vera*, a stark portrayal of life in an industrial town. We feel the empathy of the Moscow audience as they see on screen for the first time the plight of young people living in bleak housing with no prospects of escape. They laugh loudly when Vera's boyfriend asks what is her goal in life, and she replies with mock seriousness, 'In our country, Seryozha, we have only one goal, communism.' Vera learns that her mother did not want to have her but her father forbade an abortion so they could get a better apartment. She attempts suicide. The movie is shown over the objection of the head of the Soviet State Film Authority, Alexander Kamshalov, who protests that such films, 'showing intimate episodes and drinking scenes', threaten the moral health of the people. At a private screening for film-makers and critics a voice calls out, 'You should be ashamed to show such things.' Another voice replies, 'Aren't you ashamed we live like that?'

It is intriguing for Zhanna to experience this explosion of openness, not just as a party member brought up as a thoroughly Soviet person, but through the perspective of a journalist from the capitalist West. When my colleagues get to know her we are invited to dinner together in their apartments and she learns from the conversation even more about her own society, and about Western attitudes. Similarly I begin to see the world with her eyes, rather than through the distorting glass of the foreign community, where prejudice discourages positive assessments of any aspect of Soviet life.

One of the things that most offends Zhanna – and some in the foreign community – is the existence of special shops in Moscow open only to holders of hard currencies, so that we foreigners do not have to 'live like that'. These are the Beryozka (Little Birch Tree) stores, which stock items of food unavailable elsewhere. Soviet citizens are effectively barred because it is a crime to possess foreign money. The Beryozkas create consumer apartheid. As *perestroika* brings more foreigners to Moscow, the Kremlin allows the Finnish department store Stockmann to open outlets with a greater range of supermarket items, flown in from Helsinki every day. The company installs windows of opaque glass to prevent harried Moscow shoppers from glimpsing the goodies within, as they hurry by with empty string bags from one lengthy queue to the next.

There is another consumer apartheid in the Soviet system in the form of the special shops and warehouses for party functionaries, also well hidden from view. These are for *nashi* – 'our own'– and the Suvorov family have benefited from access to the *baza* special store in Krasnoyarsk. But the system is despised, even by some of those who benefit. The poet Yevgeny Yevtushenko berates a meeting of the Soviet Writers' Union for having pockets stuffed with tokens for special shops, 'as do I'.

Zhanna does her shopping at the noisy, bustling peasant markets in Moscow, where vendors, mainly from central Asia and the Caucasus, sell meat, poultry, vegetables and spices at exorbitant prices. She likes to make typical Armenian dishes, such as lamb and rice cooked in vine leaves and seasoned with herbs.

Desperate to meet the growing demand from Moscow shoppers for more sophisticated products than Soviet factories can turn out, the government resorts to emergency measures. It does not have enough hard currency to import high-quality foreign clothing so an official in the ministry of light industry persuades leading French couturier Pierre Cardin to sell his designs to Moscow. His dresses, trousers and cardigans, made in Russian factories, go on sale in a large marbled Soviet store called Lux. We go along to have a look. It is something of a sensation. Around the displays of imported Italian shoes there is a queue stretching forty metres. 'This is the most painful place in the store,' says the young chief buyer. 'People have to wait an average of three hours for service. There is a nationwide shortage of good shoes. Even if we were to give the whole store over to shoes there would still be queues.'

After we leave, we go to one of the cooperative restaurants that are beginning to open in Moscow under the economic reforms introduced by Gorbachev. There Zhanna tells me about her father, of whom she is very proud. He is a master shoemaker and designer at a shoe factory, she explains. He has just reached retirement age. If only the reforms had happened earlier he would have been a successful entrepreneur, she believes, as he made shoes just as good as the foreign models in Lux. She tells me about how hard he worked to provide for his family and how he was wrongly imprisoned for selling his car at a profit, after which the family moved to Siberia. She has never told this to anyone before. It is clear to both of us that our relationship has deepened. We are spending all our spare time together. We are now accepted by our friends as a couple. But of course, we know that our stay in Moscow is temporary and that one day soon we will go our separate ways.

CHAPTER 20

NO TO THE KGB

ONE MORNING IN April 1988 Zhanna takes the metro to the institute as normal, gets out at Krasnoselskaya metro station and walks to the entrance of the faculty of Germanic languages. A woman on security duty hands her a piece of paper on which is written an instruction to present herself later that day at the head office of the postgraduate course at Malaya Pirogovskaya Street on the fifth floor. She knows right away what is in store for her.

When she shows up, a nondescript man in his thirties, dressed in suit and tie and with a neat haircut, is waiting outside the office. He gives her a glimpse of his card, identifying himself as a member of the state security bureau. He belongs to the KGB's seventh directorate, second division, which conducts surveillance on foreign journalists and their contacts. The KGB man asks her to accompany him outside the building. They walk in silence along the narrow footpath outside, shaded by poplar trees. After a few minutes he stops and faces her.

'Do you know any foreigners?' he asks.

'Of course. There are a few in my dormitory.'

'Do you know any foreign correspondents?'

'Yes.'

He proceeds to tell her that he knows all about her background in Krasnoyarsk and why she is in Moscow and that his bosses at the KGB are fully aware of the progress of her relationship with the *Irish Times* correspondent. He provides details that shock her, as they indicate she has been under surveillance for some time.

In recent months, as we have become closer and started spending more and more time together, I have met many of Zhanna's friends from her dormitory, and I have introduced her to journalist and diplomatic colleagues, making our relationship public. We have begun to receive, and return, regular invitations to dinner. She is to them a curiosity, a real Soviet citizen and party member from a closed city who is working on a dissertation on native words in the English language. Many of the people we socialize with become good friends, among them Rupert Cornwell from the *Independent* and Xan Smiley of the *Daily Telegraph*. Xan is intrigued by Zhanna's linguistic studies and ruminates at the dinner table over the origin of words in the English language, such as 'place', which he suggests is a native English word. She takes issue with him, whereupon he consults his *Oxford Dictionary of English Etymology* and concedes gracefully that it is in fact borrowed from Latin and that the young Armenian from Siberia is right. Quentin Peel of the *Financial Times* is surprised to hear her criticize people who buy state-produced goods in one Soviet city and sell them in another at a profit, a growing practice that is causing public discontent. 'Zhanna, that is called business,' he tells her. 'That is how the market economy works.'

There are some awkward moments on these social occasions. Zhanna finds it difficult to remain politely silent when a particularly insensitive person tells anti-Soviet jokes, as happens once or twice. She can appreciate a clever anecdote about Soviet life around the table in a Russian kitchen, but the same story can be insulting when told by a foreigner. She also has to endure insinuations from casual acquaintances that she is not what she seems. Some are wary of this Soviet citizen in their midst. We are told many years later by an Irish diplomat that the French ambassador warned him that Zhanna was working for the KGB.

Now Zhanna has been targeted by the security organs because of her association with me and my colleagues. She has been half-expecting the KGB to tap her on the shoulder for some time. In 1984 a law was enacted making it an offence to help a foreigner without official permission and it is still in force. Despite *glasnost*, regular unapproved contact with a foreign correspondent still ranks high on the KGB list of subversive activities. Unauthorized contact with non-citizens makes the state so nervous that international telephone calls may only be made through an operator. Direct dialling was introduced in Moscow for the Olympics in 1980 for the convenience of foreign athletes, but discontinued immediately afterwards. The Cold War is not yet over, and the state security apparatus is continuing to act as if nothing has changed. Everything is still organized to ensure foreign reporters remain within their own bubble of relationships to keep contact with Soviet citizens to a minimum and facilitate maximum surveillance. Viktor Chebrikov, head of the KGB since 1982, is a conservative party man credited with dismantling an extensive network of CIA operatives in Russia, and his informants have instructions to report immediately any suspicious friendships.

That morning in April the agent turns at the end of the street and begins escorting Zhanna back to the faculty. His demeanour is informal, and his tone almost friendly. 'We want your help,' he says. He makes out that the KGB is only interested in finding out what is discussed at the social events which she attends with foreign correspondents and diplomats, some of whom, he warns, 'are not all you think they are and may have other duties'. He mentions as examples Xan Smiley and Rupert Cornwell.

Zhanna's contact with these two Englishmen in particular has caught the attention of the security organs. Xan is the son of Colonel David de Crespigny Smiley, a much-decorated British agent and intelligence officer, while Rupert's half-brother David

Cornwell, writing under the nom de plume John le Carré, once worked for the British domestic security service, MI5, and for the foreign intelligence service, MI6, and produces spy novels featuring a senior intelligence officer called George Smiley, reputedly based on Xan's father.

David Cornwell intrigues Russian intelligence. After years of being refused entry to the Soviet Union, he is granted a visa to visit Moscow in 1987 to do research for his book *The Russia House*. He is tailed everywhere by two KGB agents. Once they follow his brother Rupert by mistake, and on another occasion they help him back to his hotel after he leaves a boozy late-night party. The spy-fiction writer spends an afternoon in the Library of Foreign Literature, where Zhanna studies every day, and to his delight a group of students takes him to a common room to show him where they secretly watched a video of the 1979 BBC television series based on his book *Tinker, Tailor, Soldier, Spy*, and featuring Alec Guinness as George Smiley.

The KGB has every reason to believe that Zhanna will co-operate with them. They have details, evidently provided by the KGB in Krasnoyarsk, of her life as an exemplary Soviet citizen. They know that she is a highly regarded member of the CPSU, and that she served as a deputy in the Krasnoyarsk Soviet. Her family credentials seem impeccable, and they apparently never stumble upon her father's prison record back in Grozny. She once cooperated in keeping an eye on a group of Soviet citizens travelling abroad. She has just been taken under the wing of one of the most prominent lexicographers in Russia, also a party member. First in her class at university, she is about to complete a doctorate that one day will guarantee a full professorship. Moreover she will be a candidate member of the Soviet Academy of Sciences.

However, to the agent's chagrin, Zhanna expresses outrage at the invitation to spy on her new friends. She is affronted by the KGB assumption that she will work with them. 'We need the help of people like you. Think it over,' he persists, giving her a card with his telephone number. 'Meet me here a week today at the same time.'

As he opens the door of a car that has suddenly drawn up beside them, he hands her a hard-cover booklet. 'Read this,' he orders. 'You will see the type of people with whom you are consorting.'

That evening we have an arrangement to go to the theatre. Zhanna comes to my office, visibly upset. She says nothing until we are out in the open. Against the background of the traffic noise on Marksistskaya Street, she tells me what has transpired.

We don't quite know what to do. Zhanna is inclined to act as if nothing has happened. We cannot let it become common knowledge, as the KGB is capable of making serious trouble for Zhanna if she makes the approach public. Among other things they can eject her from Moscow and obstruct her doctorate.

We leaf through the KGB booklet to see who has been accused of spying. It is disappointingly out of date. One agent listed is Janet Chisholm, a diplomat's wife who acted as an intermediary for a Soviet traitor called Oleg Penkovsky, regarded as the most important Western agent of the Cold War and a model for the character of Yakov in le Carré's *Russia House*. Another is a British journalist, Edward Crankshaw of the *Observer*, who allegedly worked for MI6. The activities of these two and others who feature are already well known in the West.

Next day I take the metro across town to the Irish embassy on Grokholsky Lane and ask one of the staff I know, Judith Devlin, to come outside. While strolling in the embassy garden – in reality a few square metres of patchy grass and weeds – I tell her what has happened, explaining that the embassy should have a record of the encounter if something goes wrong – for example, if Zhanna is subject to punitive measures or I am expelled for a surreptitious reason; two years earlier five British correspondents were ejected in a tit-for-tat exchange: Dennis Blewett of the *Daily Mail*, Mark Frankland of the *Observer*, Robin Gedye of the *Daily Telegraph*, Alan Philps from Reuters, and Tim Sebastian, a television correspondent for the BBC. Nicholas Daniloff, correspondent for *U.S. News & World Report*, was arrested after being handed a package by a Soviet acquaintance, containing maps marked TOP SECRET, coincidentally a week after a Soviet diplomat, Gennady Zakharov, was detained in New York on charges of espionage. Both were freed after extensive negotiations, which was the aim all along. Ireland is not in NATO and has few secrets of interest to the Kremlin, though two Soviet diplomats and the wife of one were expelled from Dublin four years earlier on suspicion of running a clearing house for Soviet spies in Europe and liaising with the IRA in Northern Ireland.

The same KGB official as before turns up to meet Zhanna at the appointed time a week later. She does not try to avoid meeting him again as she has no choice: they know where to find her and she does not want to irritate them unnecessarily. He suggests that they walk in the direction of Novodevichy cemetery. He says that the *New York Times* and the *Daily Telegraph* often use Moscow correspondents to gather information harmful to the Soviet Union. He repeats his request, saying the KGB needs her to pass on anything she hears that might be useful to the state. 'These are people who want to damage our homeland,' he reminds her.

Again Zhanna replies that she will not pass on anything, and that it is iniquitous to ask her to betray people with whom she is friendly. She is stunned that, party member or not, with *perestroika* in full swing she has to endure this humiliating encounter and she tells him, 'I will not spy on a person I am close to.' She hands back the booklet. His tone becomes cold. He tells her that she should be more cooperative and that she will be hearing from him again.

Next day I report the second exchange to Judith in the embassy weed patch. Zhanna also confides what has happened to a Canadian friend at the student dormitory, who admits that on visits home she has been interrogated by the Royal Canadian Mounted Police about what her Soviet friends are saying about Gorbachev and their attitudes to the Soviet government, but there is never any suggestion of compromising anyone.

Another week passes. Then, as Zhanna emerges at midday from a lecture hall on the ground floor of the university, she finds the KGB man again waiting for her, this time accompanied by an unsmiling thin-faced older functionary whom she later recalls as looking remarkably like Vladimir Putin, though that KGB agent and future Russian president is serving in East Germany at this time. To her alarm they tell her to get into the back of a waiting black Volga with darkened windows, and the driver heads in the direction of the Lubyanka. She is not concerned for her safety but fears being detained for lengthy questioning. However, he turns off Gorky Street and pulls up instead at the National Hotel, a grand edifice facing the Kremlin.

It is common knowledge that state security officials like to dine at the National, where the rooms are furnished with museum-quality antiques and Lenin once had his office.

'It's lunchtime, let's eat,' says the more senior official. The two men escort her into the cavernous main dining room and call for menus. Zhanna refuses to order anything. She is furious that they think they can buy her cooperation with lunch at a grand hotel, which in their eyes is a big deal, given the severe shortages of food in the capital. It occurs to her that they think access to good restaurants is what attracts her to me, which makes her even angrier.

As they fork up their salads, the younger man, the 'good cop', renews his appeal for her cooperation. 'There are many enemies who would like to harm the Soviet Union,' he says. 'As a good

Soviet citizen, you should be aware of that. All you have to do is tell us what is discussed at these social gatherings with your friend. Like for instance the dinner two days ago at the apartment of Brian Hanrahan.' Hanrahan is a BBC Moscow correspondent, a veteran of the Falklands War, and his wife Honor Wilson is a freelance radio journalist. The KGB is obviously keeping an eye on them too.

Zhanna refuses.

The older agent suggests that she introduce them to the *Irish Times* correspondent. They would pose as important friends from Krasnoyarsk and offer to help him get exclusive interviews. What is wrong with that? It would be good for his career.

She says she will not.

The atmosphere becomes unpleasant.

'Are you going to marry him?' asks the Putin-like agent.

'Do you want me to propose for you?' she retorts.

The more they push her, the more stubborn she becomes.

'We can help you stay in Moscow if you behave,' the same agent says, implying that they will reward her for cooperation by renewing her residence *propiska* when it expires in October on completion of her PhD course.

'Do you know what?' Zhanna replies. 'My husband just died. I have a daughter at home. I'm in a different frame of mind than you think. The day for my presentation is fixed. Then I am going back to Krasnoyarsk to my daughter. Do what you have to do. I don't care.'

'We can ensure you never get your doctorate,' he says.

With that she gets up and walks out, shaking with fury. She has worked hard to make the best life for herself at home, in school, in college, in society; she has spent nearly three years separated for long periods from her daughter; she has studied diligently to prove herself worthy of her parents; she has lost her husband in humiliating circumstances, and here are these two

Cold War throwbacks threatening to rob her of her hard-earned, life-long goal for refusing to betray her new friends.

The KGB men do not follow her. She descends the escalator into the metro and takes the Tagansko–Krasnopresnenskaya line to my office. We go out into the street, away from the prying eyes of the nosey cleaner, who we now are sure is a KGB informer. The threats have to be taken seriously. Zhanna's career is in jeopardy. We discuss breaking off contact with each other, but she will not hear of it. She does not mention that they asked about marrying. At this point we are both aware that our relationship will most likely end when Zhanna goes back to Krasnoyarsk.

Next day I again take the metro to Grokholsky Lane and convey details of the exchange to Judith so that everything is on the record. I tell her about the KGB officers' proposal to meet me as Zhanna's 'friends'. Perhaps they have the mistaken impression that I might be of some assistance to them. In the early 1980s when I was *Irish Times* news editor in Dublin I was helpful to the Ireland-based TASS correspondent Mikhail Smirnov, who would ply me over lunch with questions about British–Irish relations and events in Northern Ireland. Journalists in Dublin assumed he was a bona fide journalist, or at least we gave him the benefit of the doubt, and we were critical of the fact that Smirnov was followed everywhere by members of the Special Branch. After he returned to Moscow however, Oleg Gordievsky, a KGB colonel who defected, wrote a tell-all memoir, *KGB: The Inside Story*, which revealed that Smirnov was the acting KGB station chief in Ireland and a graduate of special classes conducted in Moscow for UK- and Ireland-bound KGB agents by the Cambridge spy Kim Philby.

While apprehensive about the threats, we cannot really believe that in the new atmosphere of *glasnost* and *perestroika* the KGB will risk taking action against Zhanna which might result in unfavourable publicity about their methods. Under Gorbachev the spy agency is losing its grip on Soviet society, though it still has an armoury of coercive weapons, such as blocking promotion, denying *propiskas* or preventing the award of degrees. The irony does not escape us that because of *glasnost* the KGB can actually learn more about what is going on in Russian society from the pages of the newly liberated Moscow newspapers than from tittle-tattle around correspondents' tables. In fact our conversations are often about what we have found out ourselves from the Russian media.

Nothing does happen. Zhanna delivers her dissertation and is awarded her doctorate on 3 October 1988. She returns to Krasnoyarsk two days later to start a new chapter in her career as assistant professor, teaching lexicology at her alma mater.

After a week back in Siberia she receives another summons – would she please report to the dean's office where a young man wants to speak to her. An official of the Krasnoyarsk state security bureau is waiting. They find an empty room to talk. He seems rather uncomfortable. Her KGB case file has followed her back to Krasnoyarsk, but the local agent isn't quite sure what he is supposed to do with it. The city is small enough for him to know of the reputation Zhanna enjoys in academic and party circles. He makes a few perfunctory enquiries about her intentions. She tells him that her time in Moscow is behind her and she is getting on with her life.

Then he asks, rather bashfully, if she will meet him once or twice to help him improve his English, as he has a test coming up. Like a good Soviet citizen, she agrees. She almost feels sorry for him.

CHAPTER 21

THINGS FALL APART

STANISLAV SUVOROV IS working on the fourth floor of the
Dom Byta on 13 September 1988 when he hears sirens
and a commotion outside. Through the window overlooking
Prospect Mira he sees a smiling Mikhail Gorbachev, in suit
and tie and without a hat on this chilly afternoon, climbing
out of a black ZIL, with Raisa by his side wearing an elegant
silk scarf and a jacket with padded shoulders. Television crews
set up their equipment. Passers-by quickly form a small crowd
around them.

Stanislav goes back to work on the pair of shoes he is design-
ing for a client. Business is business. Besides, what he is seeing
below on the street is being shown live on the little television set
in his work space.

The general secretary of the Communist Party of the Soviet
Union has begun a series of visits outside Moscow to meet the
people. It is his first foray into Siberia in three years and his first to
Krasnoyarsk. He has authorized television coverage of his walk-
abouts, an unheard-of concession in a society where the imagery
surrounding communist leaders has always been controlled, and
if necessary contrived, to suit party propaganda. Central Television has already shown hours of a patient and all-knowing Gorbachev explaining to respectful crowds in different cities what
has to be done to rescue socialism.

By nature charming and garrulous, and convinced of his
ability to reform the Soviet Union through force of argument,

The calm before the storm: Mikhail Gorbachev and his wife Raisa in Krasnoyarsk in 1988, unaware of the angry reception awaiting them.

the party boss begins a dialogue with the locals. But here in Krasnoyarsk his smile quickly fades. For the first time he gets a taste of raw public anger at the worsening economic situation in the country. He is visibly taken aback by the vehemence of the criticisms he hears about shortages in state stores and high prices in new cooperative ventures.

'Go into our shops, Mikhail Sergeyevich. You will see there is nothing there.'

'We have queues everywhere – for meat, for sausages, for everything.'

'No one is doing anything about housing.'

'We have no hot water.'

'Public transport is a disaster.'

'Everything is falling apart.'

A man complains loudly about pollution, forcing Gorbachev to admit, 'The way we have been behaving with the rivers and lakes, the forests and the air itself, this has to stop.'

Beside Gorbachev, dressed in the dark suit and white shirt of the Soviet apparatchik, the balding and thin-lipped Krasnoyarsk party boss, Oleg Shenin, grimaces as if he cannot believe ordinary people are displaying such insubordination. But *glasnost* has advanced to the point where vocal street critics know they will face no consequences for speaking out, while the most hard-line communists are turning against Gorbachev because they feel he is going too far with this *perestroika* business and they are venting their anger in private.

Years of believing that nothing will change and that the leading role of the communist party is a permanent fixture of Soviet life have produced political apathy and fear in Krasnoyarsk, such as that experienced by Lyosha, a friend of Zhanna's with a PhD in economics. 'I have nowhere to live except the one room in the hostel at my enterprise,' he tells her shortly after she returns from Moscow. 'The director is a hardliner and if I get involved in anything he will throw me out. Then what do I do?'

Now, taking their cue from events in Moscow and encouraged by Gorbachev's openness, the people find their voice and small pro-reform groups start to gather in a pedestrian precinct to protest against industrial pollution. They claim high rates of cancer, respiratory diseases and miscarriages, and in particular they express their anger at the storage of uranium at Krasnoyarsk-26. *Pravda* reveals the existence of this 'beautiful metropolis of white stone buildings' shortly after Gorbachev's visit, in response to 'a new spirit of *glasnost* in international relations', and seeks to reassure Krasnoyarsk, in the aftermath of the Chernobyl catastrophe, that the site is safe. While admitting that waste from decommissioned nuclear missiles is being stored there, the party organ claims that radioactive material will not leak into the river for twenty thousand years and will by then have decayed. The admission simply heightens the outrage that a cave for spent nuclear fuel has been gouged out beneath the pure waters of the Yenisey, and at a point upstream from the city.

Such bureaucratic irresponsibility characterizes Soviet governance everywhere, and accounts for the accident at the Chernobyl nuclear power plant in Ukraine on 26 April 1986. Tens of thousands of workers sent to the scene were exposed to excessive radiation and Gorbachev later admits that the catastrophe and the attempts to deny massive incompetence enraged the people so much that 'the system as we knew it could no longer continue'. Krasnoyarsk citizens now are not of a mind to believe the reassurances of *Pravda* about the nuclear waste or to tolerate the cancerous pollution, and work under the river is stopped. The city starts to monitor the atmospheric pollution which contaminates the ice-blue Siberian sky and poisons the lungs of its people with smoke and fumes from factories, shale mines, iron and steel mills, cellulose combines and an aluminium plant. Every day the radio broadcasts terrifyingly high pollution levels.

The story of Konstantin Chernenko's concrete head is an indicator of the hesitant nature of political progress in Krasnoyarsk as compared to Moscow. Chernenko was leader of the Soviet Union for a mere eleven months. A heavy smoker who suffered from emphysema and cirrhosis of the liver, he died in March 1985 and was succeeded by Gorbachev. Oleg Shenin arranged for a bust of the short-lived general secretary to be erected on a plinth near the Lenin Museum, on the dubious grounds that Chernenko deserved the honour because he was born in a village in Krasnoyarsk Region three hundred and fifty kilometres from the city.

After *glasnost* reveals that Chernenko achieved practically nothing in the Kremlin, voiced his approval of Stalin and recommended that the name of the city of Volgograd revert to Stalingrad, someone throws paint over the bust. The sculpture is removed for cleaning, prompting speculation that Shenin might take the opportunity to quietly store it away. But the new Krasnoyarsk party boss ensures that it is returned, scrubbed clean, a visible triumph for the old ways, with a *militsia* man to keep an eye on it at night. It stays there for several months until it is removed again and consigned to storage as a result of a Central Committee decree that all memorials and place names honouring Chernenko and Brezhnev be removed, as they are publicly linked with 'the period of stagnation in the country'. Memorial plaques identifying where the two leaders were born and lived are unscrewed, and thousands of copies of Brezhnev's ghost-written biography, portraying him as a mastermind of the victory in the Great Patriotic War, are pulped or, as cynics say, moved from the non-fiction to fiction sections in state libraries.

Shenin strongly supported *perestroika* in the early years and for this reason Gorbachev promotes him to the Politburo not long after his visit to Siberia. The Krasnoyarsk boss has, however, become disillusioned with the reforms, which in his view have brought about 'the enrichment of a small group of black marketers', and Gorbachev will in time discover he has clasped a viper to his bosom.

The Suvorovs remember the last years of the Soviet Union as the era of ration coupons. The government issues books of coupons for basic items including sugar, meat, rice and clothing. No one goes shopping without a bundle of these flimsy tokens. The family manages to survive better than most because of its friends in the vegetable and meat distribution centres, although the officials are experiencing difficulties themselves in stocking the warehouses. The satirical magazine *Krokodil* publishes a drawing of Adam and Eve presenting a ration slip for the forbidden fruit. Gorbachev, blamed for the shortages, confesses in public his embarrassment at seeing a cartoon that shows Brezhnev sporting a row of medals while his own breast is covered in ration coupons. Petrol too is in short supply in a region containing some of the biggest reserves of crude oil in the world. Another sketch features a train pulling oil tanker trucks destined for the West, forced to halt at a level crossing where a car has run out of fuel.

The traditional anecdotes, those little realms of free expression in a society where outright criticism is dangerous, begin to lose their edge. It is no longer so daring to relate that a man has been jailed for revealing a state secret by shouting that the party's general secretary is an idiot, when top comrades are saying this openly, and the Soviet media is publishing the most insulting comments and cartoons about the leadership.

At the Krasnoyarsk shoe factory production becomes sporadic. The annual requisition for leather, submitted each May, is not met. Its Kalinin industrial sewing machines, mass-produced at a former Singer factory at Podolsk, are of poor quality and outdated: they are still made with pre-war machinery taken as reparations from the Singer factory at Wittenberg in Germany in 1945. Stanislav finds it difficult to source good-quality leather to make custom shoes and boots. All across the Soviet Union, even in Moscow, winter footwear is *deficit*. A woman sees a man wearing one boot and asks if he lost the other. 'No, I found this one,' he replies.

A new law comes into effect permitting 'individual labour'. Anyone who wants to work privately in a range of occupations such as dentistry, hairdressing, toy-making, taxi-driving or shoemaking, can do so and may apply to a bank for a modest loan to buy equipment. To most people it makes little difference; such activities are widespread anyway. Gone are the days when Stanislav and Marietta had to hide their cobbling and sewing tools from official eyes. Speculation is still a crime – Article 154 of the Russian Criminal Code remains in the penal code – but this law is no longer enforced.

In 1989 Stanislav reaches the mandatory retirement age of sixty and stops working at the factory. As a measure of the love

Stanislav congratulates female workers at the shoe factory on International Women's Day, 8 March 1988.

and respect for him at the Pushkin Theatre, the director continues to keep him on staff – and allows him to use the theatre workshop at the back to carry on his now perfectly legal bespoke shoemaking, on condition that the theatre has first call on his services. Stanislav has a notice placed on the wall at the entry to the theatre courtyard advertising high-quality shoe repairs and illustrated with the outline of an elegant boot. He also takes up a post teaching a new generation of shoemakers three days a week at Krasnoyarsk Technical College.

The most innovative measure Gorbachev enacts at this time is a law on cooperatives, aimed at 'saturating the market with high-quality goods and services, at making those goods and services cheaper, and at the increasingly full satisfaction of Soviet people's material and spiritual needs'. Groups of workers can set up small enterprises such as restaurants, repair workshops, garages, pavement kiosks, even shops. The Politburo approves the cooperative law mainly because of the failure of the state to provide consumer goods and services. Many factories however take advantage of the measure to create cooperatives which sell their goods at a higher price than that set by the state.

There was a spending boom in the Brezhnev years, due to the high price of oil, which brought in hard currency. It is Gorbachev's misfortune that oil prices have fallen and consumer expectations cannot easily be lowered. The Soviet leader persuades the constituent republics of the USSR to become more self-financing by going around central planning and dealing directly with international partners. In doing so he inadvertently encourages them to take the first step towards independence, which in a short space of time will become a sprint.

In four months, nine hundred cooperatives are founded in Krasnoyarsk. The most prominent are cafés and kiosks. They get a mixed reception. People know that some are spin-offs from enterprises whose managers are selling scarce stock at inflated prices. They ask, with some justification, why they should pay more for the same goods and tend to blame the cooperatives for shortages in state stores. For true believers in communism it is a retrograde step towards capitalism. They regard cooperative owners as greedy. 'Have you heard the latest anecdote about cooperatives?' 'No.' 'Give me three rubles and I will tell you.'

Ararat, Zhanna's cousin, and his comrades in the police find themselves dealing with a new type of crime. Criminals are banding together and demanding protection money from the new businesses. They usually do this by 'asking' that a cooperative take on one of their number as a member, who will not actually turn up for work, except on payday. Some of Ararat's fellow officers see an opportunity to get into the action and shake down the criminals, forcing the protectors to pay for protection – from them. Drugs have also become a big problem. Hashish is now freely available at the markets. Ararat comes across another new class of crime associated with drugs, the killings of rival gang members for control of supply chains and distribution areas.

Coop owners who do not comply with the demands of the protection gangs – known as the mafia – are simply put out of business. This is evidently what happened to the creators of a log-cabin cooperative restaurant erected on a grassy hillside within the city. Its speciality was borscht, a traditional Russian beetroot soup made with beef, cabbage, onions, potatoes and beetroot. People look up one morning and see just a heap of blackened timber where the restaurant stood the day before.

CHAPTER 22

TURNING POINT

JUST BEFORE ZHANNA leaves Moscow for Krasnoyarsk in October 1988 she receives another proposition – of marriage, from me. Up to now marriage has not been on the agenda, despite the closeness of our relationship. We never spoke about the possibility. It has seemed an impracticable prospect for both of us. I have five children in their late teens or older, most of whom Zhanna has met when they holidayed with me in Moscow, and I have just recently gone through a divorce from my former wife Della who lives in Dublin, with all the fault on my side. Zhanna is a widow with a young daughter and a position in Krasnoyarsk Pedagogical Institute as an assistant professor, with the strong possibility of rapid advancement. She would not relish the idea of attaching herself to an itinerant correspondent and moving away from her beloved family to places where her professional qualifications might not be recognized. Nevertheless I ask her to marry me as we walk along a stream-side path in the Peredelkino woods on her last day. I acknowledge there will be enormous problems and difficulties, but we can deal with them as they arise, one at a time, and with her permission I will adopt Yulia. She doesn't say yes. But she doesn't say no. Only much later do I learn that she had planned to slip away from Moscow rather than spend the last day with me as she might find it too upsetting. She now fears my proposal is impulsive. There was an element of panic on my part at the thought of never seeing her again but I have deliberately arranged for us to spend those final hours in our favourite place in the whole of Moscow as the setting for what I have to say.

We exchange several letters – all of which are undoubtedly read by the KGB, perhaps by the same young secret policeman in Krasnoyarsk to whom she gives English lessons – during the course of which I try to convince her that my proposal is serious and Zhanna explains why for practical reasons it is well-nigh impossible for her to marry me. In the end however we agree that our relationship has indeed reached the point where neither of us can contemplate spending our lives apart. She tells her mother, who is happy she has found someone else, but at the same time frets that involvement with a foreigner will get her daughter into trouble with the KGB. Zhanna does not disclose to her parents, so as not to worry them, that the secret police were already on her case. In the new year she comes back to see me in Moscow, and the matter is settled: we decide upon 29 June 1989 as the date of the wedding. During the spring break she again comes to Moscow, this time accompanied by Yulia, now eight years old. Meanwhile on a brief trip to London I purchase a wedding ring.

Frustratingly I cannot go to Krasnoyarsk to meet her family, as it is still a closed city. A foreign correspondent can travel to most places in the Soviet Union as long as the foreign ministry receives two days' notice, presumably to give the local security organs time to prepare their monitoring arrangements. However, the city of Krasnoyarsk, along with Archangelsk, Chelyabinsk, Gorky, Magnitogorsk, Omsk, Perm, Vladivostok and Yekaterinburg, remains completely off limits. I appeal to my minder in the foreign ministry, Yury Sapunov, to authorize a private visit or to let me go on a *commandirovka*, a work-related journey, to report on *perestroika* in Siberia, but to no avail.

Zhanna's parents are naturally upset at our decision to marry, not to mention members of my own family. Marietta worries that her daughter will be abandoned by this foreigner whom she has never met and whose profession means his assignment in Russia will end sooner or later. At the Krasnoyarsk Pedagogical Institute a professor warns Zhanna about marrying someone eighteen years older. She responds that she married a person of her own age and look what came of that.

Marietta, still five years away from retirement and head of the party branch in the shoe factory, is also concerned that she will be obliged to resign from the party to which she has been loyal all her working life because of her daughter's marriage to a foreigner. She goes to the district party secretary to voluntarily relinquish her membership card. The official tells her she will not have to leave the party over such a thing and she should not worry. Times are changing. Marietta retains her card.

The offer by Zhanna's mother to relinquish her party membership is made at a time when the CPSU is facing its biggest ever crisis, and when it is more concerned with keeping members than losing them. Democratic centralism, the principle which underpins its position as the ruling party, is being destroyed from within, with party intellectuals at the forefront of a campaign to remove Article 6 from the Soviet Constitution. Article 6 affirms the party to be the leading and guiding force of Soviet society, with the right to determine the home and foreign policy of the USSR and to strive for the victory of communism. Without it the communist bosses will forfeit their monopoly on power.

The Komsomol, the youth communist league, in which Zhanna was a diligent organizer and leader, is also losing its role as the model of youthful discipline. *Krokodil* shows a wide-eyed teenager about to leave for summer camp being told by her parents to take her example from Komsomol leaders, who are depicted in the background drinking, smoking and carousing.

In early June, having finished her term as an assistant professor, Zhanna comes to Moscow to prepare for the wedding. We register at the Moscow *zags*, a cream-and-green building on Griboyedov Street with the formal name of the Registry for Acts of Civil Status, and are issued with a coupon entitling Zhanna to buy a gold ring for me at a designated state store. Gold, however, is *deficit* in Moscow. It is being hoarded by people who no longer have any trust in the Soviet ruble. The assistant at the chaotic jewellery store tells Zhanna with a shrug that she can take finger measurements and place an order, but '*Bog znaet*' – God knows – when it will arrive.

As with everything in these days of scarcity, Zhanna needs someone with good contacts, so naturally she calls her parents. Marietta goes to a jewellery shop in Krasnoyarsk, tells the assistant the required size and is sold an eighteen-carat gold ring over the counter for the future son-in-law she has not yet met. She does not need a certificate of entitlement, nor does she have to use her connections. Gold is plentiful in Krasnoyarsk, where the second-largest deposits in Russia are to be found. The old saying 'In Moscow there is everything' is turned on its head, at least in this case.

Stanislav and Marietta take the four-and-a-half-hour flight to the Soviet capital for the wedding, bringing the ring and a pair of maroon suede shoes which her father has made for Zhanna to wear on the day. Xan Smiley holds a reception beforehand in his apartment, and, being a fluent Russian speaker, goes out of his way to put Zhanna's parents at their ease. 'Everybody loves Zhanna,' I say to Marietta as her daughter is engaged in conversation by my colleagues. '*Myi tozhe lyubim Zhannu,*' she replies. 'We too love Zhanna.' While Marietta is a bit guarded among Zhanna's new friends, Stanislav appears totally at ease and shows no discomfort at meeting foreign journalists and diplomats for the first time. As I am to find out, this reflects his character: he is full of humour and goodwill towards people he meets, whatever

Marietta and Xan Smiley share a joke at the pre-wedding reception in Moscow, 1989. My brother and best man, Brendan, is pictured in the mirror, holding a glass.

their status in society, and will happily share with them his own experiences of life and his strong opinions on any and every subject.

The wedding ceremony is conducted by a young woman in red evening dress who congratulates us 'in the name of the people of Moscow, the Hero City'. We have a lunch for thirty guests in the Winter Garden Room of the Praga Restaurant, which is popular with foreigners and Russians alike and is said to be under permanent surveillance by the KGB. My brother Brendan, who has come from Belfast to be best man, expresses to the guests his surprise that it took less flying time for him to reach Moscow from Belfast than for the Suvorovs to travel from Krasnoyarsk.

The KGB is now no longer interested in Zhanna; it is undergoing its own *perestroika*. Just at the time Zhanna was presenting her dissertation, the KGB chief, Viktor Chebrikov, was ousted and replaced by a sixty-five-year-old ally of Gorbachev, a former Komsomol leader and diplomat, Vladimir Kryuchkov, who promises a radical overhaul of the much-feared security organs.

Within a year Kryuchkov announces that the surveillance of dissidents has been discontinued and that the aims of the KGB have been reconfigured to include fighting terrorism, the drugs trade and serious crime, as well as combating espionage. With large pro-Yeltsin street rallies attracting scores of foreign correspondents, the idea of trying to stop Soviet citizens talking to Westerners has become ludicrous. Nor can religious activities continue to be the subject of KGB interest when the smell of incense is wafting from a restored cathedral inside the Kremlin itself. It is also futile trying to ban foreign books and newspapers when the Soviet media is full of sedition.

Kryuchkov disbands the infamous KGB fifth directorate, responsible for ideological crimes, citing its 'mistakes'. The Lubyanka assures foreign residents that our telephones are not tapped, though no one believes that. However the KGB also warns citizens that increased contact with foreigners in Moscow is facilitating the missions of foreign intelligence agencies in the USSR, whose work is 'on the rise'.

In a sign of the changed times, the foreign ministry gives permission for the shooting on location in Moscow of *The Russia House*, the film based on John le Carré's book of that name, and KGB officers fall over themselves to meet le Carré when he comes back to the Soviet capital with the stars of the film, Sean

Connery and Michelle Pfeiffer. This time they do not put a tail on him. There is no need; they are drinking vodka together. Some of the scenes are shot in the National Hotel, where the secret policemen tried to wine and dine and win over Zhanna.

Zhanna's daughter Yulia comes to live with us in Moscow and is admitted to the local school. She becomes Julia O'Clery after the executive committee of the Zheleznodorozhny District Council of People's Deputies in Krasnoyarsk approves the adoption papers and I become her papa. Now married to a foreigner, it is practically impossible for Zhanna to work in Moscow. The university from which she has just obtained her doctorate offers her a teaching post but she no longer has an official *propiska* allowing her the full rights of a Soviet citizen in the capital. She enquires about vacancies at the Anglo-American School, an independent co-educational school chartered by the US, British and Canadian embassies, which caters for foreign children in Moscow aged four to eighteen. The principal, Vera Nordal, happens to need a Russian-language teacher, and Zhanna becomes the first Soviet citizen on the teaching staff – a sign of the times.

Accustomed to the discipline and respect shown to teachers in Soviet schools, she is taken aback to find her American pupils in particular, sons and daughters of diplomats and business people, chewing gum in class and putting their feet up on the desks. She requires them to stop, and they obey, confirming her belief that children always prefer order to indiscipline, in whatever society they live.

I renew my entreaties to Yury Sapunov in the Soviet foreign ministry for permission to visit Krasnoyarsk, this time pleading my case as a private individual wishing to visit my wife's family and relatives. The country is opening up and restrictions on internal travel by foreigners are being lifted. Yury tells me that Krasnoyarsk will soon be an open city, but as of now it is still

Krasnoyarsk's folly: the world's biggest and most extravagant Lenin museum, built just as communism collapsed.

closed to private individuals. However, with a barely perceptible wink, he suggests that I make a formal application to travel to Krasnoyarsk on an official business trip, as a foreign correspondent with a programme compiled by his officials, and of course there will be no objection to me staying with Zhanna's family while I am there.

In October 1989 I am at last able to buy an air ticket and fly to Zhanna's home town, bearing a printed schedule of interviews with party officials, local journalists and heads of enterprises, and topped off with a visit to the Lenin Museum. Zhanna and Julia have to stay behind in Moscow because of her teaching and Julia's school.

The Krasnoyarsk airport terminal is a one-storey building with no air bridges. People awaiting arrivals stand in the open behind an exit gate. Stanislav has come to collect me in his silver-grey Volga. He greets me with a kiss on both cheeks. Whatever reservations he and Marietta may have about Zhanna marrying a foreigner, they do not show them, and later I overhear Stanislav, speaking of his visit to Moscow for the wedding, tell a friend, 'You should see what a wonderful, loving relationship they have.' Throughout my week-long stay I am overwhelmed with Armenian hospitality and warmly welcomed into the family by Zhanna's parents, Larisa and her husband Vova and by Ararat and Araik, who are so consumed with concern about events in Nagorno-Karabakh that they ply me with questions about Gorbachev's intentions there.

Exploring the city I find the roads are potholed, the shops are shabby and uninviting and factory buildings are in a decrepit state. I glimpse armed guards on a prison watchtower. However the River Yenisey promenade and the old buildings of Prospect Mira give Krasnoyarsk a feeling of elegance. Larisa one day takes me to visit Viktor Astafiev, the popular writer whose village stories I have come to love, at his fourth-floor apartment in the suburbs. We are followed there and back by men in a black car. He describes the mood of the Krasnoyarsk people as 'irritated'. The sixty-six-year-old Siberian, a great fan of Gorbachev, complains of shortages, even of tea, but has high hopes that Russia will pull through and is thankful to live in Siberia. 'One day in the taiga is worth a year in Crimea,' he says. 'I feel closer to God than to people there.' Things would be worse, he believes, 'but for the fruit and vegetables of the wooden dachas, the bilberries, cranberries, wild strawberries and whortleberries in the taiga, and the abundance of deer and other wildlife, which mitigate against real hunger'.

I will experience several frigid winter days here on visits in years to come, but the region on this occasion is enjoying a *babye leto*, an old women's summer, as they call an Indian summer. Stanislav and Marietta organize a family picnic in the taiga, at which I experience for myself the beauty and majesty of the vast forest. On the way there they stop at a market, buy a live lamb, truss it up and lay it in the boot. Ararat and Araik slaughter it amid the trees and roast it with aubergines, the smoke from the campfire rising into the still autumn air in columns as straight as the slender Siberian spruces.

I largely ignore my foreign ministry schedule, other than to attend a meeting with a dozen writers at the House of Journalists. They question me on how the world views *perestroika*. A neatly dressed blond-haired young man, the only one who does not introduce himself, takes copious notes. One of the others whispers to me as the meeting breaks up that the note-taker is a KGB officer, and assures me he is more interested in keeping an eye on them than on me, and it is their questions and responses he is taking note of, not mine. Things haven't changed that much yet in Siberia.

CHAPTER 23

YOU CAN'T LIVE LIKE THIS

IN AN EFFORT to accelerate reform, Mikhail Gorbachev decides to end the sham democracy of the Supreme Soviet and replace it with a 2,250-member Congress of People's Deputies, with two thirds freely elected and the remainder nominated by officially approved institutions or the party itself. For the first time since the Revolution, Soviet voters have a genuine choice of candidates. The majority of those they elect turn out to be party members. However, they are answerable not to the party but to their electors, and many have no intention of following the seventy-year routine of meekly endorsing every motion from the party leadership, as Stanislav's aunt Anna was obliged to do when she was a Supreme Soviet deputy from Grozny.

When the new deputies assemble for the first time, on 26 May 1989, Gorbachev allows television coverage, and the population tunes in to listen and watch. The session becomes a forum for the expectations, grievances, fears and outrage of millions of Soviet citizens for whom the communist party has for seven decades claimed the exclusive right to speak. An explosion of *glasnost* ends the party's monopoly on truth. Many taboos are shattered in ten days that not only shake the USSR but fracture it beyond repair.

The secret protocol to the 1939 Nazi-Soviet pact ceding the Baltic republics to the Soviet sphere of influence is exposed for the first time. With Gorbachev and the Politburo looking on impassively, Yury Vlasov, a popular Olympic gold-medal weightlifter, lacerates the KGB as an underground empire that oppresses people for thinking differently. There is a collective intake of breath in the Kremlin hall when a deputy insults Lenin. For the first time the voice of Andrey Sakharov is heard on electronic media. Speaking with dignity, the dissident nuclear scientist, not long released from internal exile, calls for the end of the party's leading role in society and attacks Red Army atrocities in Afghanistan. Sakharov is enormously respected for his integrity and scientific brilliance, but also because he never left Russia. There is an element of popular disdain for dissidents who live abroad, even if against their will, and especially for those who don't come back.

Workers in the Krasnoyarsk shoe factory listen in disbelief to the radio sets in every workshop. Hammering stops and machines go quiet at the most dramatic moments. Zhanna's mother is shocked by the assaults on Lenin. She knew when Andrey Sakharov was released from internal exile that big changes were happening, but never expects to hear him excoriating the leadership of the country on radio and television. Marietta receives instructions from the party offices in Krasnoyarsk on how to assess what they are hearing. They should understand that *perestroika* is designed fully to use the potential of socialism, and that only with a renewed and revitalized party in the vanguard and a public acknowledgement of past misdeeds can the Soviet Union move to a renewal of socialism and a bright future.

But it is too late. As Moscow party leader Boris Yeltsin says, 'Those ten days in which the country watched the desperate debates of the congress, unable to tear themselves away from their television sets, gave the people more of a political education than seventy years of stereotyped Marxist-Leninist lectures ... almost the entire population was awakened from its state of lethargy.'

The congress brings about the rehabilitation of Yeltsin, who had been severely censured by the Central Committee for criticizing Gorbachev's slow pace of reform. His outspoken manner and populistic approach to the problem of shortages, such as publicly berating shop managers for selling goods at the back door, makes him a favourite with the crowd, and he has received the single biggest mandate from the Moscow electorate. The distaste he and Gorbachev have for each other, which within two years will precipitate the end of the Soviet Union, is on full display. Marietta, who blames bad leadership for the failings of socialism, sees Yeltsin as a decent person who will change things for the better, though that impression does not last. In time she will come to regard him as a *durak*, a fool, who along with the likes of Khrushchev messed up the country.

The increasing irreverence for party leaders is on display in Moscow's Izmailovo Park, a forested estate at the end of the No. 34 tram line. Two years earlier Zhanna witnessed here how Russian artists had to lurk among the trees to display their inoffensive canvases of old churches and landscapes. During the congress the grassy expanse becomes one of the world's biggest art and junk fairs. Political busts and *matryoshka* dolls and paintings, mostly mocking party figures, along with antiques and tsarist emblems and old banknotes and coins and other bric-a-brac, are sold openly along a two-kilometre stretch of path. Stalin is mocked and vilified in pictures and cartoons, and Lenin is portrayed as a figure of fun. The best-selling items are political lapel badges, many of them proclaiming support for Yeltsin.

There are radiant faces at street demonstrations in support of the radicals in the congress and a feeling that, even as nothing changes in people's daily lives and shortages become more acute, there is hope for better times. Every week brings a new political event that maintains the heady feeling of anticipation. And in a country where aesthetics drive politics, the intellectual world is almost convulsed with joy, as censorship ends and punishments for those who have challenged orthodoxy are revoked.

In April 1989, Yury Lyubimov, the former director of the Taganka Theatre who made the playhouse a beacon of progressive thinking in the pre-Gorbachev years, and who directed Vysotsky's portrayal of Hamlet and oversaw his funeral, is able to return from exile and is given his old job back at the Taganka, thanks to his long-time disciple the actor Nikolai Gubenko, who is, astonishingly, appointed minister for culture. Soon afterwards we watch the minister himself playing the title role in *Boris Godunov* at the Taganka. The following week we attend a new staging of the Soviet underground classic *The Master and Margarita*, with Margarita appearing topless. We have a meal afterwards in the Tagansky Bar, a tiny restaurant patronized by theatre people, where a violinist and balalaika player stroll among the diners, and the conversation is full of excited optimism about the future of the arts.

Gubenko organizes one of the most emotional homecomings, that of world-renowned cellist Mstislav Rostropovich, who returns from exile with his wife, Galina Vishnevskaya, a famous Bolshoi opera singer. They enraged Brezhnev sixteen years before with their public defence of Alexander Solzhenitsyn, which led to the sacking of Rostropovich as conductor of the Operetta Theatre Orchestra. The cellist's last performance at the Moscow Conservatory, in 1971, was at a concert marking the sixty-fifth birthday of the composer Dmitri Shostakovich, also in disfavour. That year Solzhenitsyn was bundled on to a plane and sent into exile, and shortly afterwards Rostropovich and his wife were also forced to live abroad. On stepping back onto Russian soil, the cellist says, 'When I left the Soviet Union, it was a big island of lies, but now the Soviet Union is cleaning itself of lies.'

He gives his first return performance in the Great Hall of the Moscow Conservatory on 18 February 1990. There is such a crush to get in that several people fall on the icy footpath. When the bald, bespectacled figure of Rostropovich appears on stage the packed hall erupts in waves of emotional applause. The haunting strains of Dvorak's Cello Concerto become a hymn of redemption for all those repressed or forced into exile: poets such as Joseph Brodsky, the writers Viktor Nekrasov and Vladimir Maximov, the critic Andrey Sinyavsky, the dramatist Alexander Galich, and many others.

Mikhail Gorbachev gives his approval to another film which has a profound effect on the millions of people who cram into cinemas to see it in the early summer of 1990. *Tak zhit nelzya* (*You Can't Live Like This*) portrays the Soviet Union after seventy-three years of socialism as impoverished, criminalized and morally bankrupt. Gorbachev demands that the whole Central Committee sit through it. The film is an utterly bleak account of how people are forced by the system to connive and lie to have a decent life. Shots of endless ill-tempered queues are juxtaposed with people strolling around a well-stocked shopping mall in Hamburg. 'We spend our lives looking at other people's backs,' the narrator comments. Gorbachev hopes the movie will rally support for his policy of rebuilding a socialist society. However the message which cinema-goers take away is that reconstruction is futile and that the old system should be jettisoned as soon as possible.

Stalin still has his admirers but they are confronted every day with new disclosures of the horrors he inflicted. New details of his brutality are uncovered and published. The passage of time lends an academic quality to the disclosures, unless they impinge on one's life, as happens to us. Then they can become very real.

Our apartment looks out over poplar trees to the green onion domes of the Novospassky Monastery, perched on a steep bank. It is a favourite place for locals, part of a hidden Moscow

of derelict but beautiful buildings, where we like to sit looking out over the Moscow River on sunny weekend afternoons.
Inside the complex the gardens are dank and filled with rubble
and the brickwork is crumbling, but none of that is visible from
outside the walls. Trees cover the bank apart from a stretch
where only weeds grow. This area, we discover in May 1990
from historian Alexander Milchakov, holds layer upon layer of
bodies, the remains of thousands of people executed during the
terror of the 1930s. The victims were leaders of the Comintern,
the international organization set up to spread communism
throughout the world, who were ruthlessly purged by Stalin as
'enemies of the people'.

Here lie slain comrades from the United States, England, Germany, Yugoslavia, Romania, Poland and Italy, along with several
thousand other foreigners who happened to be living in Moscow
at the time. Their 'crime' was to have threatened Stalin's domi-
nation of the communist world or to have been inconveniently
opposed to fascism at a time when Stalin was doing business with
Hitler. The victims were taken to the Lubyanka, given a bath, told
to sit on a stone slab, shot through a hole in the wall, then loaded
onto trucks and thrown at night into trenches beneath where we
have been sitting. Among those dumped here were John Penner,
delegate of the American Communist Party, and Bela Kun, leader
of the short-lived Hungarian Soviet Republic in 1919.

We encounter a middle-aged woman carrying a handbag
standing alone on ground where bits of bone can be unearthed
with the toe of a shoe. 'Russia will always suffer until the full
truth is told,' she says, telling us that her ninety-year-old neighbour shocked her by saying that for *perestroika* to succeed 'we
should only shoot the right people next time'.

This discovery has a profound effect on both of us. Zhanna is
by this time wholly convinced that the system she respected, or
at least lived as part of, is indeed founded on lies and monstrous

crimes. It is no coincidence that shortly afterwards she formally cuts all ties with the party, as she has been intending for some time. She writes a letter of resignation, takes it to the party office in Marksistskaya Street and hands it to the lone, rather bored, middle-aged lady on duty. 'You too,' sighs the woman. At the age of thirty-two, the shoemaker's daughter, a model product of the Soviet system, trained to become a leading light of the CPSU, abandons the ailing monolith founded by Lenin.

She is in the vanguard. Two months later, on 12 July 1990, Boris Yeltsin gives up his membership of the party, claiming that it is not capable of reforming itself. His gesture is followed by an avalanche of defections by rank-and-file members, and terminally damages Gorbachev's hopes of revitalizing the party as the guiding force in Soviet life.

Zhanna's mother is not among those who disown the party. It provided her, the daughter of an emigrant from Nagorno-Karabakh, with status, a fulfilling career and considerable benefits. Among those benefits was stability for the place of her birth and for her former home town of Grozny. The other side of the coin for those trampling on the red flag is the inescapable fact that as the one-party state falls asunder, people are being killed and maimed in small but vicious ethnic wars that are breaking out in the parts of the world she loves. Egalitarian by nature, Marietta can acknowledge that some people were better off in Soviet society than others, but under communism everyone could get education and work. Many share her view that there are good, intelligent people in the party, but that its principles were distorted and corrupted by the wrong people at the top. She fears the emergence of a rampant consumer society in which money will be the new god, crime will proliferate and wealth will accumulate in the hands of a very few.

In the last year of Soviet communism Gorbachev is assailed by hardliners. On 14 January 1991 he is forced to appoint a conservative economist, Valentin Pavlov, as prime minister. An owlish, bespectacled veteran of the finance ministry, Pavlov faces an impossible situation. Inflation is soaring because of the printing of billions of rubles to finance a failing economy. He decides on drastic monetary reform, which deprives millions of their savings – and costs us a small fortune.

Just before Pavlov announces his measures Vova, Zhanna's brother-in-law, comes to Moscow to buy my three-year-old office Lada, as I am in the process of getting a new car for the *Irish Times* bureau. I purchased the Lada in Helsinki and drove it into Russia when setting up the office in order to avoid the delays inevitable when acquiring a car in Moscow. It is a VAZ-2107 export model, the best of the range of Ladas produced for sale abroad by the AvtoVAZ car plant in Tolyatti. Volvo has now established a service centre in Moscow and many foreigners like me are able to trade up to a Western car.

Vova has been on an interminable waiting list so I am happy for the bureau to sell him the Lada. He gathers the seven thousand rubles necessary for the purchase, flies in from Krasnoyarsk with the cash on his person, and stays in our apartment while the transaction goes through. This takes some time. It turns out that the Lada cannot be sold to a Soviet citizen as it has been registered by customs as a temporarily imported vehicle; nevertheless, I can *give* it to Larisa's husband as a present, and he can in turn give me a present of seven thousand rubles, if he so wishes. However, the car is registered with a foreign company, and it must be transferred to my name at customs before it can be given to anyone. A long-drawn-out bureaucratic nightmare ensues, with fees being charged all along the way. New number plates are required. A customs consent form is not accepted until notarized and the car independently valued, a process which takes several days. A final authorization and police permission for the transaction are obtained after much

At my Moscow apartment block, with the Lada that Vova buys and drives to Siberia.

toing and froing. Charges for these services amount to 14 per cent of the value of the car. The total cost of giving away the Lada comes to 1,340 rubles.

Finally it is done. All that remains is for Vova to deposit his seven thousand rubles into the bureau's bank account and take possession of the car. The date is 22 January 1991. That evening we relax with a celebratory glass of Armenian brandy and watch the nine o'clock news on television. Valentin Pavlov appears on the screen. He has an announcement to make. All fifty- and one-hundred-ruble banknotes are being withdrawn from circulation with immediate effect. Notes up to a total value of one thousand rubles can be redeemed for new cash, but for only one day. The measure is to prevent inflation caused by an influx of foreign currency from abroad, he claims.

Vova gasps in shock. It is as if the government has reached into his pocket and stolen most of his money. It is a financial catastrophe for him. All his money is in high-value notes. Next morning he dashes off to the banks and manages to redeem two thousand rubles' worth by pushing his way through crowds of angry Muscovites. We all pitch in to help him raise the remaining five thousand to balance the office accounts, and he eventually gets the keys of the Lada.

It will not be the last time the Suvorov family is robbed by the country's institutions as Russia faces one financial crisis after another in the rush to jettison communism and embrace capitalism.

Before he leaves Moscow, Vova wants to stock up on spare parts for the Lada, but they are as scarce in the Russian capital as in Siberia. Three months earlier they were officially classified as luxury goods, along with jewellery, natural fur, carpets, quality earthenware, cut glass, high-tech radios, electronic products, suites of furniture, delicatessen fish products, special meat cuts and imported gin, whisky and cigarettes. A telephone call to the city's biggest *zapchasti*, the official spare parts supplier, results in the following exchange. 'Do you have windscreens for a Lada?' 'No.' 'Do you have wipers?' 'No.' 'Wing mirrors?' 'No.' 'Fan belts?' Laughter.

Vova could go to the used-car market at Dolgoprudny, a district beside Sheremetyevo International Airport, but everything there costs multiples of the official price. The auto business has become criminalized. The AvtoVAZ manufacturing plant, which accounts for 60 per cent of car sales in the country, is infiltrated by criminal gangs. The mafia demands commission to guarantee the safe delivery of cars, and controls car sales, the distribution of spare parts and shipment. Criminals are even employed by AvtoVAZ managers as debt collectors.

Vova sets off for Krasnoyarsk, a journey of more than five thousand kilometres on poorly maintained roads, driving on which is like playing a video game with one's life. There is little street lighting, people tear along at manic speeds, and brakes and steering sometimes do not work because of the lack of parts. It takes him seven days but, to our relief, he makes it.

We too risk our lives on the Russian roads in the early summer of 1991, to drive from Moscow to Yaroslavl and spend a weekend at the home of Zhanna's postgraduate student friend Ira Zakharova, now a university lecturer, in the village of Krasnye Tkachi. She lives in a typical *izba*, a traditional wooden country cottage with delicate carvings around the windows and white birch logs piled high against the gable. It has four rooms, heated by the wall tiles of a centrally located wood-burning stove. It seems cosy, but a chemical pit outdoors serves as a latrine and the well is two hundred metres distant. I learn that it is easier to carry two full buckets of water than one. The shortages in the provinces are chronic. Ira has been three years on a waiting list for a new bed, and her television is thirty years old with no hope of replacement. Since our last visit two years previously the village club house, the only social centre, has burned down, symbolizing the end of an era. In an echo of Stanislav Govorukhin's film *You Can't Live Like This*, Ira tells us, 'I can't live like this.'

Another journey we make is to the Soviet Republic of Moldavia (now Moldova) to witness a little bit of history: a one-day token opening of the border with Romania, which since 1945 has separated families living only a few kilometres apart. We join busloads of excited citizens in the capital Kishinev (now Chişinău) and set out for the frontier on the River Prut, where immigration officers stand aside for a few hours to allow for some very emotional reunions and a lot of hurried commercial exchanges. We cross for a while and hasten back before the barriers come down again. Lieutenant Nerses Gukasyan passed close to this spot in May 1944 as his rifle detachment took part in an unsuccessful Red Army attack on German troops at Targu Frumos in Romania. He was deployed in defensive positions nearby for three months until the 38th Rifle Division put down pontoon bridges along the Prut and crossed to its west bank to launch a successful assault on the German and Romanian lines. As we know now, he was mortally wounded and eventually interred in the village of Glajarie. It will be many more years before we learn just how close Zhanna is, at this moment, to the last resting place of her missing grandfather.

In Moscow we regularly call at the apartment of Zhanna's old professor from the Moscow Pedagogical Institute. A distinguished academic, Yelena Borisovna has retired and is somewhat infirm, so Zhanna helps keep her apartment in order. One day her former mentor delightedly tells a caller on the telephone, 'Mrs O'Clery is cleaning my windows.' Yelena Borisovna continues her life-long work as a joint compiler of the *Müller English–Russian Dictionary*. Zhanna, who has access to native English speakers, is able to help her with new and changing definitions of English words. The elderly professor is disconcerted to learn that the word 'gay' no longer just signifies 'full of joy, merry, light-hearted', but also 'homosexual', and that a mouse is no longer merely a small rodent, but 'an input device to control on-screen objects' on a computer. She is upset that Russian is being anglicized in common speech, adopting such words as 'computer', 'supermarket' and 'shopping'. 'Such a pity,' she says. To her, the contamination of the Russian language is a metaphor for what is happening to the country, as it surrenders its ideology and succumbs to Western capitalism.

CHAPTER 24

THEY HAVE GUNS NOW

URING THE LONG hard winters in Siberia, Stanislav and Marietta sometimes think about one day returning to live in the Caucasus, with its more temperate climate, though not to Grozny, mainly because of its association with Stanislav's imprisonment and disgrace. Even if they want to it is not a good idea. As the Soviet Union begins to disintegrate, the Armenians in Grozny, including the Suvorovs' friends and relatives, are forced to contemplate leaving the city they love. The Chechens are gearing up to fight for their independence and war seems inevitable.

In May 1991, when Zhanna and I fly there from Moscow, we find that Zhanna's aunt Lena and her family still hope it will not come to that. Mikhail Gorbachev is attempting to cobble together a new union treaty which will allow the Soviet Union to survive in a looser form, while Boris Yeltsin has advised the autonomous Russian republics to 'take as much sovereignty as you can swallow'. Perhaps all will end peacefully.

Lena and her husband Volodya welcome us in traditional Armenian fashion, with a lavish lunch in our honour attended by their extended family. We eat at a long wooden table laden with plates of vegetables, pilaf and lamb in the courtyard of their house, which is shaded by thirty-year-old grape vines grown over a metal trellis. It is a glorious early-summer afternoon, with a clear blue sky and a gentle breeze that has cleansed the air of the city.

Three months before fleeing for their lives: Aunt Lena, Lena's daughter-in-law Tamara and Tamara's daughters, Anya and Gayane, pose with Zhanna in Grozny in the summer of 1991.

Typical of the Caucasus, the house consists of two separate red-brick buildings behind high walls and a metal gate, with a garden at the back where they have apricot and cherry trees and the usual plethora of fruit and vegetables, which flourish in the Mediterranean-like climate. In such idyllic surroundings it is easy to appreciate what a wrench it was for Zhanna's parents to leave, and to understand their passion for cultivating the dacha garden outside Krasnoyarsk so that they can continue to enjoy the healthy cuisine of the Caucasus. Homely and plump with an aquiline nose and thick black hair, and wearing a flower-patterned sleeveless dress and pearl necklace, Lena insists on us savouring every dish. White-haired Volodya, in open-neck striped shirt, courteously makes sure our tiny shot glasses are filled with Armenian brandy and offers a toast *za mir* – to peace. The words are echoed around the table by Zhanna's cousins Misha and Yura and their wives Tamara and Sveta, by Aram, a brother of her grandmother, Farandzem, who followed her from Nagorno-Karabakh to live in Grozny, by Elvira and Edik, children of Aram and cousins of Lena and Marietta, and by other in-laws and family friends.

It is forty years since Lena arrived in Grozny as a nineteen-year-old to live with her mother Farandzem and little sister Marietta, and twenty-one years since she was left in tears when Stanislav took them away to distant Krasnoyarsk, along with her nieces Zhanna and Larisa. Lena stayed on in Grozny and has made her life here and raised her family. They are part of a stable Armenian community that has grown from under thirteen thousand to almost fifteen thousand and is thoroughly integrated into the life of the city. In contrast to the Slavic people, who have been leaving Chechnya in great numbers, the Armenians still feel relatively unthreatened and at home in this part of the Caucasus.

In the evening Lena fetches her photograph albums. A class picture from School No. 4 shows seven-year-old Zhanna with her schoolmates, who are predominantly Russian, with a small number of Chechens, Armenians and other nationalities, reflecting the ethnic mix of what was a cosmopolitan city. Things have changed since then, says Lena, as most of the Russian children have grown up and gone to live elsewhere. The census figures, published every ten years, confirm an extraordinary shift in the ethnic balance of the Chechen-Ingush Autonomous Republic since Khrushchev allowed the Chechens and Ingush to return. In 1959 Russians made up half the population of three quarters of a million and the Chechens a third. Now the situation is reversed. There are some seven hundred and forty thousand Chechens and Ingush and less than three hundred thousand Russians. Stalin's attempt at genocide failed because of the fierce survival instincts of the Chechen people, whose families regularly number six or more children. The city of Grozny itself, founded as a tsarist outpost and developed as an oil town, still has a Russian majority with the Russians dominating the big apartment blocks in the centre, but the hinterland is solidly Chechen.

With the growth in their population the Chechens have become more assertive. In 1973 they successfully demanded more say in running Grozny, though it was not until 1989 that a Chechen, a collective farm manager called Doku Zavgayev, became the first non-Russian boss of the regional communist party. In 1990 Chechen protests over being treated as second-class citizens prompted the resignation of several unpopular Russian officials. A Chechen national congress that November sparked a movement for Chechnya to become a republic of the Soviet Union independent of the Russian Federation. Once again in their history, the Russians and the Chechens are on a collision course. Russians in Grozny greet each other with the salutation, 'Be healthy!' Now the Chechens say, 'Be free!'

Emboldened by the political paralysis in Moscow, the Chechens revive their Islamic traditions and publicly honour those who died in previous struggles with Russia. They rename North Airport, the city's air terminus, Sheikh Mansur Airport, after the eighteenth-century scourge of Imperial Russia Al-Imam al-Mansur al-Mutawakil 'ala Allah. It is an explicit message to all Russians arriving by air that the historic struggle for freedom is not forgotten – just as the city-centre statue to General Alexander Yermolov was once meant as a warning to Chechens that they should know their place. That memorial remains standing, though the inscription describing Chechens as 'the most vile and deceitful people under the sun' has long since been torn away.

The day after we arrive, and with Misha as our guide, we explore the city where Zhanna grew up. The air is full of white fluff, as the poplar trees which line the roadways are shedding their seeds; Stalin's snow, it is called, as it was he who ordered the widespread planting of poplars. The main square has been named after Nikita Khrushchev in recognition of his role in enabling the dispossessed to return. We come across the building site for a great mosque dedicated to Sheikh Mansur and financed by rich Muslim businessmen, the first to be allowed in Grozny in the near-half-century since the last *mechet* was destroyed. Until recently Chechen requests to build a mosque were rejected time after time, while a Russian Orthodox church stayed open. Central Grozny retains the physical characteristics of a typical Russian metropolis, with the usual offices, factories and concrete apartment blocks. However, Islamic music plays from tape recorders, women wear hijabs, and photographs of the Iraqi leader Saddam Hussein dangle from taxi windscreens. Groups of Chechens stand in the roads or sit at café tables discussing events in loud voices. Russians, who might not have given them the time of day a few years ago, treat Chechens and Ingush with respect and hasten about their business.

Western cars are still something of a novelty in most Russian streets, even in Moscow, but here Mercedes and Volvos jostle for space. Big money has been made by a few. Chechens possess an aggressive entrepreneurial spirit unmatched by other Soviet nationalities, which the reforms have clearly unleashed. Communism never took root among them as an ideology. Chechen villagers travel to the far corners of the Soviet Union to find work. Some get involved in the black market and in more serious criminal activity. In Moscow Chechens are becoming synonymous with the mafia.

As we drive beyond the city perimeter, past fields of 'nodding donkey' oil extraction pumps, we glimpse many new red-brick mosques in densely populated but impoverished villages. We return past the house on Pavel Musorov Street where Stanislav and Marietta lived after their marriage and where Zhanna and Larisa grew up. It is well maintained, and the apricot trees on the grass strip between the house and the road have matured to full height. Trams still rumble by every ten minutes, just as Zhanna remembers. Misha spots graffiti on apartment blocks in nearby Minutka Square, with ominous messages for non-Chechens: RUSSIANS DON'T LEAVE – WE NEED SLAVES and DON'T BUY THE APARTMENT FROM MISHA [meaning any Russian] – HE WILL BE GONE SOON ANYWAY. Our Armenian host is dismayed to see, scrawled in black paint on a factory wall, RUSSIANS BACK TO RYZAN, ARMENIANS TO YEREVAN. Such slogans shake the faith of the Armenians that the Chechens have no argument with them.

That night we hear automatic fire in the distance. 'They have guns now,' says Lena next morning at breakfast. 'They are just shooting them off, but soon they will be using them.'

To Lena and her family, *perestroika* means the unleashing of the long-suppressed national ambitions of the indigenous people of Chechnya. They are terrified of what the future might hold. Some of the families who settled here fled ethnic bloodshed in Nagorno-Karabakh, and they know that, if incited, hitherto peaceful Muslim neighbours might turn against them overnight.

The Armenian community in Grozny dates back several generations. The ruins by the canning factory of the old Apostolic church, destroyed in Stalin's anti-religion campaign in 1930, are testimony to the presence of Armenians in Chechnya before the nineteenth century. The Soviet authorities never allowed a commemoration of the 1915 Armenian Genocide in Chechnya, though there was a quiet gathering at the Armenian cemetery on its fiftieth anniversary in 1965. To acknowledge it publicly would be to invite comparisons with the genocides ordered by Stalin.

An Armenian friend of the family, a metal worker in a Grozny factory, tells us, 'My child was warned at school to stay off the streets as trouble is brewing. This is no place for us.' 'My best friend is an Ingush mechanic,' says another, an Armenian garage worker. 'He heard we planned to leave and pleaded with me to stay. I told him I have to think of my children.' He takes us to the garage to meet his co-worker. 'I want him to stay here,' says the Ingush. 'He asked me if I could give him a hundred-percent guarantee that everything will be all right. I had to say no, I couldn't.'

Three months later, in August 1991, communist party hard-liners put Gorbachev under house arrest at his Crimea holiday home and attempt to stage a coup. But it is too late to restore the old Soviet Union, and the military have no stomach for a fight with the people. Yeltsin rallies his supporters outside the White House, where the Russian parliament sits, climbs on top of a tank to display his defiance, and within four days the coup attempt is over.

In Grozny the situation quickly deteriorates. With Moscow paralysed by the subsequent struggle between Yeltsin and Gorbachev for control of the Kremlin, armed men take over key buildings in the Chechen capital, including the Supreme Soviet and the television station, and hoist green Islamic flags. Young men come in from the villages to attend large anti-Russian rallies, which fill the city streets and continue all day. The city's KGB building is overrun and its weapons store raided. Most of the fifteen Soviet republics which make up the Soviet Union are going their own way relatively peacefully, but Chechnya is part of the Russian Federation, and once the leadership issue in Moscow is resolved the new master of the Kremlin will most certainly not tolerate the disintegration of Russia itself, despite once urging provinces to grab as much sovereignty as they could.

No longer feeling welcome and with war imminent, the Armenians have no choice but to flee the city en masse. Lena and Volodya sell their house for a price considerably below its real value. They and their family members join a long convoy of cars, vans and trucks laden with whatever they can carry. There is safety in numbers. The refugees head for the Stavropol region in southern Russia, where there is already an Armenian community of seventy-three thousand living among three million Russians. Many have roots in earlier dispersals of Armenians to southern regions of Russia. In 1779 General Suvorov expelled some thirteen thousand Armenians from Crimea and forcibly settled them near Rostov-on-Don. A third perished from cold and hunger. Lena's family find temporary accommodation in Georgievsk, an industrial and university town two hundred and seventy kilometres from Grozny. The collapse of the Soviet Union causes hyperinflation, and the money from the sale of her house in Grozny becomes almost worthless. Approaching the age of sixty, Marietta's sister, who came to Grozny with nothing and made a good life for her children, finds herself again in an unfamiliar part of the world, starting over with next to nothing. They endure unconscionable hardship for years. In time Lena and Volodya and their sons will establish a small business making and selling fur garments.

Meanwhile the city from which they escaped is levelled, not once but twice, in the two vicious and bloody wars which follow in the next two decades. The shoe factory where Stanislav served his apprenticeship is left a ruined shell. Pavel Musorov Street becomes known as the most dangerous thoroughfare in Grozny because of abductions by the Russian military stationed at Minutka Square. The tram lines that run between the former Suvorov house and the Oil Workers' Block are destroyed by shellfire. The Russian Orthodox church where Baba Polina worshipped is wrecked, not by Chechens but by Russian bombs.

Ten days after the abortive coup, on Thursday, 29 August 1991, Yeltsin bans the Communist Party of the Soviet Union, which has ruled Russia since 1917. In every Russian city there is panic at party headquarters.

In Krasnoyarsk supporters of Yeltsin's decree arrive at the *raicom*, the building in the Oktyabrsky District where commu-nist party membership cards are held, order out the staff, seal the doors and leave. Marietta receives an urgent telephone call from one of the ousted officials. 'Come quickly. We are going to break the seals and get in.' As secretary of the Krasnoyarsk shoe factory branch, Marietta is responsible for the staff members' cards, which are held in the *raicom* filing cabinets. She rushes to the building where her comrades have already forced their way inside. She finds the cards of the factory workers and gathers them up for safekeeping. Officials are busy calling her counter-parts in other enterprises to come and collect their membership cards, but, she recalls, 'A lot didn't bother.' It does not matter any more. With three years to go before her compulsory retirement at fifty-five years of age, the world Marietta knows is falling apart. The communist party branch which she headed at the shoe fac-tory no longer exists.

The Russian parliament begins dismantling communist-era legislation and passing new market-friendly laws. In the autumn of 1991 it abolishes that part of the Criminal Code of the Rus-sian Soviet Federative Socialist Republic (1960) which makes speculation an offence. Defined in Article 154 as the 'buying up and reselling of goods or any other articles for the purpose of making a profit', speculation is now not only legal, but is the mainspring of the economy. One can imagine the shoemaker's thoughts as he reads about this in his newspaper, *Krasnoyarsky Rabochy* – the *Krasnoyarsk Worker*. The offence for which he did time in prison, as a result of which he uprooted his family and moved to Siberia, is no longer a crime but a patriotic act, the very foundation of the new Russia. Yet Stanislav, at sixty-two years of age, cannot help but reflect on how life has turned out well for his family in Krasnoyarsk, and that if they had stayed in Grozny they would now be refugees.

25 December 1991: Gorbachev signs away the Soviet Union – and the Suvorovs' savings.

The Soviet Union finally collapses on 25 December 1991. Mikhail Gorbachev, an urbane statesman idolized by the capitalist world but whose goal was to keep socialism alive in a reformed union, resigns as its last leader. The communist monolith known as the Union of Soviet Socialist Republics breaks up into separate states. Boris Yeltsin, an impetuous, hard-drinking democrat ridiculed in the West, becomes president of an independent Russia determined to escape as quickly as possible from the cul-de-sac into which Lenin led it seventy-four years earlier.

Stanislav and Marietta speak of the last day of the Soviet Union as the low point in the life of their adopted city. On that date, Christmas Day in the West, a headline in the nationwide edition of *Pravda* states, NO BREAD IN KRASNOYARSK. Things cannot be much worse when the staff of life itself is *deficit*. Citizens trudge despairingly from one jostling queue to another in a temperature of minus fifteen degrees Celsius. It is a frustrating time for Stanislav. Despite his contacts, the shoemaker has considerable difficulty finding basic foodstuffs to purchase for his family, let alone good leather to make decent shoes for his private customers. Never in their experience has Krasnoyarsk known such deprivation. The government has imposed rationing of meat products, butter, vegetable oils, grains, pasta products, sugar, salt, matches, tobacco products and household, bath and other soaps, 'where available'. The shortages are made worse by the knowledge that everything is going to become more expensive when the market economy arrives. It is a time for hoarding. If a consignment of salami or flour or toilet paper appears, a queue instantly forms, and people buy as much as they can. Everywhere women rush around in the freezing cold with empty shopping bags, and if they see a queue they join it, only afterwards enquiring what it's for. No matter what it is they buy it. It will cost more tomorrow.

Moscow on the last day of communism is a city of near panic with 'grim food lines, pristinely empty stores, women rushing about in search of any food for sale, dollar prices in the deserted Tishinsky market', according to Russia's deputy prime minister, Yegor Gaidar. Years later he relates to Zhanna and me in his office in the Russian capital how his wife Masha and their ten-year-old son join a line for bread at a shop in Nikitskaya Street, and when the boy gets the last *bulka*, a woman tries to snatch the loaf from him.

With Russia bankrupt and most commercial activity at a standstill, Yeltsin gives Gaidar the task of applying shock therapy. Short and chubby with a strong sense of mission, the deputy prime minister embraces the libertarian principles advocated by Milton Friedman, the American free market champion who engineered the transformation from communism to capitalism of Marxist Chile in the 1970s by training a group of Chilean economists at the University of Chicago. Gaidar forms a Russian version of the Chicago Boys to help perform what he calls 'major surgery on the economy without an anaesthetic'. He wants to make the reforms irreversible, and believes goods will quickly appear on the shelves when the market rather than the government sets prices.

For weeks suppliers and shop managers throughout Russia have been holding back, waiting for the big bang, which happens on 2 January 1992. Instantly, prices are deregulated for the first time since the Revolution. Bread appears in the shops again, and other missing products materialize on the shelves. Managers, warehouse bosses and cooperative owners unload their stock onto the nation's consumers, no longer constrained by remote bureaucrats as to the prices they can charge. Everything is suddenly more expensive. The freed-up prices start higher and keep rising. In the first month inflation increases to 245 per cent, and it continues to go up, month after month, throughout the year. Impoverished pensioners appear at the side of the road offering any possessions of value for sale so they can buy food.

Hyperinflation provides a windfall for some, in particular the heads of big enterprises who have been selling products such as crude oil and metals abroad for hard currency in the months before the red flag came down over the Kremlin, and hoarding it knowing that the ruble would soon be freely convertible and would fall in value. But hyperinflation also wipes out life savings, turning millions of Russians into paupers and stoking discontent. The money Stanislav and Marietta put aside from their state pensions and Stanislav's earnings in a Krasnoyarsk branch of Sberbank, the country's biggest savings institution, declines in value by about two thirds in the first four weeks of capitalism; within six months it is almost worthless. With her parents' savings practically wiped out and the cancellation of the banknotes Vova gathered to buy the Lada, Zhanna's family has now been robbed twice by the state. For Stanislav and Marietta, the end of the only way of life they know brings little other than disillusion and trouble. They know they are not the hardest done by; they have an income and they have produce from their dacha garden. Marietta in particular has always been a good party member: she took at face value the need for *perestroika*, but it has proved a disaster. She despairs at the collapse of a system that at least looked after the vulnerable. Now pensions have become almost worthless: old people have hardly enough money to buy bread. It is a humiliation for the generation that defeated Hitler to learn from the newspapers that war widows are getting Red Cross parcels from Germany. And worse is to come.

PART THREE

PART THREE

Chapter 25

SELLING THE NATION'S SILVER

O NE MONDAY MORNING in December 1991, the manager of human resources at the International Finance Corporation in Washington DC, Michael O'Farrell, drops into the fourth-floor office of a senior IFC official, Anthony Doran, at the organization's headquarters on I Street, not far from the White House. Doran, a Liverpool Irishman with experience of privatization in Eastern Europe, is in the process of setting up a special unit to help Russia with technical advice on making the transition from communism to capitalism. The project is in its infancy and as yet there are only half a dozen staff, mostly Harvard Business School graduates. O'Farrell is concerned that it lacks knowledgeable Russian input and needs people who are familiar with the language and culture, and he tells Doran that he got talking to a young woman from Siberia at a weekend dinner party in a Washington suburb. She is Armenian, recently arrived from the Soviet Union, a former member of a Russian regional parliament with high academic qualifications and excellent English, and is by no means an 'irredentist Marxist'. Should he ask her to call in the following week? 'Tell her to come tomorrow,' says Doran.

Zhanna found herself in conversation with O'Farrell at that dinner because my posting in Moscow has come to an end. I have been appointed Washington correspondent of my newspaper, and we are beginning to meet and make contacts in the US capital through the long-established Washington tradition of dinner parties.

We always knew that because of my profession we would have to depart from Russia at some point but when my transfer becomes real two years after our marriage, Zhanna and Julia are faced with leaving their family behind and finding their place in a new country. We fly to Krasnoyarsk to say goodbye, with promises of returning as often as we can. The last evening is particularly difficult as no one knows when we will all be together again as a family, given the constraints on foreign travel for what is still the Soviet Union. Marietta and Larisa prepare a long table of *zakuski* and serve hot dishes of meat and fish to a gathering which includes relatives and children. Ararat makes a toast wishing his cousin Zhanna and her husband well in their new life, which ensures the clinking of a dozen glasses around the table. After refilling our glasses with Armenian cognac, Stanislav makes a short speech, ending with the words from his favourite song, 'God willing, that we're drinking not for the last time.'

The Irish government waives a five-year residency qualification and grants Zhanna and Julia Irish citizenship so they can travel to North America as Irish, rather than Soviet, citizens, thus avoiding impossibly long waits for visas. We leave Russia in early August and take up residence in the Washington suburb of Bethesda where we enrol Julia in Pyle Middle School.

For all the excitement of coming to a new world of freedom and prosperity, it is a tough time for both of them. Julia finds herself in an English-speaking school knowing hardly any of the language, just as her grandmother Marietta at the same age was placed in a Russian-speaking school in Grozny with only a few words of Russian, and just like her grandmother she quickly adapts. She finds herself watching television films where the Russians are always the baddies. Zhanna, now thirty-three, has to adjust to a different social and economic system, though she has the advantage of speaking fluent English and of being married

A light moment for Julia and Zhanna during their first year in Washington DC, 1992.

to a person who is part of the Western culture and enjoys the privileges and access that go with being a foreign correspondent in the nation's capital.

In ideological terms, everything Zhanna absorbed in her previous life is turned on its head. Communism is evil, socialism is to be abhorred. The rich are respected for being wealthy. Greed is good. She is shocked by the affluence and abundance all around her. At home shoppers are frantically searching for flour; in the Giant supermarket in Washington she is confronted with bread flour, cake flour, pastry flour, whole-wheat flour, gluten-free flour, self-raising flour, stoneground flour, rye flour and organic wholegrain flour. With beef almost impossible to find in Moscow, in Washington stores entire sections are devoted to attractively packaged dog and cat food, and shelves laden down with perfect-looking fruit, which however Zhanna soon discovers to be bland if not almost tasteless. No one, it seems, grows their own. Most suburban houses have lush gardens, but rather than cultivate fruit and vegetables, as everyone does in Russia, Washington residents prefer ornamental trees and flowers and manicured lawns.

Zhanna's father had endless trouble acquiring his cars in Russia, for which he paid cash, but here salesmen at the ubiquitous car showrooms cajole customers to buy models of every conceivable kind on hire purchase, a new concept to her. She is surprised to see well-groomed old women with blue-rinsed hair driving big automobiles, and playing golf on vast expanses of grass off River Road. She finds that men often do the cooking and household chores, something almost unheard of in Caucasian and even Russian culture. She does not expect race to be such a divisive issue, and is dismayed at the vast disparity between rich and poor and by the fact that certain districts of the US capital are dangerous because of gun crime. In this land of contrasts there seem to be churches on every corner, but homeless people living on the streets, particularly near the White House.

There are many things she likes too, such as the freedom to speak one's mind, the critical reporting in the newspapers, the number of organizations campaigning without hindrance for every kind of cause, the vigour of civil society, and the ready acceptance by Americans of foreigners. She is astonished when on an expedition to buy curtains in Friendship Heights the first two passers-by she stops to ask for directions do not speak English. Not being a Russian made her sensitive to her ethnicity in the Russia-dominated Soviet Union, but here she finds that Washingtonians readily accept people of different backgrounds and nationalities in every walk of life.

Almost from the moment she arrives in Washington, therefore, Zhanna finds there are opportunities to restart her career, despite her fears that Soviet academic qualifications will be of little use. While looking for an opening, she trains as a guide with a Washington tour company, reads up on American history and politics, and is interviewed for a job at the State Department showing around Russian delegations. Then she gets a call from Michael O'Farrell asking her to drop into the IFC office at her earliest convenience, where a Mr Doran would like to talk to her.

When Zhanna does so, Tony Doran recruits her immediately to assist with translating and assessing documents, mainly from Russian into English. She discovers that the IFC is a World Bank Group entity tasked with advancing the private sector around the world, and that Doran's unit is focused entirely on the former Eastern Bloc. Soon she becomes heavily involved in the project, which ironically will lead to the privatization of her parents' shoe factory in Krasnoyarsk.

After a few weeks Doran asks her to manage a trust fund for the Russian privatization programme. 'What's a trust fund?' enquires Zhanna. 'I have no idea either,' replies Doran jokingly, 'but I need someone to deal with grants and report to donors.' Zhanna becomes responsible for processing contracts and salaries for the other consultants travelling to, and based in, Russia, Ukraine and Belarus. Along the way she takes World Bank training courses and an accounting course in Montgomery College to acquire relevant skills. The money for the trust fund rapidly rises to several million dollars, the bulk of it from the US Agency for International Development and the rest from the Know How Fund, created specifically by the British government to assist privatization, and the Canadian International Development Agency.

Just as Peter the Great looked west to modernize Russia three centuries earlier, Yeltsin has turned to the international community for help in dismantling communism. This will involve the transfer into private hands of the property of a vast industrialized country, in which practically everything, from newspaper kiosks, shops and hotels to factories, airlines and oilfields, is owned by the state. It is one of the most complex and massive challenges in the modern world and must be achieved quickly to make it irreversible should the communists attempt a comeback.

The Cold War is in abeyance, and the relationship between Russia and America is better than ever before – or since. The Russian minister for privatization, Anatoly Chubais, feels able to engage the IFC to transform one place in Russia into a model for the rest of the country to follow. The guinea pig is Nizhny Novgorod, a city of one and a half million people four hundred kilometres east of Moscow. Founded in 1221 on the River Volga, it was a major centre of commerce before 1917, and in the Soviet period became an important industrial centre, known as the Russian Detroit because of its automobile plants. Until a year previously it was a closed city and had been named Gorky, as the Soviet writer Maxim Gorky was born there, and between 1980 and 1986 it was the place of internal exile for the dissident physicist Andrey Sakharov. Its main qualification for the privatization experiment however is the enthusiasm of the region's governor, Boris Nemtsov, Russia's youngest regional boss, to push through the necessary reforms.

The first act of privatization takes place on 4 April 1992 at an auction in Nizhny Novgorod. Citizens bid against each other to purchase small businesses, including a cheese shop, a book store and a glass and crystal shop. In this and in subsequent weekly auctions open to the public, more than a third of the city's businesses are bought by the employees themselves. The Dmitriev Cheese Shop, one of the five hundred and ninety privatized stores in the city by early 1993, is promoted by Nemtsov and the IFC as a textbook example for the new consumer-oriented Russia. It is bought by Alexey Domrachev, son of a party boss, who had spurned Andrey Sakharov when they were neighbours, something he now regrets as part of his over-zealous communist past. Politicians and journalists come from around the world to sample his diverse cheeses, served by smiling assistants, and to marvel at this shining example of the new Russia. George Rodrigue of the New York *Journal of Commerce* admires how the thirty-member collective 'tossed its wooden abacuses and manual scales, cancelled the traditional two-hour lunch break and began to work weekends too. In came electronic scales and calculators.'

Soon the shelves in Nizhny Novgorod are heavy with locally produced goods. People come from afar to buy cottage cheese, sausages and yogurt. Entrepreneurs arrive to purchase trucks and get advice. The city prospers. Nemtsov becomes a national figure. The Washington IFC office produces a seventy-one-page manual entitled *Small-Scale Privatization in Russia, The Nizhny Novgorod Model*, and translated into Russian by Zhanna, Sergey Zhukov and Professor Yury Olkhovsky. It describes how shops, offices and small businesses should be privatized, and it is sent to every city in the country.

Zhanna finds Nemtsov charming, sociable, full of life and love for his country, and totally committed to wide-ranging free-market reforms. The son of a Jewish mother and Russian father, he is a brilliant physicist who first emerged as a reformer in the wake of the 1986 Chernobyl disaster, when he successfully led a protest movement against the building of a nuclear power plant beside the Volga. Nemtsov visits the IFC office in Washington, and in the summer of 1993 we look after his nine-year-old daughter, also called Zhanna, at our house in the Washington suburbs on her way to and from an American summer camp.

The International Finance Corporation and the Russian government cooperate again on the next phase of privatization – of medium and large enterprises – for which the team in Washington draws up another how-to manual. More funding is provided by the donors, and Zhanna finds herself managing a trust fund of $42 million. It strikes her as time goes by that a considerable percentage of this money goes to Western consultants, mostly American but with a few Canadians and British, whose number rises over time to a hundred and seventy in three field offices. Many of the Russian-based foreign consultants live like millionaires because of the soaring value of the US dollar against the ruble. She herself makes a number of business trips back to Moscow, staying in the pre-revolutionary Hotel Metropol, which the IFC has made its base for visiting executives. She feels uncomfortable, a recent Soviet citizen living like the foreigner she has now become.

At the Washington office she becomes known as Mama Zhanna among the staff for her kindness. A home-baked cake will always appear on a colleague's birthday. When heavy snow paralyses the city she is the only one to make it into the office, where she answers a persistently ringing telephone. The caller is Edward Nassim, the head of the European department. 'Zhanna! What are you doing there?' he cries. 'Where I come from this is nothing,' she says.

In Moscow Anatoly Chubais' team, fearful that the Russian Supreme Soviet is having second thoughts about the privatization of major enterprises and anxious to break the stranglehold of bureaucrats and functionaries over business, selects the Bolshevik Biscuit Factory for its first act of larger-scale privatization to show how it should be done. A Moscow institution, the factory is situated on six hectares of land a five-minute drive from the Kremlin. It is the biggest biscuit producer in Russia, and its dark-chocolate wafers are popular with both locals and foreigners (including me). Its transfer to private ownership will be meaningful to Russians. Founded by two French entrepreneurs in 1855, it was nationalized after the 1917 Revolution and renamed by Lenin himself.

Chubais' privatization effort here is hailed as a success. Twenty thousand people queue in the snow to acquire shares, and the factory management – now businessmen rather than communists – secure a controlling majority. It is eventually bought outright, however, by the Paris-based multinational Danone, the world's number-one producer of milk products and sweet biscuits, after Mstislav Rostropovich makes enquiries on behalf of his friend, Danone's boss and music lover Antoine Riboud.

The International Finance Corporation produces more manuals to cover the privatization of medium and large enterprises and of agricultural land. Between 1992 and 1994, seventy-five thousand small businesses and more than twelve thousand medium and large enterprises are privatized, employing half Russia's factory workers. IFC consultants assist in the privatization of twenty-nine Russian cities. Russian deputy prime minister Yegor Gaidar, speaking a year after privatization starts, credits the IFC with having a greater impact on Russia than any other international organization.

While Zhanna accepts that the work in which she is involved is necessary for the future of Russia and sees that her colleagues in the IFC are convinced they are doing the right thing for the future of the developed world, she is very uneasy at the toll that the introduction of capitalism is taking on ordinary Russians, not least her parents. The Soviet system dealt badly with her own personal tragedy but in other respects it was good to her. It gave her a reasonably comfortable life and an excellent education. She shares her parents' view that while conditions were tough there was no unemployment; everyone was literate and hardships were shared.

Zhanna in 1993 at a White House reception: President Clinton tells her he is trying to broker peace in Nagorno-Karabakh.

Zhanna is unhappy too with the triumphalism in the United States that follows the break-up of the Soviet Union, especially when President George H. W. Bush declares to cheering members of Congress in 1992, 'By the grace of God, America won the Cold War.' Nevertheless she comes to see the United States under President Bill Clinton, who takes office in 1993, as a country which at least strives to achieve decent goals in international affairs – an illusion that is shattered in 2003 with the US-led invasion of Iraq. She is impressed that Clinton uses American power and influence to attempt the resolution of conflicts overseas, even in places as remote as her ancestral home of Nagorno-Karabakh. When the president learns of Zhanna's background there during a social encounter in the White House he proceeds to tell her that he has held conversations with Armenian President Ter-Petrosyan and President Aliev of Azerbaijan in which he attempted to broker peace. He encouraged them to find common ground over the disputed region, Clinton says, displaying a close knowledge of the situation on the ground, adding that he told President Yeltsin, 'Boris, you have got to bring them together and get them to start talking.'

But events in Nagorno-Karabakh have taken an ugly turn with the fall of the Soviet Union. No one there is in the mood for talks of any kind, and Zhanna's relatives are among those who are suffering the consequences.

CHAPTER 26

WAR IN THE MOUNTAINS

ZHANNA'S UNCLE ALYOSHA Gukasyan is an accountant, and his wife Zhenya a doctor. They have a fine home in Martakert, built with the stones of the house in which Zhanna's mother Marietta and Alyosha were born. It is situated behind a high wall with iron gates, halfway along a rutted lane that traverses the town. They have a garden where fruit and vegetables grow in abundance. Intermittent fighting over the future of Karabakh has been going on for two years, since 1989. Up to now they have survived relatively unscathed, as Martakert has not changed hands at any point. In the year after the fall of the Soviet Union this is about to change.

The war in Nagorno-Karabakh is the inevitable result of *glasnost* and *perestroika*. For sixty years the territory enjoyed an uneasy peace. Then, when Gorbachev introduces his policies of openness and reconstruction in the late 1980s, Soviet citizens are allowed, for the first time since the Revolution, openly to express national grievances. On 20 February 1988 the regional soviet in Stepanakert uses this new freedom to appeal to the Supreme Soviet of the USSR to transfer Karabakh to Armenia. It is an audacious request, asking the Kremlin to take a section from one republic and give it to another. The Armenians are initially grateful to Gorbachev for the opportunity to publicly renew their historical demand, but Moscow turns them down.

With a suddenness that shocks the Kremlin, the rejection plunges the southern Caucasus into a tumult of demonstrations, strikes, ethnic clashes and mass transfers of populations, and provokes a popular movement in Armenia, where large demonstrations in support of Karabakh erupt in the capital, Yerevan. Fights break out in Karabakh towns and villages. An anti-Armenia rally in the Azerbaijan city of Sumgait on the Caspian Sea on 27 February turns violent after reports spread through the excited crowd that two young Azeri men have been killed in a skirmish with Armenians in the Aghdam district. The demonstration becomes a pogrom. Some thirty Armenians are killed, hundreds more injured, and fourteen thousand more are forced to flee Baku. Some move to Grozny, from where they will find themselves refugees again before long.

The struggle unleashes pent-up hatreds. Inter-ethnic clashes occur wherever Armenians and Azeris live together. In Nagorno-Karabakh itself the conflict escalates into sporadic warfare with sniping, ambushes and shellfire. In September Armenians are expelled from Shushi, and Azeris ejected from Stepanakert.

The twin cities of Stepanakert and Shushi have been the epi-centre of the conflict since before the formation of the Soviet republics of Armenia and Azerbaijan. In 1920 both sides regarded Shushi, one of the great urban crossroads in the southern Caucasus, as their own. Perched on commanding heights overlooking modern-day Stepanakert, Shushi had theatres, mosques and pink-marble merchants' houses, and was home to revered Azeri writers, most notably the eighteenth-century poet Vagif, who gave rise to the popular saying, 'Not every literate person can be a Vagif.' It was famous for musicians adept at playing the *gopuz*, a traditional Turkish string instrument.

To the Armenians, who made up half the forty-four thousand population in 1920, among them notable traders and famous architects, Shushi was also a religious and strategic centre, founded on the site of a medieval Armenian fortress and containing the magnificent Ghazanchetsots Cathedral, one of the biggest Armenian Apostolic churches in the world, standing thirty-five metres high and dominating the buildings around.

In early 1920 the city was convulsed by sectarian fighting. This culminated in an assault by the Azerbaijani military, who laid waste to the Armenian quarter, killing those of its inhabitants unable to flee in time. The Armenian police chief, likely a relative of Marietta's father Nerses as his name was also Gukasyan, was turned into a human torch. The cathedral was badly damaged, and the grand homes of Armenian merchants, along with schools and libraries, were reduced to smoking ruins. By the time it was over, at least five hundred and possibly several thousand Armenians lay shot or hacked to death. Even the Azeri communist Odzhakhkuli Musayev called it a 'ruthless destruction of defenceless women and children ... beautiful Armenian girls were raped and then shot'. These events have not been forgotten, indeed they remain in the living memory of Armenians and Azerbaijanis in their seventies.

People instinctively know when war is coming. Anyone visiting the region in the late 1980s, which I do as a correspondent, can sense it, as if the air itself has grown still with anticipation and foreboding that 1920 is about to repeat itself. This helps explain the great movement of peoples that occurs towards the end of 1988, when a mass exchange of populations takes place between the two republics. Two hundred thousand Azeris flee Armenia proper, fortuitously just before 7 December 1988 when an earthquake devastates parts of the country where they lived, killing over twenty-five thousand people. Two hundred and sixty thousand Armenians cross from Azerbaijan into Armenia. The Baku government blocks all rail traffic into and through Nagorno-Karabakh and Armenia, and the little railway station in Aghdam from which Lieutenant Gukasyan and later his wife Farandzem left Karabakh is forced to shut down, and is never reopened. The unrest in Azerbaijan over the future of Karabakh galvanizes a popular movement which agitates for Azerbaijani independence. In early January 1990, large crowds take over government buildings in Baku and other Azerbaijani towns as the unrest escalates into an insurrection against Soviet control. On 19 January the Red Army is sent in, and soldiers shoot dead over one hundred and fifty Azeris at street barricades in Baku before reimposing Moscow's rule.

In March 1991 Gorbachev holds a referendum asking all fifteen Soviet republics to affirm their membership of a looser Soviet Union in a new treaty. Armenia, furious at Gorbachev for backing Azerbaijan over Karabakh, boycotts the poll, while Azerbaijan's communist leader Ayaz Mutallibov manages to turn sentiment around in his republic and deliver a vote in favour of Gorbachev's new union. In return Moscow helps Mutallibov's pro-Soviet regime to regain popular support by providing television pictures of Soviet forces attacking Armenian positions in Nagorno-Karabakh at Mutallibov's request.

By this stage the Armenians living three thousand eight hundred kilometres away in Krasnoyarsk, watching events unfold on television, have become thoroughly alarmed, especially Ararat and Araik, who worry about their parents Alyosha and Zhenya and their middle brother Artur. As the struggle intensifies in 1991, Araik, who came to study in Krasnoyarsk as a teenager and is now in his mid-twenties, decides to go back and join the Armenian fighters.

When the Soviet Union collapses in December 1991, Armenia and Azerbaijan each gain independence by default. Nagorno-Karabakh, isolated within the territory of Azerbaijan, declares itself an independent state aligned with Armenia. No country recognizes its right to exist. War erupts over control of the territory, this time involving regular Azeri and Armenian forces. Both sides use weapons and tanks abandoned by, or bought from, locally based leaderless Soviet troops, many of them conscripts from Kazakhstan, Ukraine, Russia and the Baltic republics, eager to go home. Both armies use mercenaries from disbanded Soviet units.

For several months the Armenians of Stepanakert are besieged, as all access roads to the town run through heavily armed Azeri villages. In February 1992 they break out and surround the Azeri settlement of Khojali with help from Soviet armour. The residents of Khojali are prevented from leaving by Azerbaijani commanders until it is too late. On 26 February Azeri villagers trying to escape across the open ground are cut down in a hail of gunfire from Armenian fighters. The death toll reaches almost five hundred.

Stepanakert meanwhile comes under fierce attack from Shushi, now the main Azeri stronghold in Karabakh. For weeks the defenceless population of some fifty thousand is subject to shellfire from above. However, Armenian fighters manage to cut Shushi's communications and on 9 May storm the heights and eject the enemy. A week later the Armenians capture territory to the west and open up a land link with Yerevan.

By the early summer of 1992 the Armenians have expelled much of Karabakh's Azeri population and assumed control. It seems the war is over and they have won. Then on 12 June the Azerbaijani regular army launches a surprise offensive against the Shahumyan region, the most northern part of Nagorno-Karabakh, using over one hundred armoured vehicles including tanks. Armenian resistance is weak. By the end of the month enemy tanks are approaching Martakert. Alyosha and Zhenya grab a few essential belongings and join the exodus of panic-stricken residents and fighters, fleeing south, leaving Martakert to the mercy of the enemy. One of the first Azeri soldiers to enter Martakert will later tell author Thomas de Waal that the defenders deserted their homes in terror, leaving everything intact. 'When we came into town we had the impression everyone was asleep at night and in the morning they would wake up and go to work.' A graphic documentary, *My Dears, Alive or Dead*, made by the Bulgarian–Armenian film-maker Tsvetana Paskaleva, shows a stream of people, some driving cattle, making their way along unpaved roads as they flee Martakert and Shahumyan. They carry bundles and suit-cases in their hands and on their backs. Trucks grind along so overloaded with people that some are forced to hang on behind or sit on the headlamps. Women stumble along muddy paths in the house slippers they were wearing when they fled. Weeping fathers carry half-dead children into a medical centre. Men claw frantically at wrecked apartment blocks in Shahumyan and pull out bodies. Severed limbs lie on the roadside.

These graphic images are broadcast on Russian television, bringing the fate of Martakert into the Suvorovs' front room. For days there is no news of their relatives. After a week, and much to everyone's relief, Alyosha, Zhenya and Araik turn up in Kras-noyarsk, carrying the belongings with which they were able to escape. They were driven to safety by their nephew Ishkhan, son of Marietta's half-sister Greta, who lives in Voronezh and who came to get them out in the darkness as the Azerbaijani tanks were approaching. They bring news that Artur has managed to escape to Yerevan, where his wife and children have already sought refuge in his wife's parents' home.

Araik, however, has been injured in the fighting. He has frag-mentation wounds to the face and has difficulty eating. He has come back to Siberia only because he needs time to recover and is determined to return to the front. Like many young men from Nagorno-Karabakh, Zhanna's cousin is passionate about Arme-nian claims to the land, and he can recite detailed arguments and produce copies of documents proving that their ancestors lived there long before the Azeris. Ararat and Galya put up the arrivals

Zhanna's cousins Araik and Artur Gukasyan: both suffer in the war over Nagorno-Karabakh.

in their Krasnoyarsk apartment. Stanislav and Marietta also take them out to the dacha, where they stay for part of the summer.

For a year the refugees from Martakert are unable to return, and they have to endure the bitter cold of a Siberian winter. Back home the fighting surges to and fro. An Armenian counter-offensive using attack helicopters piloted by Russians is opposed from the Azerbaijani side by Russian-piloted planes which bomb Stepanakert. However, in the spring of 1993 the Armenian regular army regains the initiative, and, with the Baku government in turmoil over a leadership struggle, the limited Azerbaijani occupation collapses. On 28 June Martakert and most of the north of Karabakh is liberated, and in July the Armenians take possession of the largely undefended Azeri town of Aghdam.

In 1994 the Russians broker a ceasefire. Although skirmishing goes on, the war over territory is effectively over. The outcome is a calamity for the Azeri population of Karabakh and outlying districts. Three hundred and fifty thousand Azeris find themselves refugees in Azerbaijan after the biggest forced exodus of a people since World War II. They have never been able to return.

A combination of military support from Armenia, financial backing from the Armenian diaspora and a fierce passion to hold on to their ancient lands has given the Karabakh Armenians victory, despite being outnumbered. At the height of the war Armenia had an estimated five hundred and fifty thousand men eligible for military service compared to Azerbaijan's 1.3 million, including Chechen and Afghan volunteers. In the field Azerbaijan also had vastly superior numbers of aircraft, tanks, armoured cars and artillery. However, the Armenians were more effective fighters, and this factor also proved decisive. On both sides men gained military experience as conscripts in the Soviet army, but the Armenians were better trained because they were generally assigned to combat duties, whereas the less well-educated Muslim Azeris suffered discrimination from Slavic officers, and their military experience was often confined to mess halls and construction units. Though Russians fought on both sides, in the final stages they favoured the Armenians. The chief of staff of Karabakh's armed forces at the end of the fighting was an ethnic Russian, General Anatoly Zinevich, a former officer in the Soviet army.

Alyosha and Zhenya return home to find that the centre of Martakert has been bombed to rubble. Shops, offices, factories, distilleries and houses have been comprehensively looted. Their house is intact but that of their next-door neighbour is destroyed, having taken a direct hit from a shell. Their garden plants and trees have been stripped bare. Their best young trees have been dug up and taken away.

The indefatigable and courageous Araik goes back to join the fighters. He has the misfortune to be in a car that drives over a mine and receives serious leg injuries. His war is over and he returns to Siberia once more. He will need a total of thirteen operations which still leave him limping. Misfortune of a different kind befalls Zhanna's other cousin, Artur, who also takes part in the fighting and becomes an officer in the Armenian forces. He gets into a dispute with a fellow soldier. There is a confrontation, a shot rings out, and Artur's antagonist is killed. He serves a jail sentence of four years for manslaughter.

For the Suvorov family it is another source of personal anguish consequent on the fall of the Soviet Union, and confirms Marietta's conviction that for all its faults, the Kremlin held things together and prevented the small wars that have brought misfortune to so many of her relatives, in Karabakh and in Grozny. She grieves for the suffering endured by her beloved Alyosha and his boys. She feels fortunate at the same time that she and her own family are far away from all of this. Leaving their homeland of Nagorno-Karabakh, and then their adopted city of Grozny, has become their salvation.

The ceasefire holds, but only insofar as serious fighting is concerned. All along the one-hundred-kilometre front-line Azeri and Armenian troops face each other across trenches and minefields, occasionally trading fire. There is no war but there is no peace.

CHAPTER 27

SHOEMAKERS GET THE BOOT

Privatization is a disaster for the shoe factory in Krasno-yarsk where Stanislav and Marietta have made their living since arriving in the city a quarter of a century ago.

On 1 October 1992, as part of the Yeltsin government's plan to sell practically all state property to the public and under a scheme worked out in cooperation with the International Finance Corporation in Washington, every single person in Russia is issued with a privatization voucher worth ten thousand rubles, the equivalent of roughly thirty US dollars. Each voucher represents one citizen's share of the national wealth. The vouchers will remain valid for eighteen months, from December 1992 to July 1994. The government hopes the voucher system, rather than the open sale of state-owned enterprises, will prevent factories and large businesses falling into the hands of the mafia and the *nomenklatura*.

Citizens can sell their vouchers if they wish, and many do so as soon as they can because, at the spiralling rate of inflation, the longer they wait the less value the vouchers will have. A third of all voucher holders, finding themselves in a critical financial position, sell them without hesitation. The tokens are often bought by small-time buyers and sold on in blocks to bigger operators. By the end of 1993 the ruble has declined in value so precipitously that the buying power of a voucher drops to about six dollars.

The scheme has considerable success, however. Fifteen thousand state firms are privatized using vouchers in the first eighteen months. Some insiders manage to acquire majority stakes in individual firms and become their owners outright because of their connections, their ability to borrow from the state banks and the willingness of people to turn their vouchers into easy cash.

Marietta picks up a voucher each for herself and Stanislav at the local branch of Sberbank. They plan to invest them in the shoe factory, along with those of Larisa, Vova and their children Zoya and Valera. Most of the eight hundred shoemakers, designers, cobblers and other employees at the factory and its repair shops and in the specialized outlet in the Dom Byta, among them many acquaintances and friends of the Suvorovs, have the same idea. 'We thought we would own it and make sure it worked better,' recalls Marietta. 'We didn't know any better.'

Three options on privatizing medium-sized enterprises are outlined in the how-to guide produced for the Russian government by the team at the International Finance Corporation in

Marietta with daughters Larisa and Zhanna in Krasnoyarsk in 1993.

Washington. The manager of the Krasnoyarsk shoe factory, Pyotr Baloban, is allowed to choose the second option – the most popular – which means converting the factory into a shareholding company. Control will go to whoever owns more than 50 per cent of the shares.

The Suvorovs eventually offload their six vouchers to Baloban for fifty-eight thousand rubles. Other employees do the same. The Krasnoyarsk shoe factory manager accumulates enough vouchers to secure a majority shareholding. There is no auction. He becomes the owner, only ceding a minority shareholding to the factory accountant, who insists on her rights. Baloban asks Marietta if she too wants to be part-owner but she declines. Stanislav has had enough of the former manager and jokes to Marietta that he will pay her her factory salary if she leaves. She has little incentive to stay on. She was once head of the factory branch of the Soviet trade union which owned it, and now that is no more. She was head of the factory's communist party branch, and the party is no more. She is head of human resources but she sees that people matter no more. She is fifty-four and approaching retirement. Her association with the enterprise where she has spent her working life comes to an end.

Baloban becomes one of Siberia's first factory owners since 1917. He renames the enterprise the Mercury Shoe Factory, an appropriate title given that Mercury is the patron of financial gain in the ancient Roman pantheon, but with its old machines it is in a sorry state and cannot compete in the new cut-throat capitalist environment. It has not been modernized in its final years, and its new owner does not put any capital into the factory.

'We thought our investment would pay dividends,' recalls Marietta. 'Instead, when it was privatized he started sacking people.' Over a short period of time Baloban lays off all eight hundred workers. He sells the factory building for offices, keeping part of the premises for himself to rent out.

In factories all across Russia, workers, traditionally apathetic and distrustful of their ability to influence the outcome of events, behave passively despite having the legal right to participate in meetings of voucher holders. There is also a mistaken inclination to allow the managers they know to take ownership rather than an outsider 'off the street', who would not have their interests at heart. Russian workers experience a new phenomenon – unemployment. Four out of five enterprises in Russia fall under the control of their communist-era management, but things do not carry on as before. Many trim down the excessive workforces they inherit by keeping all their employees on the payroll but withholding wages, pleading insolvency, in the hope that some will go away and try to find work elsewhere. The era of full employment ends and being out of work is no longer considered a civil offence.

The end of central planning means that public institutions and enterprises have to secure finance from wherever they can to fund their operations. Many run out of money, and offer wages in kind to their employees. Workers at the synthetic rubber plant in Krasnoyarsk are paid in tyres, and appear at the roadside trying to sell them to passing motorists. Lumber yards pay their employees in lengths of timber. Bread shops give their bakers loaves of bread.

Larisa stops receiving her regular salary as director of the state-funded Children's Choral Studio of the Musical Society, located in a nineteenth-century building on Prospect Mira. The society can pay her only once every four to six months. They offer her food such as butter, rice and buckwheat in lieu of salary. On one occasion her 'pay' is a parcel containing twenty-four pairs of socks. In the end she receives her back salary, but the school runs out of money and ceases operating. Larisa loses her job. The building is closed for renovation and reopens as a house of weddings.

Stanislav teaching future shoemakers in Krasnoyarsk, 1990.

Since retiring as a shoe designer in 1989, Stanislav has spent part of his time teaching a class of apprentice shoemakers in a college set up by the shoe factory. He is recognized as a master in industrial education, but the market for bespoke shoes is undermined by the end of communism. Cheap footwear imported from Europe and China, infinitely better than the old Soviet boots and shoes, is available in the new shoe shops opening all over Krasnoyarsk. Stanislav continues to work at the Pushkin Theatre, where he is a much-loved and good-natured fixture in the atelier at the back, with its shelves crammed with tools and bits of leather and wax and boxes of nails and tacks, and a miniature television playing in the corner, tuned to the news channels. In the first year of privatization the theatre director cannot pay the staff their salaries. He offers them a deal: he will pay them with food, or they can hold out for their back pay when the situation improves. Stanislav opts to wait and as a result receives a tidy sum of money when the theatre becomes financially viable again.

Many factories are bankrupted through asset stripping and the seizure of capital. A steady stream of people leaves the city as conditions worsen. The birth rate declines and longevity plummets. The population of Krasnoyarsk, which by 1992 had doubled in thirty years to almost one million, falls below nine hundred thousand in the first decade of capitalism.

Krasnoyarsk Region is however a destination of choice for many aspiring oligarchs as it is so rich in natural resources. There are fortunes to be made.

One of the big winners in the battle for state assets in Krasnoyarsk is Anatoly Bykov, a former boxer. Bykov gains control of the aluminium plant, the second largest in the world, so massive that it consumes 70 per cent of the electricity produced by the Krasnoyarsk hydro-electric power station. He buys up privatization vouchers cheaply from workers arriving at the factory gates for their shifts. Like other suddenly rich Russians he also finds himself in a fierce and sometimes deadly struggle for control of the new wealth and even for his own survival. General Alexander Lebed, a former military officer who is elected governor of Krasnoyarsk Region, has Bykov charged with the murder of a crime boss, though he is not convicted.

Former stalwarts of the CPSU become wealthy capitalists overnight by seizing control of the natural wealth of the land – its oil, gold, nickel, cobalt, copper, platinum, coal and timber. Many of the new rich convert their wealth into hard currency and watch it soar in value compared to the Russian ruble, enabling them to make more purchases of national assets. In the first two years following the break-up of the USSR, the Central Bank of Russia estimates that the flow of capital out of the country reaches $100 billion, more than the combined total of inward investment and international aid.

Hyperinflation leads to the emergence of companies which promise to invest people's voucher money at an annual return of 100 per cent and more. At the peak of the privatization rush it is impossible to turn on a radio or TV in Russia without hearing the Krasnoyarsk-born actor Vladimir Permyak in the role of a simple guy, Lyonya Golubkov, claiming to have got rich by buying stock in an investment company called MMM. 'It's damn simple,' he says. MMM, run in Moscow by three people whose surnames begin with M, pulls off one of the biggest Ponzi schemes of all time. It takes in so much money that cash at its Moscow offices is counted by the roomful. When it collapses in July 1994, investors' losses run to several billion rubles. Vladimir Permyak is shunned for years afterwards.

Alexander Solzhenitsyn, who returns from exile in the United States in the summer of 1994, is credited with a saying that becomes popular: 'Everything the communists told us about communism was a lie. Unfortunately, everything the communists told us about capitalism turns out to be true.' Tens of millions of people have been impoverished and their savings wrecked by shock therapy, he says, and privatization is enacted 'with the same blind madness, the same destructive haste as the nationalization of 1917–18 and the collectivization of 1930'.

No one questions that the past is done with, but there is a nostalgia among older people for the certainty of the early Brezhnev days, when there were no wars and everyone within the Soviet Union lived at peace. As always in Russia, there is an aphorism: 'What came first, the chicken or the egg?' Answer: 'Why, in former times there was everything.' But in former times obtaining anything meant standing in long quarrelsome queues and sucking up to arrogant shop managers. People who find it hard to cope with new attitudes and behaviours tell the younger generation, 'Don't mind us, we are just *sovki* [Soviet people].' This is a pun on the term for dustpan.

'We all hate it that the most vulnerable suffer the most,' Marietta says, 'but now I don't have to humiliate myself to buy cheese.' Like everyone else she is struck by the change in attitude of once-unhelpful sales assistants who now smile and say, 'Come again!' Krasnoyarsk is flooded with foreign goods, often of inferior quality. It is intoxicating at first to enter a well-stocked supermarket or clothes shop, but the novelty quickly wears off. People become suspicious. The sell-by date on packaging convinces many that much of the foreign produce is old or surplus stock being dumped by Western suppliers.

After inflation is brought under control in the mid-1990s the Suvorovs start saving once more. By August 1998 they have enough money in their Sberbank account to contemplate buying a small apartment in Krasnoyarsk as an investment. When rumours begin circulating that month that the currency will be devalued – the ruble has been pegged at six to the dollar all year but in the last two weeks has slipped to eight – Marietta decides to withdraw her money from the bank and buy the apartment quickly. She and Stanislav go to the Sberbank branch on 30 August. The cashier has the money ready to give her, but Marietta hesitates to take it out and to risk being robbed. Stanislav persuades her at the last minute to leave it where it is until they find a suitable property.

Two days later Russia plunges into a catastrophic financial crisis. All bank accounts are frozen. Yeltsin's government devalues the ruble, which goes into free fall, and Russia defaults on its debts. When the Suvorovs' account is freed, it is worth a tenth of its former value.

Three times now the government has robbed the Suvorovs: the first when the Soviet finance minister Valentin Pavlov took most of Vova's cash, the second when Gaidar reduced their savings to kopecks, and now the third, when Yeltsin's mishandling of the economy causes a currency collapse. It is little comfort for them to reflect that they have the distinction of being ripped off by both communism and capitalism. Marietta and Stanislav are by this stage quite stoic about the blows they have to suffer. They know communism has run its course and that the country is struggling to find a new equilibrium, and it is no use being outraged. They are nevertheless deeply disillusioned. Russia has been dragged into the modern consumer era, with everything available in the stores, but it is a frightening place, with increased crime, financial chaos and no respite for the poor, while the 'new Russians' syphon off the national wealth and the former captains of communism transform themselves into the oligarchs of capitalism. They worry about what fate holds for the younger generation.

CHAPTER 28

DEATH ON THE STREET AGAIN

LIKE HIS UNCLE Stanislav and aunt Marietta, Ararat Gukasyan has done well for himself since following them from Martakert to Krasnoyarsk. At one time an uneducated army conscript with a poor command of Russian, Ararat has become a model police officer who served in Moscow during the Olympics and has been promoted, first to sergeant, then to lieutenant detective, and now, in independent Russia, to major, with shoulder boards displaying a single star between double red lines. He and his wife Galya have two children, Inna and Artur. His goal is to put them through university and give them the best opportunities in life. Like Stanislav and Marietta he has become a Siberian and a much-loved member of the small Armenian family circle in Krasnoyarsk.

Ararat spends a lot of time with the Suvorov family, at the dacha in summer or in their apartment in winter. Marietta loves him as a son, and when celebrating something or other at their home he likes to throw his arms around her and she pretends to be embarrassed by his attention.

In 1996 a Jewish couple called Delver, who reside next door to the Suvorovs on the eighth floor of their apartment block on Zheleznodorozhnikov Street, decide to move to Moscow to live with their daughter. As friends of the Suvorovs, they are more than happy to sell their apartment to Ararat, who moves in with Galya and the children to be close to Stanislav and Marietta.

Braving the Siberian cold for a family photograph at the Suvorov dacha in Bulanovka, 1999.

The two adjacent apartments are located on a short corridor running off a small landing reached by concrete stairs and a lift. Ararat's flat is on the left of the corridor and the Suvorovs' at the end. The presence of a law-enforcement officer on their floor is reassuring to Marietta and Stanislav. In the early 1970s, when they lived in the House of Actors, burglaries and break-ins were so rare that they hardly ever locked their door. In the chaos of the first post-communist years crime is so prevalent that not only do people secure their doors, they convert their homes into fortresses. Those in ground-floor apartments install metal bars on their windows, and all apartment dwellers fit security chains. Like many of their neighbours, the Suvorovs do not consider this enough, and they secure their corridor with a padded double-lock steel door. Behind such fortifications people can feel secure, but it means that in capitalist Russia the first sight of a visitor is often through a spy hole in the door.

When we visit Zhanna's parents during vacations in the 1990s Ararat is always there to make us welcome, and he and Galya eat with us at Marietta's dinner table. He rivals Zhanna's father with his toasts. We are sometimes joined by his brother Araik, who has also settled in Krasnoyarsk and is married to Gulya, a dark-haired beauty from Karabakh.

During these visits Ararat and I sometimes retreat to the long glass-enclosed balcony off the living room and, looking out over the roofs, talk about the state of affairs in post-Soviet Krasnoyarsk. Before the end of communism, he explains, drugs were available but on a manageable scale. Since then several central Asian gangs have flooded the city with narcotics, and the homicide rate is rising.* But the biggest criminals, he believes, are the Russian predators who asset-strip profitable industries, grow immensely rich and ship their billions abroad. He calls them thieves and bribe-takers. We joke about these 'new Russians' throwing their money around abroad. One asks another, 'How much did you pay for your Rolex?' 'Five thousand dollars.' 'You fool, I know where you can get the same watch for six thousand dollars.'

One day Ararat takes us on a tour of the splendid new mansions being built by the emerging oligarchs on the outskirts of Krasnoyarsk. We drive down a snow-covered cul-de-sac in the Udachny suburb to a palatial red-brick dwelling at the end constructed by Anatoly Bykov, who has gained control of the Krasnoyarsk aluminium plant. It is surrounded by a high wall with spiked metal gates and a watchtower, on which we can see an armed man silhouetted against the sky, like a sentry in a new Gulag for the rich. 'Don't take a photograph,' Ararat warns. Bykov is temporarily the shadow master of Krasnoyarsk, and his

---

* It tripled throughout Russia between 1988 and 1994 to one of the highest rates in the world.

security guards are very aggressive, he says. As we return to the city centre, an armoured Mercedes races past accompanied by a procession of fifteen high-performance cars with sirens screaming. 'That's him,' says Ararat, though he notes that, as the car windows are blacked out, no one can be sure he is in the convoy, and that sometimes Bykov travels incognito using the limousine as a decoy.

A number of Bykov's rivals have met a violent death, says Ararat. Rarely is anyone arrested. One of the most feared mobsters in the city is a man with a tic in his eye, which earns him the nickname Pasha Strobe Light. His real name is Viktor Struganov and he will commit several contract murders before he is finally put behind bars in 2015.

Many of the crime victims in Krasnoyarsk are *kommersanty*, business people who find themselves at the mercy of criminals prepared to use brutal methods to enforce the collection of debts or escape paying their own debts. 'If you owe someone money it's easier to have them killed than to pay it back,' explains Ararat as we contemplate the powdery snow falling on the rooftops one Saturday afternoon. In one criminal case he dealt with, a businessman who owed his partner eighty thousand rubles got rid of the debt by paying a contract killer six thousand rubles to kill him. Yura, an Aeroflot pilot and family friend, who has joined us, jokes that the country is heading for an Italian solution: 'Either Sicily or Mussolini, or both.'

By coincidence we are in Krasnoyarsk one day visiting Zhanna's family when the street outside becomes the scene of one of the most horrific crimes in the history of the city. We watch on television news, aghast, as a newscaster reports that the head of a small boy has been found in a rubbish bin where a path links Zheleznodorozhnikov Street with busy Bryanskaya Street. We walk by the rubbish bin some hours later on our way to Prospect Mira. Apart from a small knot of people peering at the metal box there is nothing to indicate that this is a crime scene. The head has simply been removed and taken away. The assumption is that the killer drove along Bryanskaya Street during the night, stopped, got out of his car, dumped his parcel in the nearest receptacle and drove off. Ararat fears a serial killer is at work. It is the second boy's head to turn up in three years. More body parts have been discovered in other districts, and two years later five boys aged between nine and twelve are found murdered in a sewage pipe in Krasnoyarsk's eastern Leninsky suburb.

Stanislav and Marietta associate the increase in crime with the fall of the Soviet Union. In years gone by they could look out of their apartment window and see children playing in the narrow tree-lined park outside. Since the gruesome discovery in the bin the park has gone quiet and children only appear with their parents. We learn from Ararat that the police in Krasnoyarsk are demoralized by the lack of professional training and equipment to cope with the crime wave that has followed privatization.

Brave new world: security firms advertising protection in post-Soviet Krasnoyarsk, 2004.

They do not get their salaries regularly and have to accept gifts of cars and radio equipment from rich businessmen seeking their protection. Some of his colleagues are leaving to join the private security companies such as Okhrana (Security) or Uragan (Hurricane) whose billboards decorate the city bus stops.

Around the same time that he moves into the apartment beside the Suvorovs Ararat himself begins to provide security for a fruit and vegetable importer at Krasnoyarsk market as a sideline to his police work. The produce business is conducted in cash; credit cards are still a novelty, and market vendors are vulnerable to extortion. He takes us to meet his partner, a Tajik with a large flowing moustache, at a stall laden with every conceivable kind of fruit, vegetable and spice.

Two years later Ararat decides to leave the police and go into business for himself providing security for all the market vendors. Stanislav and Marietta try to talk him out of it. He has every prospect of advancing further in the ranks of the Krasnoyarsk Region police force; he is a senior officer of the CID; he could soon be a lieutenant colonel. But he resigns from the force on 1 January 1999 to become a businessman.

Ararat prospers in his new role and joins the ranks of the nouveau riche. When we visit Krasnoyarsk in the spring of 2003 he takes us to see another mansion, this time his own. It is a high two-storey-over-basement structure of red brick, with green-tiled roofs and a projecting first-floor balcony with brick arches on white pillars. It isn't quite finished. Without fixtures or fittings the rooms seem enormous. From below we take pictures of each other standing on the balcony. Ararat plans to move his family into the house within a few months. He invites us back for a celebration to mark the occasion.

It never takes place. At 7.30 a.m. on Wednesday, 11 June 2003 Ararat leaves his apartment to fetch his black Volkswagen Passat,

Ararat at his almost complete house, in 2003, three months before the assassin strikes.

which he has parked nearby. His daughter Inna is due to sit an examination and he is planning to take her to the university. He steps into the tiny lift on the eighth floor, closes the wooden flap, pulls shut the concertina metal doors and descends to the entrance hall. He emerges onto the street and walks along the side of the apartment block. As he approaches his vehicle, a man

The house Ararat is building after leaving the police force to go into private business.

gets out of a white car and walks towards him. Ararat apparently recognizes him or realizes what he intends. He tries to run, but the man shoots Ararat at close range and stabs him as he lies on the ground.

Zhanna's father Stanislav, who at the age of seventy-four still goes every day to his leather workshop in the Pushkin Theatre, steps out of the apartment block a few minutes later and walks in the same direction. He comes upon a small crowd of people. In their midst he sees Ararat's body, his life blood seeping away, the keys of his car still clutched in his hand. Horrified he pushes his way through to see if anything can be done but it is no use. Ararat is beyond help. People tell Stanislav there were two men in the car which drove off at high speed.

We get the news in the middle of the night in New York, where we are then living, in a phone call from Larisa's son Valera. We know immediately something is wrong from his voice. Zhanna turns deathly pale as she hears him say, 'Ararat is dead.' She has lost the nearest to a brother she ever had in what, from Valera's description, seems to be a professional killing.

We find out later what happens after the murder. The *militsia* arrive very quickly and in large numbers. One of the first things they do is to race up the concrete steps to search Ararat's eighth-floor apartment. The police do not say what they are looking for, but afterwards there are rumours, never substantiated, that Ararat had a tape-recording that might incriminate someone. Ararat's body is taken away for a post-mortem examination.

Vova and Larisa drive to the dacha to break the news to Marietta, who has been staying there to tend the garden. They bring her back. She and Stanislav are profoundly shaken and find it difficult to come to terms with the fact that the young man whom they nourished and encouraged and who was at the centre of their lives is dead.

Ararat's remains are brought to his apartment so Galya and his children Inna and Artur, his brother Araik, his aunt Marietta and uncle Stanislav from next door, and other members of the family and his friends can mourn his passing. His parents Alyosha and Zhenya arrive after a day-long journey by road and air from Martakert. Their grief is compounded by the fact that Ararat will not be buried in the family grave in Karabakh, but here in his adopted Russian city. They will say their final good-byes as he is lowered into the cold earth of Siberia rather than in his native soil.

The killing makes news across Russia. It is broadcast on Channel 1 television out of Moscow and in the national print media. The newspapers report, in summary, that former police officer Ararat Gukasyan, chief of security at Krasnoyarsk market, was killed by a man who fired two shots, that the crime was committed right by his home in Zheleznodorozhnikov Street, that a homicide investigation has been started, and that the investigation is being led by the Krasnoyarsk Region prosecutor. They disclose that Ararat Gukasyan was one of the main witnesses in an investigation into the revealing of state secrets by Nikolai Khamsky, chief of the state agency combating illegal narcotics, a charge denied by Khamsky.

Nothing comes of the investigation and three months later Khamsky is transferred to head the military criminal investigation division of Sverdlovsk Oblast, a district in the Urals whose administrative capital is Yekaterinburg.

Ararat is given a full-dress police funeral, with uniformed personnel and senior officers lined up along the road outside his apartment as the body is carried out to the hearse. Police cars, their blue lights flashing, escort the cortège to the Badalyg cemetery. A rifle salute is fired over his grave. All expenses are paid by the Internal Affairs Agency of the Krasnoyarsk Region.

The killing of Ararat takes a heavy toll on the family. Stanislav, his hair cropped to a bristle, loses the twinkle in his eye and his ready smile, and begins for the first time to show his age. Marietta, Zhanna and Larisa are heartbroken. Araik is devastated. The whole family connection is in despair. Their disillusion grows with a society where yet again a member of the family has been killed and no one is held to account.

Seven years pass. On 24 September 2010 the Siberian news agency krsk.sibnovosti.ru reports that the crime has been solved. A thirty-six-year-old known criminal, Gamet Gurbanov, a native of Azerbaijan, has confessed. He claims that as Gukasyan knew about his criminal past he 'reacted negatively' to the former police officer's frequent appearances at the market and decided to kill him with a gas pistol which he had modified for use with lethal ammunition. Gurbanov is sentenced to fifteen years in a strict-regime prison colony for Ararat's murder. No mention is made of a second assassin.

Gravestone (on left) for Ararat in Martakert, though he is buried in Krasnoyarsk; beside it is the grave of his father Alyosha, 2016.

Whether or not there was more to it than that, we will never know. The case is officially closed. His relatives are left to reflect on the tragic irony that Ararat, an Armenian who left Nagorno-Karabakh and, unlike his brothers, did not fight in the war against the Azeris, should have been killed so far from his birthplace by a native of Azerbaijan.

CHAPTER 29

WAR WITHOUT END

ONE SPRING DAY in 2014 Zhanna finds herself on a Russian-made military helicopter flying from Armenia to Nagorno-Karabakh. As it approaches their destination, the Armenian pilot warns nonchalantly that they might be fired at but not to worry: 'Shooting happens.' The guns on the ground stay silent.

Zhanna hasn't planned to visit Karabakh. Indeed the fact that she is in this part of the world at all, on her way to the remote and disputed land of her ancestors, is an extraordinary twist of fate arising from her career trajectory since leaving Russia for the United States in the year the Soviet Union collapsed.

Her work on Russian privatization as a consultant at the International Finance Corporation in Washington continues for five years, and then in 1996 my editor sends me to Beijing, where Zhanna works as director of development for an international school, the Western Academy. In January 2001 I am given the title of international business editor and transferred to New York where Zhanna is appointed head of development at the International Baccalaureate, the non-governmental organization which provides international-standard educational programmes for schools and has its fundraising headquarters in the city. We witness the 9/11 attacks – our forty-second-storey apartment in Chambers Street is two blocks away – and experience the horrible aftermath for months as bodies are discovered and taken out beneath our windows, and the debris is dumped into barges on the Hudson beside our building.

We finally settle in Dublin in 2005. Zhanna's career comes full circle: having always aspired to a life in academia, she finds herself back in a university, albeit not in a teaching capacity but as associate director of development at Trinity College Dublin raising funds for medical research.

Then the former Soviet Union calls on her again. In 2013, when the former board chair of the International Baccalaureate Fund, Michael Obermayer, is asked to name someone with Western expertise in fundraising to help develop an international school in Armenia, he immediately recommends Zhanna. She has proved her abilities at the International Baccalaureate and is of Armenian extraction. The school is the project of an Armenian-Russian entrepreneur and philanthropist, Ruben Vardanyan, and his wife Veronika Zonabend. The couple are making a number of philanthropic investments with social impact to help life in Armenia. Zhanna agrees to assist on a part-time basis until the school is up and running, and she subsequently makes a number of trips to Armenia over a period of four years while on leave from Trinity.

On one of these visits, six months before the completion of the school in the town of Dilijan, Vardanyan and his wife take a group of a dozen guests and Zhanna on a long road trip to visit the ninth-century Tatev Monastery, perched on a basalt plateau in south-eastern Armenia. They leave the cars and approach the site using a cable car opened in 2010 with financing from Vardanyan, and certified by Guinness World Records as the world's longest non-stop double-track cable car. A helicopter is waiting for the group after their tour of the monastery. It flies low through valleys and over mountain villages, and after a short time lands in Stepanakert, capital of Nagorno-Karabakh.

One of the passengers is Tatiana Shahumyan, the Moscow-based granddaughter of the Bolshevik hero and friend of Lenin, Stepan Shahumyan, who was executed by counter-revolutionary forces in 1918 and after whom Stepanakert is named. Vardanyan leads the group to a statue erected in his honour, showing him facing his executioner with courage, where Tatiana places a bouquet of flowers.

Zhanna is unprepared for the emotions she feels at finding herself in the territory where her mother lived as a child with Zhanna's grandparents, Nerses and Farandzem Gukasyan, until their lives were so dramatically changed by Nerses' death in World War II. Her grandfather was also, like Shahumyan, a product of the Bolshevik era and gave his life in the Soviet cause. She feels a strong connection to her family here, and the personal stories of her grandmother and mother. What would have happened if her grandfather had not been killed in the war and her grandmother had stayed in Karabakh? She is overwhelmed by a sense of how history has been so cruel to the people from which she sprang and how, like the Israeli-Palestine conflict, there seems to be no solution.

Six months later, in October 2014, Zhanna returns to Armenia for the opening of the international school. It is one of sixteen United World Colleges, the first of which was established in Wales, with the aim of uniting 'people, nations and cultures for peace and a sustainable future'. It is a significant occasion for Armenia and is attended by the presidents of Armenia and Nagorno-Karabakh and the head of the Armenian Apostolic Church. The gathering is addressed via a video link by the Prince of Wales, former president of United World Colleges.

On this occasion I am also in Yerevan, having flown in with Zhanna from Dublin, and Marietta too joins us, having travelled from Krasnoyarsk. The three of us plan to make a proper visit to Nagorno-Karabakh and stay a few days with Marietta's sister-in-law Zhenya and her nephew Artur. It is sixty-four years since Marietta left Martakert as an eleven-year-old with her mother to start a new life in Grozny. Other than a holiday visit when she was sixteen, she has not been back.

While Zhanna is busy at the school in Dilijan, Marietta and I explore Yerevan. It is her first time in the Armenian capital and she struggles to make her Karabakh dialect of Armenian understood by the locals. Yerevan bears little resemblance to a Soviet-era city. It was created a century before by the Russian-born architect Alexander Tamanyan, who transformed a small town into a neoclassical jewel when it was chosen as the capital of Armenia. At its heart is Republic Square, an extensive and elegant plaza surrounded by pink and grey buildings with traditional decorative carvings, and a dancing fountain at its centre. We walk from there towards the smaller Freedom Square, on the way pausing on the pedestrian link for a coffee and to observe Yerevan's smart society strolling past the high-end stores and restaurants.

In Freedom Square Levon Ter-Petrosyan, president of Armenia from 1991 to 1998 and now an opposition voice, is addressing a large political rally on the opera house steps. I recall for Marietta how I met Ter-Petrosyan in Yerevan in November 1989, when he was leader of the pro-Karabakh protest movement. A Syrian-born scholar fluent in Armenian, Assyrian, Russian, French, English, German and Arabic, Ter-Petrosyan told me then that there were two moments in the history of Armenia when they could have been wiped out, in 1918, when most Armenian men were at the Western Front, and in 1943, when a majority of the male population were fighting the Nazi invaders and Turkish forces were massing on the Armenian border.

After the Soviet Union broke up Ter-Petrosyan and his government looked longingly to the West for a new identity, but ever mindful that Armenia is surrounded by unfriendly neighbours – to the west Turkey, to the south Iran, to the east Azerbaijan – and that to antagonize Moscow would be to give a hostage to fortune, they prevaricated. Indeed two weeks after our visit, Armenia bows to Kremlin pressure and, along with Belarus, Kazakhstan and Kyrgyzstan, signs up to a Russian alternative to the European Union, the Eurasian Economic Union, which comes into effect on 1 January 2015.

We walk on to Yerevan's famous Cascade and ride a series of elevators to the immense statue of Mother Armenia, who carries a large, unsheathed sword. From here we glimpse Mount Ararat, sacred to Armenians and reputed in Christianity to be the resting place of Noah's Ark. While it is actually in Turkey, Armenians have made it their cultural property, a symbol of the nation, reproduced on banknotes and postage stamps, framed in pictures in every home, and given as a first name to countless young Armenian males, like Marietta's murdered nephew.

The only way for the three of us to travel to landlocked Nagorno-Karabakh next day – without the benefit of a helicopter – is by road from Yerevan, a seven-hour drive. The rail connection from Baku has been blocked for twenty-seven years by Azerbaijan, leaving Karabakh with two hundred and forty kilometres of disused railway lines. Azerbaijan still controls the airspace over its lost territory and threatens to shoot down any passenger plane approaching from Armenia.

We hire a taxi in Republic Square. The driver turns out to be an embittered veteran of the war against Azerbaijan who makes racist comments about the 'dirty, treacherous' Azeris and overcharges us for the privilege of listening to him.

For the first fifty kilometres after leaving Yerevan our route runs parallel with the Turkish frontier on our right, and we can see Mount Ararat up close in all its majesty. The road continues through rugged terrain and arid canyons with fantastic rock formations. Nearing our destination, we are stopped at a passport control post where an Armenian immigration officer instructs Zhanna and me to call at the foreign ministry in Stepanakert to obtain tourist visas. As a Russian passport-holder, Marietta can enter freely. The final sixty-five-kilometre stretch of road, once a mountain track largely unusable in winter, is a black ribbon of smooth tarmac funded by a ten-million-dollar gift from the Armenian diaspora. We pass small peaks strung with nets to deter enemy helicopters, drive through a neck of captured Azerbaijan territory and past the sad ruins of Shushi, then descend to Stepanakert, the capital of the Republic of Nagorno-Karabakh.

At the foreign ministry polite young officials speaking fluent English and Russian stamp our passports and wish us a pleasant stay. They are happy to welcome visitors to their nominally independent country, which they call Artsakh. It has all the trappings of statehood: its own government departments, its own parliament, its own police force and its own Artsakh postage stamps featuring wildlife, musical instruments, mountain scenes, and images of a giant statue of an elderly Armenian couple carved from volcanic tufa with the national slogan, 'We are our mountains.'

Throughout history Armenians have adjusted to whatever conditions they were forced to endure in often hostile surroundings. For the first time in many centuries they have now acquired and defended their own land rather than acquiescing to foreign rule. The enclave has become the core of Armenian identity. One meets many Armenians like Vardanyan who say they must move on from the past and from commemorations of the genocide and look to building a viable future, and Nagorno-Karabakh is essential to that.

Yerevan pays lip service to Artsakh's independent status and stops short of annexation for fear of international repercussions but treats Karabakh nevertheless as an extension of itself. Its currency, the Armenian dram, circulates, and financial support comes in the form of domestic loans. Armenia provides Karabakh residents with passports, it pumps in gas for heating, it supplies military equipment, and it sends recruits to protect the borders.

Nagorno-Karabakh has become one of a small club of largely unrecognized statelets left stranded by the Soviet Union's collapse, the others being Abkhazia, a supposedly independent Black Sea resort region that the world considers part of Georgia but is under de facto Russian control; South Ossetia, also officially part of Georgia but occupied by Russian troops; and Transnistria, a sliver of Soviet nostalgia wedged between Ukraine and Moldova that is a protectorate of the Russian army. Nagorno-Karabakh/Artsakh is officially part of Azerbaijan, but that country has not been in a position to exercise its sovereignty since 1994.

Marietta marvels at how Stepanakert has been transformed from the old Caucasian city she remembers into a small, elegant metropolis, rebuilt since its part-destruction by Grad missiles in the 1990s. We explore fashionable shops, carpet stores, art galleries and cafés with free Wi-Fi, and pause to listen to a brass band in the central park, before hiring another taxi to our final destination, Martakert, fifty kilometres to the north.

We set out across a grassy plateau with occasional patches of oak and linden trees. Along the highway army vehicles jammed with young soldiers and flatbed trucks carrying T-72 tanks lurch around each other to avoid deep potholes and flocks of sheep. The road runs parallel with the Azerbaijan border, and we see many deserted and wrecked settlements, the biggest being Aghdam. I visited Aghdam as a correspondent in May 1991, when it was a thriving town of forty thousand mainly Azeri people. I tell my travelling companions that, approaching the town from the direction of Baku through small steep valleys with poppy-strewn vineyards and sheep pastures, I came across little mountain hamlets, both Armenian and Azeri, damaged by shellfire.

I recall in particular an Azeri stone-cutter, Faisal Aliev, who told me the villagers used to be friendly with each other. 'We were like that,' he said, holding his two forefingers together. He guided me to the deserted settlement of Airu, where the lane leading to the nearby Armenian village was blocked by a telegraph pole and a tree trunk. The Armenians had fled villages such as Dashbulag, where Azerbaijani army units and *militsia* were busy destroying the Armenian church with explosives. Aghdam that day in 1991 was under intermittent fire from Armenian batteries and there too families were beginning to leave. Now it is a ghost town. We gaze wordlessly, kilometre after kilometre, at a desolate landscape of roofless houses systematically wrecked to prevent the Azeris returning and plundered by Armenians for building materials. Only the twin minarets of the abandoned Aghdam mosque are left intact.

Karabakh tourist officials do not regard the ethnic cleansing of Aghdam as something to be ashamed of; in Stepanakert they encourage visitors to take guided tours of the 'abandoned city'. Meanwhile many of the former inhabitants of Aghdam live in wretched, makeshift homes in Azerbaijan, which refuses to give them proper housing as that would be to admit the loss of Aghdam is permanent. Marietta, her eyes heavy with sadness, recalls how she and friends used to attend school concerts in Aghdam. Her childhood memories of the blighted town are of harmony, not strife.

After an hour we arrive in pouring rain in Martakert. Yellow gas pipes loop over the lanes and side roads to allow traffic to pass beneath. With difficulty the driver finds the house we are seeking, one of several situated behind high walls along a lane so rutted that the taxi leaps and bounces almost out of control.

Zhanna's aunt Zhenya and her cousin Artur are waiting for us. Zhenya, long since retired as a doctor, is in her eighties and in poor health due to arthritis. They make us welcome with a meal of *dolma* and *lavash* bread stuffed with herbs. Raising glasses of their home-made red wine, we toast family and the memory of Zhenya's husband Alyosha, Marietta's half-brother, who died in 2005.

The suffering of her life lies heavily on Zhenya's weary body. Her eldest son Ararat left home to live in Siberia, and was murdered. His children – her grandchildren – live there, far away. Her son Araik, twice wounded in the fighting, is also living in Siberia with his wife and four children. She sees them only on holiday visits. They want her to move to Krasnoyarsk but it is too late now, she says. Artur, fifty-five, remains at home. His wife and three children live in Yerevan, while he looks after his mother in Martakert where he works in construction.

It is a sad homecoming for Marietta, not helped by the chilly rain. Her happy childhood memories of a 'blossoming place' are overlaid with the reality of modern Martakert, run-down and war-damaged, deprived of so many able people who have emigrated to find a better life elsewhere.

Next day Artur drives us in his battered jeep to the family grave at the top end of an unkempt, topsy-turvy cemetery. We stand in silence by a headstone he has erected in memory of Ararat, which bears a ceramic picture of his brother smiling, etched from a photograph taken by me at the dacha outside Krasnoyarsk in happier days. Beside it stands his father's gravestone. Ararat's body is not here, of course, but in Krasnoyarsk. The Gukasyan family plot is missing another body, that of Marietta's father, whose grave in Romania we will not locate for another three years.

In the mornings some male neighbours and relatives drop in for breakfast and a glass of *tutovka*, the sweet local vodka made from mulberries. In the evenings we watch Russian television stations if there are no electricity blackouts. Most people in Martakert understand Russian, a legacy of Soviet times, when Armenians and Azeris shared a common political system and language. Russian is still taught in the schools, a recognition of both geopolitical realities and of the fact that Karabakh Armenians, because of low wages and unemployment, often end up making their lives in the Russian Federation.

The ceasefire between the two sides came into force twenty years ago, on 12 May 1994, but the war has not ended for Martakert. The town lies close to the front line between two well-equipped armies. We are a mere three kilometres from the frontier, which is marked by concrete bunkers, sandbags and camouflage netting. At night shots ring out in the darkness, and during the day an occasional boom echoes around the low hills, a noise so commonplace that no one pays much attention. Hardly a day goes by without fusillades of bullets cracking across no-man's-land. In the week we are there twenty thousand shots are reported fired across the lines in both directions – the number is regularly logged – and an Armenian officer and two Azeri soldiers are killed. There is no formal contact between the enemies, not even a telephone line, though we hear of local conscripts who exchange shouts rather than shots across the lines, and sometimes cigarettes.

Since both gained independence in 1991 Armenia and Azerbaijan have set unity with Karabakh as the non-negotiable limit of their national ambitions. Bill Clinton could not broker a peace treaty. Vladimir Putin has attempted mediation between Baku and Yerevan, but Russian arms dealers supply weapons to both sides, thus maintaining Russian influence over the southern Caucasus. If it were not for the passionate support of the Armenian diaspora, life in Martakert and other front-line towns would be more wretched than it is. Believing that the loss of Karabakh would be a catastrophe for the whole race, Armenians abroad, particularly in France and the United States, have donated millions of dollars to the Hayastan All Armenian Fund to improve living conditions and the region's infrastructure. As the most isolated sizeable town in northern Karabakh, Martakert is vulnerable to sudden attack, and its security is being enhanced with the construction of a second road from Armenia funded by Hayastan. One hundred and sixteen kilometres long, it begins at the city of Vardenis in the Lake Sevan region of Armenia.* The fund is also helping rebuild Martakert with support for agriculture, water supply, healthcare and schools.

We are driven back to Yerevan by a taxi driver from Martakert who charges us a quarter of the fare we had to pay the driver who brought us.

No one knows for sure why the war suddenly reignites on 2 April 2016. Without warning Azerbaijani forces launch attacks along the line. Shells fall on Martakert in the early hours, damaging houses and fracturing the gas pipeline. Later a drone is launched by Azerbaijani forces and strikes a bus as it passes through Martakert, half a kilometre from Zhenya and Artur's house, killing seven Armenian volunteers. The drone was manufactured by Israeli Aerospace Industries and has never before been used in battle. The use of military drones which can hover for six hours and travel a thousand kilometres is a frightening new reality for those living within their reach. As the front line is strengthened with a hundred and seventy volunteers from the town, many residents head for safety further away or take to air-raid shelters. There is no mass evacuation, as happened during previous alarms; nevertheless, along with scores of vulnerable neighbours, Artur and his mother again temporarily abandon their home, this time for the safety of Yerevan.

Perhaps President Aliev is looking to distract the Azeris from domestic setbacks by seeking to regain lost territory, or he wishes to put the issue back on the international agenda. Some Armenians suspect Turkey has incited the conflict;

---

* It has since opened with smooth tarmac, proper signage and snow-removal facilities.

others see the hand of Russia, intent on reimposing itself as the arbiter of peace and war in the region. Or maybe someone wanted to test new weapons. Conspiracy theories and paranoia are as common in the Caucasus as mulberry trees.

The 'war' ends after four days with Azerbaijan seizing a small strip of territory. Some three hundred and fifty people, military and civilian, are killed. Several houses in Martakert are destroyed by missiles. Zhenya's house survives intact. The town's mayor, Misha Gyuriyan, a burly white-haired veteran of the 1992–4 war, assures the population that water, light and gas are working and that all is now safe. Zhenya and Artur return home, but they begin planning to move to Armenia proper permanently, where Artur's wife and children already reside. By now Marietta's three half-sisters have also died. In Karabakh nothing will be left of the once-thriving Gukasyan family of Martakert, other than the engraved faces on the headstones looking out on a tortured graveyard.

EPILOGUE

SIPPING AN AMERICANO in the marble-and-glass Planeta shopping mall in Krasnoyarsk and watching elegantly dressed people browse in stores like Zara and Adidas or tap on their iPads, or settle their café bills by Android Pay, it is difficult to imagine that we are in the same distressed city I first visited in 1989. Opened in 2008 and spread over 1.5 million square feet, the mall has palm trees, a multiplex cinema, bowling alley, restaurants and all the fancy outlets one might expect in any big Western shopping centre.

Krasnoyarsk is today a modern European city. People laugh out loud and staff fall over themselves to be nice to customers. The nineteenth-century buildings on Prospect Mira have been renovated and painted afresh in shades of blue, yellow and brown. Lexus and Mercedes automobiles cruise by. The shabby old Soviet-era stores have been transformed into delicatessens, boutiques, jewellers, cake shops, sushi bars, Irish pubs, vape rooms and pet-food kiosks, and the concrete exterior of the biggest city-centre prison has long since been faced with red brick. Hugo Boss and Armani have established downtown outlets. Roadside billboards advertise new restaurants. A Villeroy & Boch salon has opened near the restored Orthodox Cathedral of the Protection of the Virgin, which in Soviet times was a run-down museum. Glamorous women sweep along the freshly tiled pavements in ankle-length fur coats and fashionable shoes.

A rather forlorn-looking Lenin in Krasnoyarsk, 2018.

Where once the only decent shoes in Krasnoyarsk were supplied by Stanislav Suvorov and other bespoke shoemakers, now there are shops, boutiques and galleries selling every kind of high-quality, fashionable footwear, much of it made in China. Irina Yaroslavtseva, creator of a series of fashionable outlets called Shagal ('made a step') which retail patent-leather shoes, stilettos, sports shoes, slip-ons, lace-ups, ankle boots, high boots and house slippers, boasts of having three hundred pairs of shoes at her home and advocates that women in Siberia should own fifty to a hundred pairs of shoes to cope with every weather condition and social occasion.

The city has fallen in love with fountains. With one hundred and forty cascades of every shape and size, Krasnoyarsk is third in Russia by fountain count. The one in Theatre Square is a continuous concert of music, colour and dancing water spouts around a three-metre-high statue of Father Yenisey holding a boat, with a bevy of scantily clad females representing the river's tributaries. Here there is also one of the three clock towers in Krasnoyarsk that look remarkably like Big Ben in London. The Lenin Museum is now a palace of the arts. People no longer worship at the shrine to Lenin but in the Orthodox churches. The city has witnessed a revival of religion. On Easter Sunday passers-by greet each other with 'Khristos voskres' – 'Christ is risen' – and the reply, after three kisses on the cheek, 'He is indeed risen.' The Orthodox Paraskeva Pyatnitza chapel, which looks out over the city, has been reconsecrated and is a place of pilgrimage for newly married couples. A sketch of the chapel decorates the Russian ten-ruble note. Nearby a cannon is fired every day precisely at midday, a practice begun in 2001 to celebrate City Day. The boom is heard all across the west bank of the city and the reverberations sometimes set off car alarms.

On Molokova Street, just a block away from Planeta, is a yellow-painted church with three conical towers. Consecrated in May 2003 by the head of the Armenian Apostolic Church, Catholicos Karekin II, the Church of St Vargis is the first Armenian place of worship in all of Siberia, catering for a far-flung population of just over ten thousand.* To judge by the Suvorovs and their family and friends, the Armenians of Krasnoyarsk are not very religious, but great store is still put on having infants baptized.

In common with dozens of Russian cities a statue of the popular folk singer Vladimir Vysotsky has been erected in Krasnoyarsk. Titled *A Hunt for Wolves*, it is a metaphor for the Stalin period. One comes across fun pieces of street art too, including a bronze drunkard leaning against a lamp post with a dog doing its business on his shoes.

---

* Armenians form 0.37 per cent of the 2.8 million people living in the Krasnoyarsk Region according to the 2010 Russian census.

Zhanna and I try out one of Moscow's new coffee shops, on a visit in 2002.

Young people have adapted quickly to a new lifestyle. The Komsomol and the lofty ideals of Soviet youth belong to their parents' and grandparents' generation. They watch MTV, which competes with five Russian music channels, and they dress and wear their hair the way the performers do. They are highly computer literate. They plan foreign holidays and study to be lawyers and economists. They expect instant service in shops. They have no memory of the misery and insults their parents and grandparents suffered in Soviet stores, queueing to order substandard goods from surly assistants, queueing again to pay the cashier, and standing in line a third time to collect their purchase. Coffee shops and restaurants abound, and pavement billboards advertise bars with names like 'Striptiz'. Russian spoken in the city is saturated with English words. A resident might carry a 'smartphone', discuss 'traffic' on the 'web', spend 'money' in a 'boutique', have 'lunch' in a 'pub', spend time in a 'music club', or go 'shopping' for 'shoes'. Zhanna's PhD professor, who jointly compiled the popular *Müller English–Russian Dictionary* and was horrified at the contamination of the language she loved even when the Soviet Union still existed, is undoubtedly turning in her grave.

Some things, however, have not changed. In the mall we leaf through the *Krasnoyarsk Gazette* as we linger over our Americanos and experience a feeling of déjà vu. With old Soviet-era blandness the broadsheet reports the visit to Krasnoyarsk the day before of Vladimir Putin. It was in Krasnoyarsk that Mikhail Gorbachev was first subjected to the anger of the people when he went for a walkabout on Prospect Mira. Their comments were covered extensively in the media then. There is no stroll along the boulevard by the leader of the new Russia. No criticisms are voiced or heard. Nor is there any opportunity.

At one point it seemed that Boris Nemtsov would become president of the Russian Federation. The champion of reform in post-Soviet Russia rose to the rank of deputy prime minister in the 1990s after his successes in Nizhny Novgorod, and Boris Yeltsin for a time favoured him as the next occupant of the Kremlin. Yeltsin introduced Nemtsov to Bill Clinton as his successor but opted instead for Vladimir Putin at the final moment. It was a critical choice, determining that Russia would not opt for a democratic law-based society, but for one that followed the Chinese communist model in which citizens can do as they like – make money, travel, build mansions – as long as political authority is not challenged. During the next decade Nemtsov became an outspoken critic of Putin, organizing demonstrations and accusing the president and his allies of corruption and embezzlement on an industrial scale and of turning Russia into an authoritarian state. He formed a political party, the Union of Right Forces, to promote democracy, the rule of law and a functioning civil society.

In the 2007 parliamentary elections in Krasnoyarsk, Larisa – who never joined the communist party in Soviet times – decided to support Nemtsov's candidates and travelled to his regional party headquarters in Kansk, two hundred and thirty kilometres east of Krasnoyarsk, only to find a Soviet-era mentality among officials, i.e., that there is one ruling party and that is the one headed by Putin. Nemtsov supporters were not allowed to canvass voters, collect their election material from the printers or use premises for meeting candidates and deputies. Larisa had her passport temporarily taken away and her identity noted.

On 27 February 2015 Boris Nemtsov, who once embodied the hope for an open, democratic Russia, was assassinated on a bridge near the Kremlin. He was about to publish a report demonstrating that Putin sent Russian troops into eastern Ukraine to assist rebels there, which the Kremlin has denied. In June 2017 five Chechen men were tried and convicted by a Moscow court of the murder, which they say they carried out for a fee of a quarter of a million US dollars. The person who paid them has not been identified.

After retiring, Stanislav and Marietta spend as much time as they can at the dacha, often with family members and friends. Each year their strip of land has gifted them with a prodigious variety and quantity of fruit and vegetables. The tomatoes and cucumbers are pickled, the potatoes stored in the cellar, and the fruit used to make jams and compotes, though plastic-wrapped variants of such produce can be purchased in the hypermarket on the road back into the city. Everyone helps out, hoeing between the rows of onions and potatoes, planting out seedlings and exchanging gardening lore. On holidays we enjoy a sauna afterwards in the wooden *banya*, and a leisurely dinner in the still-light evenings, raising our glasses to friendship, to family, to

Good connections: Stanislav in 2004 with meat factory director Ivan Kasyanovich and railway yard stock controller Boris Arutyunyan.

health and to Stanislav's wish that we are not drinking together for the last time.

Unfortunately modern consumer society has brought problems of rubbish disposal. A well-trodden path behind the dacha now leads to a fly-infested clearing filled with twisted plastic bottles and wrapping and obsolete household goods dumped by the villagers, who use the road carved through the undergrowth by the military when there was a nuclear missile deployed here. The village of Bulanovka has not benefited from the rush to modernization, although mobile phone transmitter masts can be glimpsed above the coniferous trees. The city people in the dachas communicate by text, email, Snapchat, Twitter, Facetime, Facebook, Instagram and every other social media innovation, and read world newspapers and books on mobile devices. The taiga is wired up, and 'roaming' has also been incorporated into the Russian language.

Stanislav and Marietta with great-grandchildren Jessica, Artem and Timur at the family dacha in 2013.

Julia keeps in close touch with the Russian-Armenian family who cared for her until she was nine years old. She lived in Washington and Beijing with us, then studied at university in London. Now married to Joey Halliday and with two children, Jessica and Jason, she resides in Wiltshire, in England.

Stanislav and Marietta are made Russian citizens after their Soviet travel documents are replaced with Russian passports. They become *Rossiyane*, the term used in tsarist Russia for 'citizens by naturalization' regardless of ethnicity or mother tongue, which has come back into fashion in the post-Soviet media to embrace all citizens and not just *Russkiye*, or ethnic Russians. The Russian embassy in Dublin insists that Zhanna apply for a Russian passport, so that now on visits back to Krasnoyarsk she enters Russia on her Russian passport as a *Rossiyanka*, and leaves on her Irish passport as an Irish citizen.

After fifty years living in Krasnoyarsk, Stanislav and Marietta have become something more than *Rossiyane*; they are Siberians. They went into voluntary exile in Krasnoyarsk to escape the stigma of Stanislav's prison sentence and to forge a new life, economically and professionally. They endured harsh winters and tough conditions, but they prospered and gave their daughters a good education and start in life. The collapse of communism came too late for the master shoemaker to realize his full potential as a businessman, though he did better than most under the Soviet system.

Deep in concentration: Stanislav in his theatre workshop in 2007.

In the grand scheme of things they consider that they have been blessed. As Marietta sees it, 'We had a good life in the Soviet Union and we were happy. Many things were unfair under communism but nowadays they are one hundred times worse. In Soviet times those prepared to work hard could provide for themselves. There was free healthcare, free education and free housing. Everyone was equal. Everybody had a piece of bread. Yes, there was disparity, but nothing like what we have now. Yeltsin and the others sold off the country. Today the rich are getting richer but one in ten people live in poverty and the children can't go out and play outside like they used to because of criminals.'

All through his seventies and into his eighties the shoemaker from Grozny continues to work late into the evenings in the workshop behind the theatre, where he always has sweets or something more fortifying for customers, theatre workers, actors and friends who drop in. He continues to bring home a treat of some sort in his 'doctor's' briefcase, though the novelty of producing a *deficit* item from its interior is gone. Now there is everything – at a price.

On evenings spent at home or at the dacha he puts on his large reading glasses after dinner and peruses the *Krasnoyarsky Rabochy* from cover to cover, or immerses himself in a book and then falls asleep in his chair. In 2009 he develops stomach pains and is diagnosed with cancer. His doctor recommends the removal of part of his stomach. Against everyone's advice he goes into hospital for the operation but when told that his whole stomach has to be taken out he calls Marietta to bring his clothes, signs himself out and goes back to work. He endures the pain, and it does not get any worse, possibly due to his robust nature and a diet rich in herbs.

We travel to Krasnoyarsk in February 2014 to take part in the celebrations for his eighty-fifth birthday. At a gathering of family

Stanislav makes a toast to world peace at his eighty-fifth birthday dinner in 2014.

and friends in a hotel restaurant he makes his usual speech and sings his Caucasian drinking song and several others, some from his army days. As always he toasts our health, peace and '*Za zhenshchin!*' ('To the women!')

On 26 February 2015 Zhanna calls her father to wish him a happy eighty-sixth birthday. 'Thank you, *moya zolotaya* [my golden one],' he replies. These are the last words the shoemaker speaks to his daughter. When Zhanna's mother comes on the line moments later she tells Zhanna that her father is not well and that when he asked Marietta why she was not preparing a birthday party as always, she told him, 'What party? You are sick.'

Stanislav has contracted a virus, and two days later he is admitted to the state hospital in Oktyabrsky District known colloquially as the one-thousand-bed hospital. He makes a brief

*A shoemaker is buried here: grave in Krasnoyarsk of Stanislav
Suvorov, 2015.*

recovery and returns to work but collapses again within days and
is readmitted to hospital. He berates visitors who do not bring
him newspapers and, to the amusement of other patients in the
ward, asks Larisa to make sure when she returns to have the sixth
volume of the works of Victor Hugo, which he has been reread-
ing at home. Though never a communist party member, it is a
measure of the man that he finds comfort on his deathbed in the
works of an advocate of a better world.

On 4 April 2015 Larisa's daughter Zoya contacts Zhanna and tells her to come immediately. Her father is in intensive care and is dying. Zhanna happens to be in Armenia. She catches a flight from Yerevan to Moscow and from there to Krasnoyarsk. Zoya picks her up at the airport. On the morning of 6 April Stanislav Suvorov dies in his sleep from internal bleeding. Technically he never stopped working until the day he died, aged eighty-six, as he was on official sick leave from the theatre.

His memorial service is packed with members of the ensemble and staff of the Pushkin Theatre, where he provided everyday shoes, ballet shoes, platform shoes, walking boots, riding boots, Cossack boots, sandals and slippers, as well as leather bags, belts, gloves, straps and coats, to several generations of thespians. One of them tells Marietta that he dropped into Stanislav's workshop not long before and found him in a contemplative mood. He

Zhanna, Marietta and Larisa, reunited for New Year in Krasnoyarsk, 2018.

recalls what the shoemaker told him then: 'I have a loyal wife, wonderful children and a job that I love.' The deputy director pays a warm tribute, saying that Stanislav, who worked at the theatre for forty-seven years, was known fondly as the night director. One of the actresses, speaking on behalf of the performers, describes him as a legend of the theatre. The service finishes in theatrical style with a round of applause.

Stanislav Suvorov, master shoe designer, provider of bespoke footwear to Soviet royalty, stage actors and family and friends, is laid to rest on a south-facing slope in Badalyg cemetery on the edge of the city, in a section for war veterans in recognition of his teenage wartime work in the Grozny shoe factory and his military service in Chukotka. The Pushkin Theatre provides a memorial for the grave in the form of an elegant boot shaped from a strip of black enamelled metal hanging from a stand, so anyone passing by will know that a shoemaker is buried there.

BIBLIOGRAPHY

Alexievich, Svetlana, *Second-Hand Time*, London: Fitzcarraldo Editions, 2016

Anderson, Richard, *Russia, Modern Architectures in History*, London: Reaktion Books, 2015

Applebaum, Anne, *Red Famine, Stalin's War on Ukraine*, London: Allen Lane, 2017

Astafiev, Viktor, *To Live Your Life and Other Stories*, Moscow: Raduga, 1989

Barnes, Andrew, *Owning Russia, The Struggle over Factories, Farms and Power*, Ithaca, New York: Cornell University Press, 2006

Beevor, Antony, *The Second World War*, London: Weidenfeld & Nicolson, 2012

Bennett, Vanora, *Crying Wolf, The Return of War to Chechnya*, London: Picador, 1988

Conradi, Peter, *Who Lost Russia? How the World Entered a New Cold War*, London: Oneworld, 2017

De Waal, Thomas, *Black Garden, Armenia and Azerbaijan through Peace and War*, New York: New York University Press, 2003

De Waal, Thomas, *The Caucasus, an Introduction*, Oxford: Oxford University Press, 2010

Eaton, Katherine B., *Daily Life in the Soviet Union*, Westport, Connecticut: Greenwood Press, 2004

Gall, Carlotta, and de Waal, Thomas, *Chechnya, A Small Victorious War*, London: Pan Books, 1997

Glinkina, Dr Svetlana, *Distributional Impact of Privatization in Russia*, Russian Academy of Sciences: Moscow, 2003

Gordon, Michael R., 'Krasnoyarsk 26', *New York Times*, 18 November 1998

Grossman, Vasily, *Life and Fate*, London: Vintage, 2006

Haywood, A. J., *Siberia, A Cultural History*, Oxford: Signal Books, 2010

International Finance Corporation, *Small Scale Privatization in Russia: The Nizhny Novgorod Model. A City Official's Guide*, International Finance Corporation, 1992

Jaimoukha, Amjad, *The Chechens, A Handbook*, London: Routledge, 2014

Kaminskaya, Dina, *Final Judgement, My Life as a Soviet Defence Lawyer*, London: Harvill Press, 1983

Klumbyté, Neringa, and Sharafutdinova, Gulnaz (eds), *Soviet Society in the Era of Late Socialism 1964–1985*, Lanam, Maryland: Lexington Books, 2013

Kotkin, Stephen, *Stalin, Waiting for Hitler 1928–1941*, London: Allen Lane, 2017

Leno, John Bedford, *The Art of Boot & Shoemaking*, Mansfield Centre, Connecticut: Martino Publishing, 2010

Lewin, Moshe, *The Soviet Century*, London: Verso, 2016

Lieven, Anatol, *Chechnya, Tombstone of Russian Power*, New Haven, Connecticut: Yale University Press, 1999

Mandelstam, Nadezhda, *Hope Against Hope*, New York: Penguin Books, 1975

Merridale, Catherine, *Ivan's War, The Red Army 1939–1945*, London: Faber and Faber, 2005

Naimark, Norman M., *Stalin's Genocides*, Princeton, New Jersey: Princeton University Press, 2012

O'Clery, Conor, *Moscow, December 25, 1991, the Last Day of the Soviet Union*, London: Transworld, 2011

Orlov, Igor, *The Soviet Union Outgoing Tourism in 1955–1985*, Moscow: National Research University, Higher School of Economics

Rand, Robert, *Comrade Lawyer*, Boulder, Colorado: Westview Press, 1991

Schwartz, Charles A., 'Economic Crime in the USSR: A Comparison of the Khrushchev and Brezhnev Eras', *International and Comparative Law Quarterly*, Vol. 30, No. 2 (April 1981), pp. 281–96

Smith, Kathleen E., *Moscow 1956, The Silent Spring*, Cambridge, Massachusetts: Harvard University Press, 2017

Spufford, Francis, *Red Plenty, Inside the Fifties' Soviet Dream*, London: Faber and Faber, 2010

Taubman, William, *Gorbachev, His Life and Times*, London: Simon & Schuster, 2017

von Bremzen, Anya, *Mastering the Art of Soviet Cooking*, London: Doubleday, 2013

Westwood, J. N. (ed.), *Endurance and Endeavour, Russian History 1812–2001*, Oxford: Oxford University Press, 2002

Woll, Josephine, *Real Images, Soviet Cinema and the Thaw*, London: I. B. Tauris, 2000

Yurchak, Alexei, *Everything Was Forever, Until It Was No More*, Princeton, New Jersey: Princeton University Press, 2005

PICTURE ACKNOWLEDGEMENTS

All images courtesy of the author and the Suvorov family unless otherwise stated.

P. 14 Martakert photograph by Sergey Advalian; p. 95 Roman Rudenko © ZUMA Press, Inc./Alamy Stock Photo; p. 102 Leonid Brezhnev © ITAR-TASS/Archive; p. 184 Vladimir Vysotsky © ITAR-TASS News Agency/Alamy Stock Photo; p. 244 Gorbachev and his wife in Krasnoyarsk © TASS/Getty Images; p. 283 Gorbachev resigning as General Secretary © Vitaly Armand/ Getty.

ABOUT THE AUTHOR

Conor O'Clery holds a unique perspective on the former Soviet Union, as resident *Irish Times* correspondent during the last four years of communism and as a frequent visitor since then, having married into a Russian-Armenian family in Krasnoyarsk. After Moscow he was a foreign correspondent in Washington, Beijing and New York. He has been twice awarded Journalist of the Year, for his dispatches from Moscow and for his reporting of the 9/11 attacks in New York. He is the author of several books including *Melting Snow*, on the fall of the Soviet Union; *The Greening of the White House*, about the Clinton presidency; *The Billionaire Who Wasn't*, a biography of the philanthropist Chuck Feeney; and *Moscow, December 25, 1991*, an account of the last day of the Soviet Union.